The Victorian Ghost Story and Theology

Zoë Lehmann Imfeld

The Victorian Ghost Story and Theology

From Le Fanu to James

Zoë Lehmann Imfeld
University of Bern
Bern, Switzerland

ISBN 978-3-319-30218-8   ISBN 978-3-319-30219-5 (eBook)
DOI 10.1007/978-3-319-30219-5

Library of Congress Control Number: 2016940610

© The Editor(s) (if applicable) and The Author(s) 2016
This work is subject to copyright. All rights are solely and exclusively licensed by the Publisher, whether the whole or part of the material is concerned, specifically the rights of translation, reprinting, reuse of illustrations, recitation, broadcasting, reproduction on microfilms or in any other physical way, and transmission or information storage and retrieval, electronic adaptation, computer software, or by similar or dissimilar methodology now known or hereafter developed.
The use of general descriptive names, registered names, trademarks, service marks, etc. in this publication does not imply, even in the absence of a specific statement, that such names are exempt from the relevant protective laws and regulations and therefore free for general use.
The publisher, the authors and the editors are safe to assume that the advice and information in this book are believed to be true and accurate at the date of publication. Neither the publisher nor the authors or the editors give a warranty, express or implied, with respect to the material contained herein or for any errors or omissions that may have been made.

Cover illustration: © Illustration by Gustave Doré from Edgar Allan Poe's 'The Raven'.
Rare Books and Special Collections Division of the Library of Congress, Washington, DC.

Printed on acid-free paper

This Palgrave Macmillan imprint is published by Springer Nature
The registered company is Springer International Publishing AG Switzerland

And the fallen human soul, at its best, must be as a diminishing glass, and that a broken one, to the mighty truths of the universe round it; and the wider the scope of its glance, and the vaster the truths into which it obtains an insight, the more fantastic their distortion is likely to be, as the winds and vapors trouble the field of the telescope most when it reaches farthest.

John Ruskin, *Stones of Venice*

Acknowledgements

The research for this book was made possible by a Marie Heim-Vögtlin Grant from the Swiss National Science Foundation (SNSF). The MHV grant is aimed at female scholars who are balancing an academic career with family commitments. As the mother of very young children, I cannot describe the value of such a grant, and I think it should be considered the jewel in the crown of the Swiss academic system.

I give my enduring thanks to Virginia Richter, who when I turned up on her academic-doorstep took me under her wing, and has provided guidance and support ever since. Her advice and insight have been invaluable from the conception of this research idea to its final manuscript. I am also indebted to Alison Milbank, whose careful and thoughtful advice at various stages of this book made me examine and re-examine both my literary criticism and use of theology to produce something sound.

This book has also benefited from many and repeated readings by my colleagues at the University of Bern, who were incredibly generous with their time and offered comments and suggestions that greatly improved the resulting work. Likewise thanks go to my 'Emeritus-RA', with whom many a theological discussion has taken place over 'extraordinary' afternoon teas in Oxford. Long may they continue.

I must of course also give my sincere thanks to William Desmond and Charles Taylor, whose writings provide fundamental background to my theoretical claims, and both of whom were kind enough to provide feedback and suggestions to early parts of this book.

I am very lucky to have been on the receiving end of a great deal of support from Ben Doyle and his team at Palgrave Macmillan. My thanks also to Francesca Lehmann and Lobsang Gammeter for carefully proofreading the manuscript.

Last but of course not least, this book would not have been possible without the support and patience of my husband Bruno, and my children Toby and Sophie, who will hopefully one day read ghost stories with as much glee as I do.

Contents

1 Introduction: Rethinking the Victorian Ghost Story   1
   Rethinking Victorian Agnosticism   2
   Rethinking Victorian Society   4
   Reviving Theological Ghosts   6
   A Journey through the Stories of Machen, MRJ,
      Le Fanu and Henry James   7

2 Haunted by the Ghost of God—Reading Theologically   13
   God as Ghostly: The Relegation and Return of Meta-Narrative   14
   Being as Ghostly: The Christian Meta-Narrative of
      the Ghost Story   26

3 'Strangely mistaking death for life': Arthur Machen   39
   Anglo-Catholicism and Arthur Machen's Sense of Mystery   41
   Machen's Thomist Anthropology   46
   'The White People'   47
   Man without Christ in 'The Great God Pan'   55
   Aesthetic Nihilism in The Three Impostors   59
   Conclusion   70

4 'What is this that I have done?': M. R. James   79
   M. R. James, Anglican Dogma and the Moral Authority of Text   80
   MRJ's Theological Anthropology   84

'Canon Alberic's Scrapbook' and 'Count Magnus' — 86
'Mr Humphreys and His Inheritance' — 94
Conclusion — 100

5 'These devils have made quite a saint of you': Sheridan Le Fanu — 107
Le Fanu and the Irish Protestant Establishment — 109
Le Fanu's Augustinian Journey—Doubling and Transformation — 110
Mimetic Crisis as Gothic Horror in 'Spalatro' and 'Borrhomeo the Astrologer' — 115
From Horror to Terror: Incomplete Resurrection in 'The Haunted Baronet' — 120
Terror Brought to Actuality in 'The Mysterious Lodger' and 'The Familiar' — 126
Conclusion — 133

6 'He's there from the moment he knows somebody else is': Haunted by Paralysis in the Stories of Henry James — 141
Henry James' Non-Theology — 142
Henry James and Teleology — 143
Becoming and Stasis in 'The Beast in the Jungle' — 144
Aesthetic Creation in 'The Altar of the Dead' — 148
Conclusion — 155

7 Conclusion: 'This supernatural soliciting cannot be ill, cannot be good' — 159
Return to the Gap — 161
Reader Doubling — 164
Response as Participation — 166

Bibliography — 169

Index — 183

CHAPTER 1

Introduction: Rethinking the Victorian Ghost Story

Writing in 1894, the psychical researcher and literary anthropologist Andrew Lang noted that the ghost had become 'a purposeless creature', with 'no message to deliver'.[1] Lang was writing at a time in which discourse on the supernatural sought to categorise and explain phenomena within an empiricist and Cartesian understanding of the world. In fact, for those seriously interested in the supernatural as measurable phenomena, such as members of the Society for Psychical Research, such a project could be a means through which man could ultimately rediscover the extent of his relationship with God's created world, and through which the Christian revelation would be better understood.[2]

This book aims to explore this relationship between supernatural narrative and religious hermeneutics by rereading and rediscovering fictional ghost stories as theological texts. The best recent scholarship has involved refocusing the twenty-first-century lens through which we read Victorian literature in general and the Victorian ghost story in particular. There are two aspects of this refocusing which have laid a ripe foundation for a theological approach to the ghost story. The first of these has been a shift in our understanding of Victorian agnosticism, and the second has been a move away from inwardly directed readings of the ghost story, heavily influenced by psychoanalysis, to refreshed social contextualisation of the texts.

Rethinking Victorian Agnosticism

Recent scholarship of Victorian theology has gone far beyond conflating Enlightenment discourse or scientific empiricism with what was so long assumed to be an agnostic panic. Timothy Larsen has led the charge in this area, revisiting the role of Christian apologetics in Victorian discussions of science and secularity by arguing that 'the nineteenth-century story is really one of contested Christianity rather than the ebbing of the sea of faith'.[3]

James C. Livingston has described the period between 1860 and 1890 as the 'Age of Agnosticism', and in *Religious Thought in the Victorian Age* gives a detailed account of the origins of agnostic discourse, such as that of T. H. Huxley in the empirical philosophical tradition. Crucially, however, the crisis of such agnosticism was not over the existence, necessarily, of God, but of how to know such a God within the limits of human knowledge.[4] Certainly such a crisis did lead to the withdrawal by many thinkers from practised religion, and this was reflected in the literature of period. George Eliot (Mary Ann Evans) has often been used as exemplary of a paradigmatic shift from Evangelical faith to scepticism, and her supernatural tale 'The Lifted Veil', gives an insight into this sense of 'crisis' which provides an important counter-balance to the tales which follow in this volume. In this story, a man is cursed with visions of his own future, including a life of unhappiness with the woman he loves and of his own death. The visions are a curse as they steal from the man any sense of an unknowing but faithful hope. He tells us: 'I had begun to taste something of the horror that belongs to the lot of a human being whose nature is not adjusted to simple human conditions.'[5] The protagonist's narrative, which nonetheless mirrors 'the soul's path [...] through the thorny wilderness' described by a Christian teleology, draws its horror not from a *failure* to participate in community and human relationships, as we shall see in the stories of Henry James, but in the affliction of seeing into the inner self of others whose natures are 'in radical antipathy' to one's own.[6] Texts such as 'The Lifted Veil' are important to a theological reading of supernatural tales, not only as they remind us that the theological story being told is not univocal, but also as they establish a position of doubt from which a teleological journey such as the one described in the following chapters can begin.

Timothy Larsen, however, has argued that claiming narratives such as Eliot's as paradigmatic has led to an over-estimation of a 'crisis of faith' in

Victorian England. Indeed, Larsen argues that literary studies themselves have contributed to this distorted emphasis on a loss of faith.[7] He follows, perhaps, Bernard Lightman's warning that our sense of familiarity and commonality with Victorian agnosticism can 'lead us to flatten down the diverse and protean quality of Victorian agnosticism into a completed picture'.[8] Instead, Larsen convincingly argues for a Victorian Britain in which religious 'doubt' contributed to a resituating of Christian thought, rather than undermining it.[9] It is this narrative of a Victorian Britain in which Christian teleology was being reconsidered that provides the framework for my rereading of the supernatural tales which follow. This also follows Michael Wheeler's description of a Victorian interpretative project which was shared by writers, philosophers and theologians alike. Wheeler points out that our common understanding of creative writing as 'reflecting' theological questions falsely suggests a gap between the writing and the theological conversation itself.[10] In such a climate, ghost stories responded not only to a theological conversation in which faith was undermined by scepticism, but to one in which challenges to Christian orthodoxy demanded reinvention and re-engagement with faith.

What is crucial, however, is that this imaginative task took place at a time when the *language* of theological conversation was being reshaped by sceptical discourse and empiricist formality. In what Shane McCorristine calls a 'cross-pollination' of ghost fiction and ghost 'fact', ghostly discourse in literature became itself haunted.[11] The language of scepticism shaped a discourse which nonetheless sought to describe some sort of metaphysics of life and afterlife. Ghost fiction, just as much as ghost 'fact', was haunted by the uneasy hope that behind Victorian empiricism lay the promise of revelation, and it is the nature of Victorian ghostly discourse which lends this sense of unease.[12] Susan Navarette, for instance, notes that Arthur Machen's weird-tales make use of the very language of the natural sciences and scepticism to which they respond.[13] It is no surprise, then, that today's scholarship of the Victorian ghost-story genre continues to rely on an approach in which the supernatural tale is seen as an expression of uniform agnostic anxiety. Unlike explorations of theology in the gothic genre, the theological voice of the Victorian ghost story remains only a whisper behind theories of secular disenchantment or psychoanalytical disturbance.

In this book I aim to challenge the presumption that the supernatural tale lifts a veil only to a void, absent of theological ontology, and will seek to place the theological import of the supernatural tale alongside that of the gothic and the grotesque in fiction.[14] I will suggest that the authors considered in this book contributed to a movement in Victorian theological discourse which sought to reaffirm Christian orthodoxy while at once reinstating the role of medieval mysticism to religious experience. As shall be seen, however, each of our authors approached this discourse from very different theological backgrounds and perspectives. For this reason space is given in each chapter to the religious and theological discussions which informed their stories. At the end of this chapter I will briefly consider the ways in which the different religious traditions from which each author came communicate with each other, and reflect the climate of 'conversation' which was made possible by using Scripture as what Northrop Frye calls 'The Great Code'.[15]

Rethinking Victorian Society

In his book *A History of the Modern British Ghost Story*, Simon Hay recognises the reductive effect that a concentrated perspective has had, particularly with its inevitable focus on psychoanalysis.[16] Hay recognises that the spectrality of the stories and the sense of return symbolised by the apparition lend the ghost story to psychoanalytical readings, and he posits this as a reason for the dominance of psychoanalytic readings in criticism. In its place, Hay offers a valuable picture of the social concerns motivating the genre, and joins Andrew Smith in seeing the ghost story as '*the* form in which conventional cultural assumptions about identity politics were challenged'.[17] Smith in particular acknowledges the background of religious debate in nineteenth-century ghost discourse, but ultimately both Hay and Smith focus on firmly situating the ghost story as a voice for social and cultural preoccupations.

In light of the challenges to identity politics which Smith identifies, the authors represented here may seem like a narrow choice for a book that claims to draw on socially informed ghost-story scholarship. Their religious backgrounds are disparate, from Anglo-Catholicism, to Irish Protestantism, to Henry James, whose main engagement with theology is understood by many to have been a strict avoidance of it. Theologically at least, this group would not consider themselves to be homogenous. Nonetheless, it is impossible not to notice that the authors here are a group of middle-class, middle-aged men in a time when the ghost-story form was breaking down barriers to publication. For the rereading of supernatural tales as social documents, the supernatural fiction of women writers in particular is a gold mine. Diana Wallace includes ghost-story fiction as part of the Female Gothic, which she claims is 'perhaps par excellence the mode within which women writers have been able to explore deep-rooted female fear about women's powerlessness and imprisonment within patriarchy'.[18] Edith Nesbit's tales of the uncanny, for instance, are perfect examples of the chill that can suddenly descend when the supernatural disrupts a domestic setting, and her stories are rightly being rediscovered by scholars and publishers. A perfect example is 'The Mystery of the Semi-Detached', in which the striking simplicity of a vision of a foreseen death is played out in a generic suburban house.[19]

This is not to say that the ghost stories of female writers are limited to their socio-historical value. Suzanne Raitt's biography, *May Sinclair: A Modern Victorian*, offers a fascinating and detailed insight into Sinclair's struggles with her own faith, and how this related to her engagement with philosophy.[20] May Sinclair's attention to the relationship between faith, reason and Idealism run through her stories from the early twentieth century as well as her philosophical writings, and her tale 'The Finding of the Absolute' is examined further in the next chapter. (It will also be interesting to read Sinclair's stories in light of Henry James' supernatural tales, given the modernist inheritance in Sinclair's work. Further discussion of this can be found in chapter 6.)

While all four of the authors considered in detail in this book can make claim to being figures of great influence in the genre, the choices made for this book are not intended to privilege their authority over other authors, nor claim them as comprehensively representative of the genre. Rather, the hope is to describe a way of reading the texts theologically which sees the approach as being hospitable to other texts and theological perspectives.

Such recent re-evaluations of Victorian supernatural fiction as Hay and Smith's have been invaluable in allowing us to read the texts as if in their contemporary climate. Indeed, Hay recognises the unique place of the ghost story in re-establishing this relationship between past and present: 'The ghost's primary role is to signify what can no longer be experienced directly, a lived relationship to the past.'[21] It is this approach to a sort of temporal bridge-building which likewise informs this project. In *A People of One Book: The Bible and the Victorians*, Timothy Larsen calls the Scriptures 'the common cultural currency of the Victorians', including in agnostic or sceptical discourse.[22] As we reread the Victorian ghost story in light of their social climate, the centrality of theology to Victorian discourse makes a reintroduction of this currency into circulation in ghost-story scholarship a crucial part of this bridge-building.

Reviving Theological Ghosts

The ultimate concern of this book, in fact, is to expand the historical reconsideration of Victorian theological discourse in order to rediscover the theological language of the tales for today's readers. There is a specific sense in which the ghost story or supernatural tale offers a unique perspective to Wheeler's 'theological conversation', as much to today's theological conversation as for Victorian scholarship. Several of the tales considered in this book draw on ideas of apocalypse as revelation—a moment of crisis in which a complete understanding can occur. Northrop Frye sees the literary form of the Book of Revelation in this way: 'The vision of the apocalypse', explains Frye, 'is the vision of the total meaning of the Scriptures, and may break on anyone at any time.' Indeed, Frye's description of Revelation, while using terms of 'breaking down' rather than 'building', is noticeably similar to the temporal bridge-building envisioned by recent socio-historical scholarship: 'What is symbolized as the destruction of the order of nature is the destruction of the way of seeing that order that keeps man confined to the world of time and history as we know them.'[23]

The supernatural tale takes up a specific and privileged space in literature which hopefully takes the value of the readings performed here beyond an exercise in theological commentary.[24] The momentary confrontations of these tales suspend ontology, and open a space in which theological truth claims are doubly immanent and other. Specifically, this suspension provides a space in which a theological meta-narrative can be explored by what I will term 'non-theological' readers. In describing such a reader, I do not intend a diametric secular opposition to the theologian, but rather mean those literary readers who come to the texts from the discipline of literature without a specifically theological framework or agenda. In 1941 Dorothy L. Sayers went some way to identifying such a reader in her book *The Mind of the Maker*, in which she also successfully managed to withdraw herself and her own theological perspective (a withdrawal which I also make in this book). Sayers describes a generation of readers for whom the language of Christian philosophy is alien to the point of being 'a confused jumble of mythology'.[25] While I am certainly not as pessimistic as Sayer about the non-theologian's subsequent 'proved inability to read', I do believe that the readings which follow can recover a metaphysical language that currently haunts the discipline of literature as a secular task.

The theological readings offered within these chapters describe a confrontation to the protagonists in which they are challenged not only to reconsider their world-view, but to move, or change their way of being in light of this consideration. My sense, however, is that to recognise and follow this confrontation within the tales is to undertake a repositioning for the reader also. With this in mind, the core chapters of this book are framed by a description of the hermeneutic 'journey' taken by the non-theological reader. Chapter 2 will begin by establishing a position from which such a reader can embark on his journey through the tales, and in chapter 7 I will return to find out where the reader finds himself situated at the end of the journey.

A Journey through the Stories of Machen, MRJ, Le Fanu and Henry James

The following core chapters (chapters 3, 4, 5, and 6) have been designed in such a way as to chart the journey on which the ghost-story reader is taken. Through the tales examined here, this journey adheres to an Augustinian teleology in which the breadth of possible human 'being' is explored.

As shall be seen in the chapters, my assertion is that the tales are reflexive, each contributing to a coherent theological progression. The initial difficulty in making such a claim lies in the apparent disparity of religious traditions from which these four authors draw. Certainly from a purely literary perspective their influence over the genre warrants a close reading of their works for a better understanding of the genre as a whole. H. P. Lovecraft mentions all four authors as masters of their craft in *Supernatural Horror in Literature* (though admittedly he pays little attention to Le Fanu).[26] Likewise they are known to have influenced each other.[27] In their theological backgrounds, however, they represent a spectrum of Christian religious traditions, sometimes to the point of seeming mutual-exclusivity. Arthur Machen's mysticism, for instance, is situated firmly in an Anglo-Catholic orthodoxy, in stark contrast to Sheridan Le Fanu's Huguenot inheritance.

In this spectrum lies the very spirit of conversation described by Larsen and Wheeler in which the theological explorations taking place in these tales are based. Le Fanu is perhaps the best example of this, who in his tales often struggles with apparent contradictions within his own Protestant tradition. Victor Sage has drawn attention to this conflict in several works, including *Le Fanu's Gothic* and *Horror Fiction in the Protestant Tradition*, arguing that Le Fanu's Irish-Protestantism struggles with a resurgence of Catholic 'superstition'.[28] In chapter 5 I will suggest that by reading Le Fanu's stories in the context of the other tales presented here, Sage's description of theological conflict can be further unpacked to reveal the seeds of a theological reconciliation in Le Fanu's work. Indeed, all the stories which follow engage both with the anxieties of faith and doubt, and offer potential models of resolution, even when that resolution is not offered to the characters.

Arthur Machen seemed an appropriate author with whom to begin, in keeping with the argument that terror as cathartic religious experience can only occur after paralysing horror. Machen's weird tales expose the nihilism of being without divine creation, or rather, the non-being of profane creation. For Machen, Christianity has the power to reveal to man the mystery of divine creation of which human being is part. Tales such as 'The Great God Pan', 'The White People', and *The Three Impostors* portray attempts by their characters to bring something into being outside the miracle of divine creation. The result is that nothingness is given horrific form.

M. R. James uses many of the same motifs in his vivid depictions of the demonic—of nihilism given form. Just as Machen's demonic humans return to primordial states of non-being, MRJ's demons are creatures for whom the vestiges of humanity are enveloped in bestial form. Each one is given their horrific quality by being 'nearly' human. Where Machen's protagonists stare into the abyss, MRJ's protagonists respond to 'being without humanity' with blind confusion. Their survival, both spiritual and physical, relies on their ability to navigate a path back to their own Christian teleological journey. In this way MRJ's stories show this journey to be not a linear path, but labyrinthine and unnavigable without guidance. As the hunters of Abbot Thomas' treasure are reminded, '*Oculos habent, et non videbunt.* (They have eyes and shall not see.)'[29]

MRJ's protagonists stand in mazes which lead both to the *Imago Christi* and (in)humanity as demonic. This doubling effect of man as *actually* fallen but *potentially* saved reaches its fullness in the short stories of Sheridan Le Fanu, which is why he comes at the end of the three, despite pre-dating both MRJ and Machen in publication. In his supernatural tales, Le Fanu creates spaces in which man's condition as both fallen and saved can be played out. Through various forms of suspension, the moment of numinous realisation can be extended into a journey in which spiritual transformation is possible. By exploring the double nature of the human condition, Le Fanu allows for that doubling to be reconciled, and thus for his protagonists to come through terror and into transformative grace. The stories explored here enact a fulfilment of the Anglo-Catholic mysticism suggested by Arthur Machen—only the more striking in the context of Le Fanu's otherwise Lutheran and even Calvinist theology.

Having thus accompanied the ghost-story protagonist on a labyrinthine journey from the abyss to grace, the final chapter uses two stories by Henry James to explore ghost stories which arguably portray 'failed theology'. The teleological journey taken through Machen, MRJ and Le Fanu's stories serves to highlight the tragedy which permeates stories in which the haunted protagonist remains static, or only recognises his own fallen condition too late, thus damning himself to remain haunted.

At its inception, this book was intended as a historical engagement with Victorian theological preoccupations. It soon became clear, however, that while the theological narrative described above was certainly informed by Victorian post-Enlightenment preoccupations, it was not restricted by it. Rather, these tales provide a privileged space within which to explore a wider theological meta-narrative. The theological significance of Arthur Machen's early weird tales, for instance, is often neglected by scholars due to the wealth of non-fictional theological writings which Machen himself composed and reflected in his later fictional writings. Indeed Mark Valentine, one of Machen's most prolific critics and biographers, not only emphasises this 'change in direction', but situates the weird tales firmly in their time by placing Machen amongst his Decadent contemporaries. Valentine writes that in his most clearly apologist works (such as *The Secret Glory*) 'it is as if Machen was turning his back on any further evocation of images of evil, in the manner of Huysmans or Beardsley making their peace with the Catholic Church at last'.[30] Here, I suggest that a forensic adherence to historicised reading can mean that categorisations into theological or denominational 'schools' can drown out the nuanced philosophical voices in the works. Such a departure on my part, however, is not intended to undermine historicised readings of the authors considered here. Rather, my hope is to allow specific tales to contribute to a larger theological journey through the confrontation of the supernatural.

Notes

1. Andrew Lang, *Cock Lane and Common-Sense* (Cambridge: Cambridge University Press, 1894), 95.
2. Another founding member of the Society for Psychical Research, Frederic W. H. Myers, dedicated much of his writing effort to reconciling the SPR's empiricist approach with a Christian understanding of the self. See, for instance, *Human Personality and its Survival of Bodily Death* (New York: Longmans, Green & Co., 1903), 284sqq.

3. Timothy Larsen, *Contested Christianity: The Political and Social Contexts of Victorian Theology* (Waco TX: Baylor University Press, 2004).
4. James C. Livingston, *Religious Thought in the Victorian Age: Challenges and Reconceptions* (London: T&T Clark, 2006), 20–31.
5. George Eliot, 'The Lifted Veil', in *Silas Marner, The Lifted Veil, Brother Jacob* (Boston: Estes and Lauriat, 1895), 268. (Originally published 1859).
6. Eliot, 'The Lifted Veil', 280, 289.
7. Timothy Larsen, *Crisis of Doubt: Honest Faith in Nineteenth-Century England* (Oxford: Oxford University Press, 2006), ch. 1. In this book, Larsen distinguishes 'doubt' from 'loss of faith', through the stories of various Victorian sceptics who reconverted to Christianity.
8. Bernard Lightman, *The Origins of Agnosticism: Victorian Unbelief and the Limits of Knowledge* (Baltimore: Johns Hopkins University Press, 1987), 3.
9. See Larsen, *Crisis of Doubt*, and *Contested Christianity*.
10. Michael Wheeler, *Heaven, Hell and the Victorians* (Cambridge: Cambridge University Press, 1994), 3, 8.
11. Shane McCorristine, *Spectres of the Self: Thinking about Ghosts and Ghost-Seeing in England, 1750–1920* (Cambridge: Cambridge University Press, 2010), 16.
12. Other scholars have seen the Victorian ghost-story tradition (both 'real' and fictional) as a challenge to Max Weber's disenchantment theory, describing them as secular re-enchantment. See Joshua Landy and Michael Saler, 'Introduction', 2, and Nicholas Paige, 'Permanent Re-Enchantments: On Some Literary Uses of the Supernatural from Early Empiricism to Modern Aesthetics', 159–180, in *The Re-Enchantment of the World: Secular Magic in a Rational Age*, eds. Joshua Landy and Michael Saler (Stanford: Stanford University Press, 2009). See Max Weber, 'The Social Psychology of the World Religions', 290, and 'Religious Rejection of the World and their Directions', 350, in *From Max Weber: Essays in Sociology*, trans. H.H. Gerth and C. Wright Mills (Oxford: Oxford University Press, 1946). Also, *The Sociology of Religion* (London: Beacon Press, 1963).
13. Susan Navarette, *The Shape of Fear: Horror and the Fin de Siècle Culture of Decadence* (Lexington KY: The University Press of Kentucky, 1998), 182.
14. For examinations of theology in the gothic and grotesque, see Alison Milbank, several works, including *God and the Gothic: The Dark Imagination* (forthcoming), 'The Sleep of Reason: Reason, Gothic and the Grotesque', in *The Grandeur of Reason: Religion, Tradition and Universalism*, eds. Conor Cunningham and Peter M. Chandler (London: SCM Veritas, 2010), 432–43; Also Victor Sage, *Horror Fiction in the Protestant Tradition* (New York: St Martin's Press, 1988), 1–25, 36–70. (For Victor Sage and Alison Milbank's handling of Sheridan Le Fanu's tales specifically, see Chap. 4.)

15. Northrop Frye, *The Great Code: The Bible and Literature* (Orlando FL: Harcourt Brace Jovanovich, 1981).
16. Simon Hay, *A History of the Modern British Ghost Story* (Basingstoke: Palgrave Macmillan, 2011), 5.
17. Andrew Smith, *The Ghost Story, 1840–1920* (Manchester: Manchester University Press, 2010), 4. Original emphasis.
18. Diana Wallace, 'Uncanny Stories: The Ghost Story as Female Gothic', *Gothic Studies*, 6.1 (2004), 57–68, 57. Wallace, together with Andrew Smith, explores the specifically female mode of the gothic in their introduction to *The Female Gothic: New Directions*, ed. by Diana Wallace and Andrew Smith (Basingstoke: Palgrave Macmillan, 2009), 1–12. Recently, Melissa Edmundon Makala has extended this exploration of the female gothic into the ghost-story genre, in *Women's Ghost Literature in Nineteenth-Century Britain* (Cardiff: University of Wales Press, 2013). For functions of femininity in the gothic and ghost story, see Alison Milbank, *Daughters of the House: Modes of the Gothic in Victorian Fiction.* (Basingstoke and London: Macmillan, 1992), and 'Gothic Femininities' in *The Routledge Companion to Gothic* (Abingdon: Routledge, 2007), 155–163.
19. Edith Nesbit, in *Grim Tales* (London: A.D. Innes & Co., 1893), 67–76.
20. Suzanne Raitt, *May Sinclair: A Modern Victorian* (Oxford: Clarendon Press, 2000).
21. Hay, *History*, 18.
22. Timothy Larsen, *A People of One Book: The Bible and the Victorians* (Oxford: Oxford University Press, 2011), 2.
23. Frye, *The Great Code*, 136.
24. Something should be said about my choice of the term 'supernatural tale' for this set of texts. In his volume of criticism on Arthur Machen, amongst others, S. T. Joshi adopts H. P. Lovecraft's term 'weird tale', arguing that although 'ghost story' may be in wide usage, 'to me, "ghost story" can mean nothing but a story with a ghost in it' (*The Weird Tale: Arthur Machen, Lord Dunsany, Algernon Blackwood, M.R. James, Ambrose Bierce, H.P. Lovecraft*, Austin: University of Texas Press, 1990, 2). Several of the tales included here go beyond depictions of ghosts as apparitions, and thus using the term would open itself to Joshi's criticism. Only the stories of M. R. James really fit this terminology. I have also avoided 'story' where possible, as this term is used here in relation to the theological narrative described through the texts. I have followed Joshi in using 'weird tale' where appropriate, but have broadened this to 'supernatural tale', taking the opportunity to explore the treasure-chest of meanings which the term 'supernatural' can reveal.
25. Dorothy L. Sayers, *The Mind of the Maker* (London: Methuen, 1941), Preface, N. pag.

26. H.P. Lovecraft, *Supernatural Horror in Literature*, ed. by S.T. Joshi (New York NY: Hippocampus Press, 2000), 13, 48, 68–69, 81–87, 92–96.
27. See, for instance, M. R. James, 'The Novels and Stories of J. Sheridan Le Fanu', Ghosts and Scholars 7. Web; James Machin, 'Arthur Machen and J.S Le Fanu', *The Green Book*, 5 (2015) 34–39.
28. Victor Sage, *Le Fanu's Gothic: The Rhetoric of Darkness* (New York: Palgrave Macmillan, 2004); *Horror Fiction in the Protestant Tradition*.
29. M.R. James, 'The Treasure of Abbot Thomas', in *Ghost Stories of an Antiquary* (London: Edward Arnold, 1905), 256.
30. Mark Valentine, *Arthur Machen* (Bridgend: Seren, 1995), 56. The English illustrator Aubrey Beardsley and the French novelist Joris-Karl Huysmans were both artists associated with the Decadent movement who would convert (or in Huysmans' case return) to Roman Catholicism in later life.

CHAPTER 2

Haunted by the Ghost of God—Reading Theologically

The notion of living in a secular age, as Charles Taylor has termed it, at least within the academic humanities, is crucial to the literary scholar's understanding of herself as reader. Academic theologians have long recognised the value of literary texts to their task, but to the meta-modern secular literary scholar there seems to be a discomfort in the prospect of using theology as a hermeneutic tool. To read theologically, it is supposed, must be to commit to the univocity of a Christian Truth, with a capital T, which sits uneasily in an academic sphere that, as Charles Taylor would describe it, is 'emptied of God, or of any reference to an ultimate reality'.[1] Within these pages, I hope to describe (and perform) a form of theological reading in which the secular literary scholar can participate, which nonetheless refuses to reduce theological hermeneutics to a set of 'literary tools'. To identify a 'theological' and a 'secular' reader is, of course, to create a false dichotomy, and such a dichotomy as is suggested here is based very much on an understanding of theology and literature as fields defined by academia. Of course a readership is instead something of a spectrum. Perhaps, then, it would be better to identify a 'non-theological' reader. Such a description refers not to a reader who identifies as secular and frames their reading as such, but one for whom theology is not the starting point of their reading journey.[2] Such participation means inhabiting a hermeneutic space which is hospitable to both theological and secular ontological commitments, but which is also confrontational in that it demands a repositioning of the reader. Moreover, participation in the privileged space of the supernatural tale *effects* such a repositioning. I will try to map this hermeneutic space in this chapter.

Taylor describes the modern mode of being as 'bounded' or 'buffered', a self which is aware of the possibility of disengagement from its surroundings. The buffered self is constructed entirely by a Cartesian cogito, and that cogito is understood to remain stable regardless of what it encounters in the world, neither affected nor effected. For Taylor, however, the result of living within this 'immanent frame' is not freedom or power, but a malaise of immanence. He writes of 'a sense of ourselves as divided, cut off from a great stream of life without'.[3]

This malaise provides a perfect description for the protagonists of many a Victorian ghost story. These stories are filled with beacons of post-enlightenment Victorianism who, when faced with the spongy and porous world of the supernatural, have no tools with which to encounter it. In the stories examined here, the ghosts and demons confront the characters with an inherent and necessary anti-structure, something which Taylor claims is missing from the secular world. Through this confrontation, the constructs of the modern buffered self are disintegrated. The characters are, as it were, confronted by their porous selves. With this in mind, I would suggest that the ghost story is not only a confrontation to the modern buffered characters, but to the modern scholarly reader also. To read theologically is to allow the assumed constitutive power of readership to be reversed.

In this light, we find ourselves concerned with two 'subjects'. The readings of each supernatural tale examine the experience of the supernatural event as theologically charged for the protagonist. Central to this examination is the supernatural as an agent on the ontological position of each protagonist. Such readings are framed, however, by an interest in the experience of reading the supernatural as theological for the non-theological reader. Such reading demands a repositioning which is crucial to participate in tracing the journey of our protagonists. Thus, this chapter has two foci. The first is to establish or 'map out' the reading space for the non-theological reader, before joining the protagonists on their theological journey in the sections following.

God as Ghostly: The Relegation and Return of Meta-narrative

The ghost story form, for Northrop Frye, is that in which the supernatural is most comprehensively relegated to the 'outside', exiled there by a 'skepticism which extends only to low-mimetic conventions'.[4] To maintain this sceptical exile in theological reading is in many ways to classify the supernatural as a metaphor, perhaps representing a (hypothetical) spiritual unknown. It is certainly the case that metaphor or allegory provide substantial frameworks for the readings performed in this project. However, what I will call the 'in-between' space of participatory reading does not allow for exiling. That which it represents must be contained within it. By definition, the appearance of the supernatural is super-natural because it challenges the 'natural', and it is this challenge which allows theological stories of the supernatural to go beyond metaphor. The challenge, however, is not to the natural order, as constructed by a Cartesian cogito, but to the 'natural' self. The supernatural tale *participates in the possibility* of a super-natural mode of being. By readjusting the 'natural' of supernatural to refer to being, rather than order, the supernatural event goes beyond allegory and becomes constitutive. As Frye describes it: 'we can see that literature has an upper limit, a point at which imaginative vision of the eternal world becomes experience of it'.[5]

Why, however, should this experience be understood within the terms of theology? The answer is in the double confrontation of the supernatural event. The haunted protagonist of the story and the reader likewise are confronted with the *possibility* of the supernatural and the *actuality* of the supernatural at the same time. The event points not only to a transcendence of the immanent frame, but suggests that this transcendence has already taken place. The reader has been repositioned. Nicholas of Cusa describes God in these very terms, using *possest*, combining *posse* and *esse*, to describe actualised possibility.[6] Actualisation is not here the completion of possibility, but the concurrence of all possibility and the actualisation of that possibility at the same time. In the supernatural event of the ghost story, the possibilities of the natural as ultra-natural have been thrust insistently upon the reader.

In this repositioning, the familiar has become foreign. Later, in regards to the stories of Sheridan Le Fanu, I will discuss the concept of dread itself as part of a theological journey, following Kierkegaard, but for now, in the context of a hermeneutical mapping, it is the repositioning itself which causes dread. Removed from Taylor's immanent frame, we are first confronted with the otherness of the supernatural. If the world beyond the natural frame is like this, then what of God? And more importantly, what of us? The Catholic philosopher William Desmond acknowledges this insecurity in describing the otherness of God:

If God is unlike, 'person' must also mean something other: either a meta-personal or non-personal otherness beyond all finite manifestation. This makes us very uncomfortable, for this otherness cannot be faced directly. We cannot put a face on it, and this renders us deeply insecure.[7]

Again, it emerges that the supernatural challenges not 'natural' as order, but 'natural' as being.

In the secularisation of the modern ghost story, God as the 'super' or 'ultra' of the supernatural has been relegated to the underlying insecurity which the stories evoke. However, the possibility of *being* as supernatural continues to haunt. As Desmond notes:

> Why should only the faces of beauty show the divine? Startling us, sometimes monstrous faces seem truer masks of the divine, for even in the revulsion they call forth a reckless consent. The divine is there in the grotesque, disproportionate to our sense of finite harmony, shattering the concord of our finite measure of love. There is excess to the repulsive we cannot stand, but the ultimate stands with the monstrous too, and we must look at the monstrous differently to be with the ultimate differently. We need agapeic beholding of the beauty in the ugly, the eyes of God in the scabby countenance.[8]

The terror of the supernatural reminds us that the *excess* of God need not be contained or accommodate itself to be recognisable. Rather, '*we* must be with the monstrous *differently* to *be with the ultimate* differently'. The aim of the chapters which follow is not to demand that this change takes place, but to show what such a difference might look like.

The Haunted House: Creating a Space for Theological Reading

In Wilkie Collins' short story 'Mrs Zant and the Ghost', a man and his daughter come across a woman in Kensington Gardens, whose demeanour so frightens the little girl that she is sure the woman is mad. The father, convinced his daughter is describing a blind woman, approaches to offer help. In fact, the woman is in the midst of a supernatural experience, feeling the presence of her dead husband. The manifestation of this (invisible) presence between this woman and the father and daughter separates her from them entirely, although they are all standing in close proximity to each other:

It was impossible to realise such a state of things; but the strange impression that she had already produced on him was now confirmed. If he could believe his senses, her face did certainly tell him that he was invisible and inaudible to the woman whom he had addressed![9]

In his wish to help the woman Mrs Zant, the father must enter the world of her supernatural experience; he must 'speak her language'. This space 'in between' which the supernatural inhabits is also the space in which secular literary scholarship and theology meet. Just as for Wilkie Collins' characters, the taking up of this space, or the negotiation of it, becomes a question of language and communication. It is my intention in this section to attempt to locate this hermeneutic space, and explore how the non-theological literary scholar can step into it.

The purpose of this project is to enable the literary scholar to 'read' the ghost of God which haunts the tension between faith and modern, secular rationalism. For this I will follow Jürgen Habermas' declaration that 'it makes a difference whether we speak with one another or merely about one another'.[10] This demands a form of reading which is necessarily theologically participatory. The supernatural tale will show itself to offer a privileged space for this task, in which truth claims are at once suspended and insisted upon. If we as readers are to inhabit this space, however, we must be able to locate it. Much of Jacques Derrida's philosophical and philological project has concerned itself with the seeming evasiveness of this space. He writes:

> How is it that philosophy finds itself inscribed, rather than inscribing itself, within a space which it seeks but is unable to control, a space which opens out onto another which is no longer even *its* other. [...] How is one to name the structure of this space?[11]

The first question, then, is one of language. It is not enough to say that we can participate in theological language games. Rather, we must position ourselves in a language which is communicative and dialogic.

In his decision that he must help the woman in Kensington Gardens, Mr Rayburn, the father of Wilkie Collins' tale, hears her story, in which she explains that the spirit of her dead husband has somehow been imparting on her his continued love and protection, with the warning that his brother in some way intends her harm. Mr Rayburn must decide whether to accept her reports of supernatural intervention, and with it the implication that Mrs Zant is under threat from her brother-in-law, or to see them as evidence that she is mad, and entrust her to the care of that very brother-in-law. Notably, however, he is not required to 'believe' Mrs Zant's story, but simply to accept that it *may be* true:

> At any time his habits of life and his ways of thinking would have rendered him unfit to weigh the arguments, which assert or deny supernatural revelation among the creatures of earth. But his mind was now so disturbed by the startling record of experience which he had just read, that he was only conscious of feeling certain impressions—without possessing the capacity to reflect on them. That his anxiety on Mrs. Zant's account had been increased, and that his doubts of Mr. John Zant had been encouraged, were the only practical results of the confidence placed in him of which he was thus far aware. In the ordinary exigencies of life a man of hesitating disposition, his interest in Mrs. Zant's welfare, and his desire to discover what had passed between her brother-in-law and herself, after their meeting in the Gardens, urged him into instant action.[12]

Responding to the 'doubts' which Mrs Zant's story inspire, Mr Rayburn follows her to a seaside retreat, where he saves her from her brother-in-law and a forced marriage. For this happy ending, Mr Rayburn must *suspend* the language of madness and brain-fever, and participate in the *possible truth* of Mrs Zant's story. In this story communication has strikingly become action. If the non-theological reader of supernatural tales is to follow Mr Rayburn's example in this communicative action, and participate in the theological 'story' in the same way, what suspension or repositioning is necessary?

The first step of this repositioning must be what Taylor has called a 'semantic readjustment'. If we continue to think in terms of locating a participatory space, then it is helpful to think of this semantic readjustment as visiting a foreign land. Such a visit involves recognising that language is manifold, and also to accept the validity of these manifold languages. Both Habermas and Paul Ricœur locate the hermeneutic act as taking place on a horizon or border between the familiar and the foreign.[13] Ricœur describes this location as 'to understand oneself in front of the text'.[14] Crucially, however, the 'readjustment' necessary for the taking up of this hermeneutic position applies to both the foreign terrain in front of us, and the familiar behind us.

To take this position 'between' lands then, is to accept that the familiar has been cloaking the foreign. As readers we become like the characters of a ghost story, confronted by the 'presence' of a truth claim which challenges our secular ontological commitments. The negotiation of this space requires a hospitable response to these truth claims, as part of our 'semantic readjustment'. This is arguably a readjustment *from* a Cartesian hermeneutics in which the text comes under the control of the reader. 'The motive of Cartesian hermeneutics', claims Gerald Bruns, 'is to preserve alienation as a condition of freedom from the text'.[15] Alienation is here not a response to exclusion, but an anti-communicative act, a distancing or withdrawal from the foreign space. Desmond goes further, claiming that the in-between space unmasks this freedom as counterfeit. The result of the assertion of this autonomous power is 'ontological tyranny on ourselves'.[16] Freedom through participation, by contrast, lies in the *transcending potency* of the in-between. The transcendence of this freedom implies movement, in this case movement towards the other, and also change. Moreover, the nature of movement and change mean that inhabiting the in-between is to recognise that it is unstable. It is a 'potent' space. The in-between, then, reveals not only the transcendental possibilities of the self, but the possibilities of transcendence *itself*.

I have suggested, however, that this space for secular theological reading is a space 'between' literature and theology. The non-theological literary scholar is not asked to visit the theologian where he is 'at home'. What, then, are the semantic readjustments required for the theologian's participation in this space? The readings of ghost stories which are performed in the following chapters point towards a teleological meta-narrative which is identifiably and forcefully Christological. Contemporary theology offers two contrasting approaches to such a meta-narrative. The first is one of Radical Orthodoxy, in which the Christian theological meta-narrative need not be translatable in a space outside its own terms. The theologian John Milbank tells us that 'Just as, for the structuralists, a novel is ultimately "about" its self-constitution as a novel, so theology has only ever really been "about" its own possibility as theology, as "divine language".' Moreover, Milbank situates not only the language of theology as firmly within theology, but also the conditions for the communication of that language. The 'possibility' of communication must be the formal possibility of theological truth.[17]

I will shortly consider Mikhail Bakhtin's contribution to reader-repositioning in the form of dialogue. Milbank's model is especially complex in this regard in that he problematises even the dialogic, arguing that 'dialogue' can only be said to occur between those who share basic values and truth claims. Milbank instead suggests that 'dialogue' be replaced with 'mutual suspicion'. As the aim of my own 'reader-repositioning' is to replace the idea of suspicion with that of hesitation, Milbank's approach is problematic for the non-theological reader. However, as a representative of Radical Orthodoxy, Milbank's approach is worth examining in more detail, not least because it ultimately reflects an orthodoxy in which the reader is asked to participate in the following chapters. For the purposes of my reader participation, the same essay does balance 'suspicion' with 'conversation'. Milbank (on inter-religious dialogue) writes:

> With an extreme degree of paradox, one must claim that it is only through insisting on the finality of the Christian reading of 'what there is' that one can both fulfill respect for the other and complete and secure this otherness as pure neighborly difference. Then, at last, a conversation is established, which is itself the goal of true desire, and not a debate about truth, in the manner of 'dialogue.'[18]

Such a conversation, for Milbank, cannot 'mean anything other than continuing the work of conversion', and must ultimately aim to subvert the denial of otherness by remaining Christocentric. Again, such a model appears to leave little room for a suspended or hesitant space. There is one reading, however, which is potentially important to my question as to what semantic readjustments are required of the theologian.

In his essay, 'The Finality of Christ', Rowan Williams writes that the Christian Church should be committed to the 'questionability and the ambiguity' of 'all attempts at finished religious ontologies'.[19] If we take this questionability to lie at the heart of the theological 'conversation', then Milbank's 'continuing conversion', applies potentially just as much to the conversing theologian as to the 'other' whom he encounters. Milbank himself argues that such a conversation could 'set free a spiritually "different" response', albeit a Christocentric one. The theologian is, through such encounters, constantly 'reconverted' and 'repositioned'. Such a reading speaks to the repositioning of the theologian, not perhaps, into a suspended space, but certainly into a space in which engagement with the 'suspended' non-theologian is possible.

The participatory journey on which we will embark, however, demands a 'working through' for the inherent sense of insecurity and otherness which must accompany the act of reading literature, especially supernatural literature. A kerygmatic approach ultimately remains an either/

or model. 'Mrs Zant and the Ghost' contains a prologue in which the implied author recognises just such a hesitation:

> The record of this event will of necessity produce conflicting impressions. It will raise, in some minds, the doubt which reason asserts; it will invigorate, in other minds, the hope which faith justifies; and it will leave the terrible question of the destinies of man, where centuries of vain investigation have left it—in the dark.[20]

By anticipating this hesitation, the readers of this story are sent on a journey with Mr Rayburn. Rayburn's insecurity in the face of Mrs Zant's narration is the reader's insecurity. Rayburn's acceptance of the narrative's insistence as a *possible* narrative is necessarily the reader's acceptance also. In the same way, the literary scholar performing a theological reading encounters both the 'invigoration' and 'doubt' which the prologue describes. It is just this *hesitation* which paradoxically forces the reader to *participate* in the confrontation of the supernatural narrative.

The second theological approach, in contrast with the totalising orthodoxy of Milbank's project, is to identify a shattering of meta-narratives in modern Christianity. Anthropological projects such as that of Michel de Certeau are suspicious of all claims to universality, recognising the other as a disruptive element to the mapped order of a meta-narrative.

In his essay 'Walking in the City', Certeau describes various topographical positionings for the reader, two of which are useful to my 'topography'. The first is to take a position 'above' (and here Certeau uses the analogy of the 107th floor of the World Trade Centre). 'The person who ascends to that height', writes Certeau,

> Leaves behind the mass that takes and incorporates into itself any sense of being either an author or spectator. [...] His altitude transforms him into a voyeur. It places him at a distance. It changes an enchanting world into a text. It allows him to read it; to become a solar Eye, a god's regard.[21]

Certeau soon exposes this perspective, however, as a fiction. 'The city-panorama is a "theoretical" (i.e. visual) simulacrum.' Moreover, the inevitable return 'down' turns this distance into alienation. A contrasting positioning is the pedestrian, walking the topography of the city. For Certeau, the act of walking is to the city what the speech act is for language. Certeau's walker not only travels through the space, he *realises* it.

While the spatial order allows possibilities, the walker actualises some of those possibilities and ignores others. By creating new routes, the walker 'transforms every signifier into something else. [...] Thus he creates *discontinuity*'. If we adopt this metaphor as the non-theological reader walking through a theological space, we see that he has become the disruptive other.

In contrast to Milbank's claims, in which the other frames the delineated theological perspective, for Certeau the transformations to the signifying order imposed by the non-theological reader means it is ultimately the theologian who stands in 'another country'.[22] For Certeau, the other constantly undermines the truth claims of theology. For this reason, just as Milbank's totalising meta-narrative can be inaccessible to the secular scholar reading theologically, so too is Certeau's fictionalising of meta-narrative also inappropriate to the task. The secular literary scholar and the theological literary scholar cannot meet in the 'in-between' space of communication, as for Certeau, *neither* the secular reader *nor* the theologian occupies that space. If, as I have suggested (and upon which I shall elaborate), the participation of theological reading is to be constitutive to the reader, then the recognition of otherness must be one in which otherness is 'worked through'. The other thus serves, as Ricœur suggests, to enlarge and *effect* the reader who encounters it, by contributing to a readjustment of position. This is in stark contrast to an other which undermines or fragments readership positioning altogether.

The philosopher and literary critic Mikhail Bakhtin goes some way to reconciling the acceptance and maintenance of otherness with an openness to the constitutive effect of the other—what he calls an 'open totality'. To allow for this, however, Bakhtin situates the literary scholar in yet another location on the hermeneutic horizon. 'In order to understand,' writes Bahktin, 'it is immensely important for the person who understands to be *located outside* the object of his or her creative understanding—in time, in space, in culture.'[23] Such a positioning potentially answers both the possible buttressing against the other of Milbank's self-contained meta-narrative, and the instability of the theological model which the other poses to Certeau. The hermeneutic act is both a recognition of the other as other, and to be other oneself. Located 'outside' as in Bakhtin's model, the non-theological literary scholar recognises *himself* as other in order to contribute to understanding. Thus, the exchange becomes dialogic.

Dialogue, however, is not the same as the fullness of participation. Ultimately, Bakhtin's literary scholar is a charitable and friendly tourist. With Habermas' scholar boldly entering the foreign land, Bakhtin's remaining outside, and Ricœur's standing on the border looking in, I return to the suggestion that *participatory* reading creates an 'in-between' space which develops and fulfils the 'possibilities' of Habermas and Ricœur. The location of this in-between space is not 'neither/nor' but 'both/and'. The validity of truth claims and the veracity of meta-narratives are *both* in suspension *and* insistent.

'The play's the thing': Supernatural Literature and Suspended Space

The theologian Charles Taylor describes modern man as living in a secular age, a 'bounded' self, living within an immanent frame, which he contrasts with the pre-modern, 'porous' self.[24] This provides a useful set of terms to describe the literary reader attending to theology. For Taylor, the sense of an external constitutive agency on the self was integral to the pre-modern porous way of being. There was no boundary between the physical and emotional, the natural and supernatural. The modern Cartesian self, however, has the possibility of distance, which provides a 'buffer' against external agency. Crucially, Taylor does not argue that this buffer must be permanent. Rather, that the bounded self has the *possibility* to remain within an immanent frame, and that this possibility was not part of the porous existence. Charles Taylor's secular reader therefore not only stands outside the foreign land, but builds a wall around himself.[25] The space created by Taylor is thus 'either/or': The secular reader can choose to remain within the walls of his immanent frame or leave them, finding himself in a land in which there is no border within or without which to step.

This porous world is an understandably fearful place to be for the bounded self. Taylor describes the bounded self as inherently melancholic and dissatisfied; 'haunted', in other words, by our porous selves. However, in a space in which buffered constructions of the self collapse, there is always the danger that one becomes the ghost. The insistence of a porous meta-narrative is thus a potential barrier to participation. It is to avoid this 'either/or' dilemma that I would like to reconsider the in-between not as a separate space, but as an excess, or rather, an *extension beyond* the bounded space.[26] It is in this space that a meta-narrative is *both* true *and* suspended, in a tension which goes beyond the dialectic. It is this move beyond the dialectic which I believe is necessary for participatory literary reading. This is the space of insistent haunting, in which the reader stands both on the border of the foreign land, and enters it. The taking up of this in-between space then, is not so much a stance as a journey, a participation in the transcendent potency of the in-between.

The 'both/and' nature of the in-between space, what William Desmond calls the 'metaxological', means that it is full of doublings. The in-between is both immanent and transcendent through its *transcendent possibility*, and it is this concurrence of the immanent and the possible which is crucial to the theological readings in this project. This concurrence is possible because the in-between is both a journey and a moment of suspension. Just as in the moment of the appearance of an apparition the haunted character 'realises' the narrative behind the ghost story, so the metaxological moment contains a journey of recognition within it.[27]

That the in-between space allows a symbol to be both transcendent and 'in the midst of', brings a monstrous quality to experience. In Grant Allen's story 'Pallinghurst Barrow', Rudolph Reeve visits the eponymous pre-historic barrow on the evening of the autumn equinox. As he watches the sunset, he is suddenly aware of invisible presences grabbing and pulling him. Back in the safety of his hostess's home, he learns of the legend that the barrow is haunted. Later that night (after a generous dose of 'cannabis indica' for a headache), Rudolph returns to the barrow. What he finds there is the epitome of metaxological monstrosity:

> For, O God! looking round him, he saw, to his infinite terror, alarm, and awe, a ghostly throng of naked and hideous savages. They were spirits, yet savages. Eagerly they jostled and hustled him, and crowded round him in wild groups, exactly as they had done to the spiritual sense a little earlier in the evening, when he couldn't see them. But now he saw them clearly with the outer eye. […] They were savages, yet they were ghosts. The two most terrible and dreaded foes of civilised experience seemed combined at once in them. Rudolph Reeve crouched powerless in their intangible hands; for they seized him roughly with incorporeal fingers, and pushed him bodily into the presence of their sleeping chieftain.[28]

Recognising these beings as pre-historic humans, they horrify Rudolph by being both insistently present and yet remaining ghostly. Their physical presence makes them *recognisable* to Rudolph, but this recognition does not diminish their spectrality. Again, the participation of the character in the supernatural event is framed by language. Rudolph can 'instinctively' understand the speech of these creatures, 'because he and his ancestors had once passed through it', but they cannot understand him. Rudolph is *positioned* in the event as it is part of who he is.

The world of the ghost story is a privileged framework from which to explore the in-between space. I would want to argue that the *fantastic* is a privileged framework, or at least locate the ghost story within the genre of the fantastic, but this becomes complicated as I attempt to describe a suspended space within contemporary literary terminology. Tzvetan Todorov, in his seminal structural approach to the fantastic as genre, identifies the fantastic as a world which is recognisable, within which occurs an event which cannot be accounted for by the rules of that world. Within the moment of that event, the person who experiences it is in suspension:

> Either he is the victim of an illusion of the senses, of a product of the imagination, and the laws of the world remain what they are; or else the event has indeed taken place. [...] Either the devil is an illusion, an imaginary being; or else he really exists, precisely like other living beings—with this reservation, that we encounter him infrequently.[29]

For Todorov, the fantastic requires that the reader reject both the 'poetic', in which the fantastic images pose no challenge to the familiar world, and the 'allegorical', in which the reader realises that he need not take the supernatural elements literally. The fantastic lasts for as long as the reader hesitates between these two. For the Victorian ghost-story genre, this suspension ostensibly is only momentary. The shock of the confrontation of the supernatural lasts only as long as it takes for the reader to choose to accept the apparition as part of the 'story'.

The in-between space of the supernatural tale, however, with its concurrence of shock and journey, in fact allows this fantastic moment to expand and encompass the whole narrative. This expanded moment of hesitation, both vast and close, provides a unique space for participation in a theological meta-narrative even if it is foreign. It is such a space which can accommodate a meta-narrative which claims that God is *both* 'in the midst of' *and* beyond, and in which man is *both* immanent *and* transcendent.

In the ghost-story readings which follow, the supernatural events do not destroy or usurp the frame of the immanent world. Rather, the supernatural event expands the frame to *allow for the possibility* of a theological meta-narrative. The events show the characters to themselves, a sort of *anamnesis*, or 're-remembering'. Characters recognise something a priori in themselves. Indeed, this sense of *anamnesis* is crucial, as it at once allows for and contains the fantastic. This sense of recognition also contributes to the experience of the reader. The suspended space is different from the space defined by non-theological ontological commitments, but it is nonetheless a recognizable space. When the supernatural comes to represent the super-natural, or the supernatural self, then the reader need not question its nature because of its recognisability. Through a sense of *anamnesis*, the supernatural moves towards what Ricœur describes as the 'symbolic function' of myth, with 'its power of rediscovering and revealing the bond between man and what he considers sacred'.[30]

As Rudolph Reeve stands captured in Pallinghurst Burrow, it is this *anamnesis* which both frames and facilitates the supernatural experience. The experience is for Rudolph both shocking and familiar: 'New sights floated over him; new worlds were penetrated; new ideas, yet very old, undulated centrically towards him from the universal flat of time and space and matter and motion. [...] Everything was changed, *and he himself changed with it.*' Through this repositioning, Rudolph recognises himself in the event: 'Even in the agonised horror of that awful moment, Rudolph knew why he understood those words, unheard till then. They were the first language of our race—the natural and instinctive mother-tongue of humanity.'[31] This sense of *anamnesis* plays a central role in the theological meta-narrative revealed in the ghost stories discussed here. The repositioning of the secular reader into the in-between space allows for the *possibility* of this meta-narrative, but the truth claims of the narrative itself are insistent.

Being as Ghostly: The Christian Meta-narrative of the Ghost Story

This repositioning brings with it the insistent return of a theological meta-narrative of being, in which natural being contains within it the possibility of supernatural being. The themes of possibility and actuality which have brought us to the hermeneutic space for reading ghost stories theologically, are the very themes which frame this narrative of being. Just as the repositioning or readership is at once a stance and a journey, so this Christian theological understanding of being is at once a state and movement. This mode of being will be used throughout this work as the lens through which to read the literary texts, and as such it is worth fully unpacking it before we begin.

The readings performed in this book proceed on the understanding that the supernatural events of the stories confront their protagonists with *themselves* as theological beings. The events challenge the protagonists to recognise themselves within a theological and Christological narrative of being. Furthermore, three of the primary authors considered here all reveal a recognisably Augustinian theology, centred on the human condition as fallen.

This condition, however, is not static, but rather a condition which stands somewhere along a journey of 'becoming'. This notion of becoming is rooted in Aristotle's metaphysics of potency and act, which is central to the theological anthropologies of both SS. Augustine and Aquinas. As theological beings, created by God in the image of God, we contain the potential to *become* the fullest theological versions of ourselves. At the same time, we are *actually* fallen, and in the condition of universal sin. May Sinclair addresses just this theme of human potency and divine actuality in her 1923 story 'The Finding of the Absolute'. Sinclair's protagonist, a philosopher called Mr Spalding, loses his belief in the Absolute when his wife leaves him for another man. Eventually, Mr Spalding's grief over the apparent metaphysical impossibility of an Absolute is replaced by a fear that there might be an Absolute from which he would remain cut off through his imperfect human condition: 'That was hell, the continuance of the filthy state.'[32] Mr Spalding dies with this fear, but finds himself in heaven, met by his former wife and her lover. They explain that it is those parts of themselves which were most fully actualised which earned them their place in heaven. For Spalding's wife it was her love of her partner, Paul; for Paul, his poetic appreciation of eternal beauty, and for Spalding his passion for truth.

Slowly (and with some elucidatory help from the appearance of Emmanuel Kant), Spalding begins to realise that he can participate in the Absoluteness of God and God's creation: 'He passed from God's immanent to his transcendent life, in the Absolute.' The story ends with the spirit of Spalding joining in the creative actuality of God: 'When he came out of his ecstasy he was aware that God was spinning his thought again, stretching the web of matter through space and time. He was going to make another jigsaw puzzle of a universe.' Made in the image of God, our *telos* is to return most fully to that image. In Christ, or the *Imago Christi*, humanity becomes the *Imago Dei* in its most actual form. And, just as happens to the spirit of Mr Spalding, God, who is pure act, can act upon man through grace, to bring about that transformation.[33]

While our natural inclination is towards God, however, we are chased by our basest, fallen selves. In turning towards God, claims the Augustinian tradition, we are fleeing from nothingness. This struggle is seen repeatedly in Augustine's own description of his theological journey, *Confessions*, in which his attempts to reach towards God are repeatedly thwarted as he is dragged back down by his own spiritual insufficiency. In the Victorian ghost story, the human condition in its basest state, as without God, takes horrific physical form and appears in order to remind the protagonists that they are on this theological journey. The characters are haunted by the shadow of the worst of themselves. The Catholic writer Robert Hugh Benson captures this external manifestation of an internal condition in his short story 'The Watcher', from 1903. In it, a priest remembers a shooting holiday when he was eighteen. The priest describes finding himself in a wood which he recalls with theophanic awe. The young man then catches sight of a small bird coming in to roost, 'his head lifted and his whole body vibrating with the joy of life and music'. This theophanic imagery is shattered, however, by the young man's apparently instinctual response: 'There came on me a blinding desire to kill him. All the other creatures had mocked me and run home. Here at least was a victim, [...] and I had no excuse—no excuse.'[34]

Having shot the bird, the man notices a rhododendron bush nearby, and realises that a disembodied face is looking out from it, witnessing the scene. An earthy and animalistic form which recalls Arthur Machen's primordial demons, the face 'smiled with sheer delight, not at me, but at the thrush's body. There was not change of expression so long as I watched it, just a silent smile of pleasure petrified on the face.' The young man is immediately filled with shame, and turns to the rituals of the Church to make amends, burying the bird with the words of the funeral rites. It is through this ritual that the young man attempts to restore the unblemished nature of the scene. He takes comfort in knowing that now 'no evil thing could mock the defenceless dead out there in the clean meadow where the wind blew and the stars shone down'.[35]

The power of Benson's story, ultimately little more than a vignette, comes from the recognition of the demonic face as figurative. The priest's guilt is *manifest* in the pleasure which it brings to the face, and it is this manifestation which prompts his repentance. It is in this way that the ghoststory form reveals and explores a paradox that is central to the Christian and particularly Augustinian concept of evil. The demonic here is both the opposite of being, and shockingly and effectively present. As will be seen in the discussions which follow, it is in this way that the ghost-story form is demonstrably fulfilled by a theological reading.

The Demonic

Augustine, in his treatise *City of God*, explains his privation theory of evil: 'For evil is not a positive substance: the loss of good has been given the name of evil.' As to the presence of evil within the world, then, Augustine's privation theory situates the origin of evil firmly within the self, as coming from man turning in the wrong direction on his teleological path:

> For when the will leaves the higher and turns to the lower, it becomes bad not because the thing to which it turns is bad, but because the turning is itself perverse. It follows that it is not the inferior thing which causes the evil choice; it is the will itself, because it is created, that desires the inferior thing in a perverted and inordinate manner.[36]

Negativity or absence, however, is not equated with passivity. Augustine is here describing a choice to turn away from God. Evil is the result of that choice. Moreover, for Augustine our fallen condition means that we are drawn to this 'perversion'. Edgar Allan Poe would call this 'the imp of the perverse', and Arthur Machen explores the consequences of this perverse instinct in the stories discussed in chapter 3.

Evil described as negativity or absence, however, is problematised when reading ghost stories, in which the demonic appears with such radical and insistent presence. Such an incongruity reflects a paradox within the Judeo-Christian tradition. If God is the Ultimate Being and the Ultimate Good, evil is the absence of being. Through God, being and the good are inextricable. For the demonic to be manifest then, as radical evil, is paradoxical. Again it is the both/and which gives the ghost-story form its power. The demonic supernatural is both nihilistic and insistently immanent. The ghost-story demon is given its horror because it cannot *be*. And that horror is doubled by the recognition that the demon is manifest from the self. The demon is at once impossible and recognisable.[37]

A Christian orthodox theological approach to the demonic allows for, and indeed embraces, this paradox. The theologian Karl Barth describes terror as integral to the religious journey. 'Religion', for Barth, 'is an abyss: it is terror. There demons appear.'[38] To accept a Christian teleology; to see oneself as journeying towards God, is to recognise the full landscape of that journey. God may lie in one direction, but as Barth describes, the abyss lies in the other. To recognise God as 'real' is to recognise the abyss as 'real', as dangerous.

Kierkegaard's development of this journey through terror is explored fully in chapter 5, as we follow the journey of Sheridan Le Fanu's characters. However, it is worth mentioning here as it has something to say to the experience of the ghost-story reader. For Kierkegaard, as was recognised by Augustine, the demonic and the good, at least in terms of experience of them, are inextricable from each other. The sinful man, *dreading the good*, creates a condition of 'shut-upness' in which he can hide from himself. Such a shutting off, however, is impossible, as the man has shut himself up with himself: 'The demoniacal does not shut itself up *with* something, but shuts *itself* up; and in this lies the mystery of existence, the fact that unfreedom makes a prisoner precisely of itself.'[39]

It is not the demonic, then, which intrudes upon man's self-created fortress (what Taylor would call his immanent frame), but the good, which in doing so reveals the demonic and offers in its place redemption: 'The demoniacal becomes thoroughly evident only when it is touched by the good, which now comes to its confines from the outside.'[40] To experience the demonic, for Kierkegaard, is to experience the possibility of salvation from it.

This reconciliation of the demonic paradox comes full circle in the ghost-story form. Such a theological anthropology fulfils and gives meaning to the feeling of dread which comes from participation in the supernatural tale, as the narrative gives tangible form to the Christian paradox of evil as both 'nothing' and 'something'. And it is for this reason that full participation in the supernatural tale as *horror* fiction means participating in a theological anthropology. Robert Louis Stevenson, whose novel *The Strange Case of Dr Jekyll and Mr Hyde* provides perhaps one of the most striking depictions of the internal demonic, recognises the role of reader participation in a letter from 1886. Stevenson had read another of the great novels depicting the demonic self, Dostoevsky's *Crime and Punishment*, and responded as follows:

> Many find it dull: Henry James could not finish it: all I can say is, it nearly finished me. It was like having an illness. [Henry] James did not care for it because the character of Raskolnikoff was not objective; and at that I divined a great gulf between us, and on further reflection, the existence of a certain impotence in many minds of to-day, which prevents them from living in a

book or character, and keeps them standing afar off, spectators to a puppet show. To such I suppose the book may seem empty in the centre; to the others it is a room, a house of life, into which they themselves may enter, and are tortured and purified.[41]

Stevenson's description of the participating reader as 'tortured and purified' is important, as it acknowledges that the participant will emerge changed. It also acknowledges that such participation is terrifying, but also necessary, the alternative being emptiness. Stevenson's readers who stand far off, spectators to a puppet show, have more than a little resonance with Kierkegaard's sinners locked up in their self-protective fortresses. Moreover, Stevenson sees the process as one which 'purifies'. To experience is to vanquish, both for the reader and the protagonist.

The stories which are examined in this book endorse an orthodox Christian structure for this anthropological meta-narrative. In various ways, the characters rely on the voices of Christian orthodoxy for guidance towards redemption from their desperate positions. The outcome for each protagonist is tightly bound to their ability to recognise themselves as fallen and desperate beings. While the alternative for Stevenson's reader may be disappointment or dissatisfaction, the alternative for the protagonists of the upcoming tales is a nihilistic abyss.

The Haunting Abyss: Nihilism and Orthodoxy

In his 1987 survey *Haunted Presence: The Numinous in Gothic Fiction*, S. L. Varnado places Rudolf Otto's concept of the 'numinous' as central to that supernatural fiction which 'can best be described as an ontological challenge'.[42] Varnado's study took an important step in halting the spread of Otto's concept as a generic literary term and maintaining its philosophical nuances. The numinous quality of the supernatural fiction discussed here, however, serves not simply as an ontological challenge, but to *signify* an ontological challenge to which the authors provide a theological response. As shall be seen, the Victorian post-Enlightenment 'melancholia' described by Charles Taylor, which itself provides the context for the development of the numinous, reveals two alternative responses to an encounter with the numinous: metaphysical nihilism or theological orthodoxy. (In anticipation of the indignation that such a suggestion would rightly inspire in post-modern or liberal theologians, it is better said that these are the alternatives presented within our supernatural tales.)

Rudolf Otto's search for a meaningful description of preternatural intuitive experience is most comprehensively laid out in *The Idea of the Holy* (1923). The essay is an attempt to restore the validity of such an experience within the framework of a Kantian model of human experience, despite the Kantian insistence on the impossibility of apprehending the 'thing as itself' through such an experience. Otto describes the holy as something which remains apart from the rational, 'in the sense that it completely eludes apprehension in terms of concepts'.[43] By resisting categorisation by reason, however, Otto finds that the experience of the holy as 'feeling' can escape the Kantian limits of reason. Using the vocabulary of Schleiermacher and Fries, he writes:

> The Infinite for us is still the Incomprehensible. But what the comprehension cannot achieve we may achieve in the Feeling. Feeling, with Knowledge and Faith, gives a third kind of real knowledge, one which combines and unifies both of these—"Ahnen".[44]

Without needing to rely on the rational self to interpret religious or supernatural experience, we can recognise it as 'wholly other'. The 'numinous' expresses our response to the wholly other. Indeed, Otto uses the example of ghosts and ghost stories to point to the un-naturalness of the experience, and the way in which that un-naturalness is revealed in our response. Only as the numinous feeling is heightened and clarified, do we come to describe the wholly other as super-natural.

Otto, in his attempt to describe a post-Enlightenment mystical theology, was clearly trying to restore a sense of participation in the supernatural for post-Enlightened man. Charles Taylor would no doubt argue that he was responding to the 'malaise of modernity' which struck the nineteenth century. The sense of the self as being cut off from some great supernatural and creative force. The teleology of Otto's *mysterium tremendum* is to rediscover the human spirit as transcendental, and thus numinous itself:

> Inasmuch as the nature of our spirit is above our understanding, it has here an exact resemblance to the all-sublime, representing by its own unfathomableness the incomprehensible Being of God.[45]

In affirming the *Imago Dei* as wholly other, Otto also anticipates the sacred as the opposite of the profane.[46] Religious consciousness, therefore, occurs when the holy passes through the sublime into the numinous, and it is this description of the numinous which Varnado identifies in the gothic genre. Such a descriptive interpretation, however, lacks participation in this wholly other. By remaining wholly other, Otto's description of the spirit as numinous cannot be actualised. By contrast, it is in the gothic tradition that the wholly other is collapsed, along with distinctions of sacred and profane. The profane hides behind the sacred, and the sacred reveals itself in the apparently profane.

Lewis' *The Monk* is a complex example of this. The physical form of evil as it appears to the priest Ambrosio, entirely mirrors the priest's choice to turn away from God. Having summoned a demon in order to help seduce Antonia, the demon appears to him as an erotic and youthful figure, 'more beautiful, than Fancy's pencil ever drew'. Just as Ambrosio is enchanted with the idea of seducing Antonia, so this figure enchants him. Later, however, after Ambrosio has gone on to drug, rape and murder Antonia, and feels himself 'doomed to perdition' (with good cause, given that he has been caught by the inquisition), Lucifer appears to him again. Again the vision is a reflection of Ambrosio's own condition, now hopeless and broken: 'He appeared in all that ugliness, which since his fall from heaven had been his portion.'[47] (This motif of the 'real' Lucifer revealing himself to a man once he has chosen damnation is repeated in Le Fanu's *Borrhomeo the Astrologer*, discussed in chapter 5.)

In this way, the super-nature of God is absorbed into the fabric of a preternatural environment, becoming not a distant and wholly-other Creator, but part of Ambrosio's chosen path. In the following passage, Ambrosio is first tempted by Matilda to raise a demon to help seduce Antonia, the object of Ambrosio's lust. Matilda mocks Ambrosio's fear that this will lose him his salvation.

> 'Shall I renounce for ever my title to salvation? Shall my eyes seek a sight which I know will blast them? No, no, Matilda; I will not ally myself with God's Enemy.'
> 'Are you then God's Friend at present? Have you not broken your engagements with him, renounced his service, and abandoned yourself to the impulse of your passions? Are you not planning the destruction of innocence, the ruin of a Creature whom He formed in the mould of Angels? If not of Daemons, whose aid would you invoke to forward this laudable design? Will the Seraphims protect it, conduct Antonia to your arms, and sanction with their ministry your illicit pleasures? Absurd! But I am not deceived, Ambrosio! It is not virtue which makes you reject my offer: You *would* accept it, but you *dare* not.'[48]

In this scene, the profanity lies not in Matilda or her demonic master, but in Ambrosio's choice to turn away from God; to no longer participate in his own *telos*. The portrayal of a world in which the distinction of natural and supernatural collapses allows the experience of God to be part of the fabric of that world. And as shown in *The Monk*, the return of a supernatural God into the natural world is most acutely portrayed when the source of supernatural events are shown to be embedded in the self.

The character of Ambrosio demonstrates a tension between what Otto calls the compelling 'energy' of a 'living God', and Augustine's claim of man's instinctive perversion, his desire to turn towards his basest self. Such a tension is only resolved if God and being are understood to be the same. Otto accommodates this in his 'feeling' of the numinous, in which 'mysticism at the same time retains the *positive quality* of the "wholly other" as a very living factor in its over-brimming religious emotion'.[49] Man's perversion, then, is to turn away from 'life' and towards nihilism.

Of the authors discussed in these pages, Arthur Machen in particular is conscious of the nihilistic void as a human possibility, and is joined by M. R. James and Sheridan Le Fanu in turning to Christian orthodoxy as a spiritual safeguard against it. These authors anticipate the school of Radical Orthodoxy in their assertion that 'any alternative configuration perforce reserves a territory independent of God. The latter can only lead to nihilism.'[50] A world in which the supernatural remains beyond or other than the natural creates a space in which a supernatural God is necessarily absent. If, as argued by Augustine and later Aquinas, God is understood to be *the same as* being, then a space in which God is absent is nothingness. The protagonists of our ghost stories are confronted by visions of this space. By then collapsing a world in which 'natural' and 'supernatural' are delineated, however, these authors ultimately force their protagonists to participate in a world in which the natural is saturated by the supernatural, one which belies the counterfeit autonomy of a divided self.

The form of Christian orthodoxy represented in these works can best be understood by looking briefly at an early nineteenth-century movement which sought to restore the language of pre-Enlightenment mysticism to the Christian framework. Just as writers of the gothic novel such as Radcliffe and Lewis drew their language from Romanticism, it is from High-Church orthodoxy that Machen, M. R. James and Le Fanu draw their theological discourse. In the first quarter of the nineteenth century the Oxford Movement (so called because of its origins amongst members of the university) 'was one part of that great swing of opinion against Reason as the Age of Reason had understood it and used it'.⁵¹ Members of the Oxford Movement, worried that the evangelical language of Reformation Protestantism might lead Christians to forget the need for salvation through grace, wrote of a catholic Christianity which both embraced the Romantic language of mystical experience and reinforced the necessity of the Church in interpreting that language. The authority of the Church as protection against the fallen individual mind was indeed a foundation of the Oxford Movement. John Henry Newman (later Cardinal) writes of such a need with respect to the interpretation of Scripture in a lecture from 1849:

> I would not deny as an abstract proposition that a Christian may gain the whole truth from the Scriptures, but would maintain that the chances are very seriously against a given individual. I would not deny but rather maintain, that a religious, wise and intellectually gifted man will succeed: but who answers to this description but the collective Church? There, indeed, such qualifications might be supposed to exist; what is wanting in one member being supplied by another, and the contrary errors of individuals eliminated by their combination.⁵²

Certainly some of the writers considered in this project could be more obviously aligned with the Oxford Movement as a statement of Anglo-Catholic doctrine (Arthur Machen, for instance). For each of the authors, however, Victorian Anglo-Catholic theology provided a language through which the ghost story could be given a Christian framework. By recognising the need for fear and trembling in the experience of grace, yet containing this within the authority of Church tradition, such a framework turns the theological supernatural tale from a gothic experience of the numinous to a journey through the numinous into a Christian revelation of self.

Notes

1. Charles Taylor, *A Secular Age* (Cambridge, MA & London: Harvard University Press, 2007), 2.
2. It is this framework to which I refer when I occasionally rely on the more convenient term of 'secular reader'.
3. Taylor, *A Secular Age*, 381.
4. Northrop Frye, *Anatomy of Criticism* (Princeton, NJ: Princeton University Press, 1990), 50.
5. Frye, *Anatomy of Criticism*, 45.

6. Nicholas of Cusa, 'De Possest', §6sq.
7. William Desmond, *God and the Between* (Chennai, India: Blackwell, 2008), 197.
8. Desmond, *God and the Between*, 197.
9. Wilkie Collins, 'Mrs Zant and the Ghost', in *Little Novels* (New York: Dover Publications, 1977), 3.
10. Jürgen Habermas, 'An Awareness of what is Missing', in *An Awareness of What is Missing: Faith and Reason in a Post-Secular Age*, ed. Jürgen Habermas et al., trans. Ciaran Cronin (Cambridge and Malden MA: Polity Press, 2010), 16.
11. Jacques Derrida, 'The Time of a Thesis: Punctuations', in *Philosophy in France Today*, ed. Alan Montefiore, trans. Kathleen McLaughlin (Cambridge: Cambridge University Press, 1983), 45.
12. Collins, 'Mrs Zant', 12.
13. See Jürgen Habermas 'On Hermeneutics' Claim to Universality', in *The Hermeneutics Reader*, ed. Kurt Mueller-Vollmer (New York: Contiuum, 2002), 294–319; Paul Ricœur, *From Text to Action: Essays in Hermeneutics II* (London and New York: Contiuum, 1991), ch. 3.
14. Ricœur, *Text to Action*, 84.
15. Gerald L. Bruns, *Hermeneutics Ancient and Modern* (New Haven and London: Yale University Press, 1992), 149. Bruns uses this definition to describe Spinoza's reading of Scripture in *Tractatus Theologico-Philosophicus*.
16. Desmond, *God and the Between*, 21. I am unable here to do justice to Desmond's complex model of transcendences, although I will return to it in the concluding chapter. For more detail see *God and the Between*, p. 22sqq. and 'Being Philosophical: On Metaphysics as Metaxological', in *The William Desmond Reader*, ed. Christopher Ben Simpson (Albany NY: SUNY, 2012), 195–228.
17. John Milbank, *The Word Made Strange* (Cambridge MA: Blackwell, 1997), 111.
18. John Milbank, 'The End of Dialogue', in *Christian Uniqueness Reconsidered*, ed. Gavin D'Costa (Maryknoll NY: Orbis, 1996), 177sq., 189, 190.
19. Rowan Williams, 'The Finality of Christ', in *On Christian Theology* (Oxford: Blackwell, 2000), 100.
20. Collins, 'Mrs Zant', 1. For further discussion of Radical Orthodoxy as an either/or model, see John Milbank, 'The Theological Critique of Philosophy in Hamann and Jacobi', in *Radical Orthodoxy: a New Theology*, ed. John Milbank, Graham Ward and Catherine Pickstock (London: Routledge, 1999), 32.
21. Michel de Certeau, 'Walking in the City', in *The Certeau Reader*, ed. Graham Ward (Malden, MA: Blackwell, 2000), pp. 101–118. I am not only ascribing the appellation of 'reader' to the object of Certeau's essay, which he does not

do, but use it here specifically in terms of the literary scholar. However, I think that this is an appropriate use of Certeau's thesis.
22. Michel de Certeau, 'Is there a Language of Unity?' *Concilium*, 1 (1970): 73–93, 91.
23. M.M. Bakhtin, *Speech Genres and Other Late Essays*, ed. Carl Emerson and Michael Holquist, trans. Vern W. McGee (Austin TX: University of Texas Press, 1986), 7. Original emphasis.
24. Taylor, *Secular Age*, 38, 40. Title quotation: William Shakespeare, *Hamlet*, Act 2 scene 2.
25. While I prefer to identify a 'non-theological reader', Taylor's book makes explicit reference to the non-theological as secular, and so I use Taylor's term here.
26. For this conception of the in-between as excess I am indebted to the work of William Desmond. Desmond describes such a space as 'metaxological', an excess of being which goes beyond univocity, equivocity and dialectic, and in doing so fulfils the promise of each. See William Desmond, *Being and the Between* (Albany, NY: SUNY Press, 1995), and other works.
27. See Desmond, *God and the Between*, 123.
28. Grant Allen, 'Pallinghurst Barrow', *Ivan Greet's Masterpiece* (London: Chatto and Windus, 1893), 67–89, (83, 86).
29. Tzvetan Todorov, *The Fantastic: A Structural Approach to a Literary Genre*, trans. Richard Howard (Ithaca, NY: Cornell University Press, 1975), 25.
30. Paul Ricœur , *The Symbolism of Evil*, trans. Emerson Buchanan (Boston MA: Beacon, 1967), 5. See also 'The "Adamic" Myth and the Eschatological Vision of History', 232–278, and 'The Myth of the Exiled Soul and Salvation Through Knowledge', 279–246.
31. Allen, 'Pallinghurst Barrow', 82, 83–4. My emphasis.
32. May Sinclair, 'The Finding of the Absolute', in *Uncanny Stories* (Ware: Wordsworth, 2006), 163. While I use this story here to show the fullness of human actuality, it is worth noting that Sinclair's stories as a corpus offer a more ambivalent examination of the supernatural in light of Kantian and Hegelian models of knowledge. In his introduction to the Wordsworth edition of *Uncanny Stories*, Paul March Russell suggests that the redemptive image offered in this story may be 'designed to ameliorate the waste of human life that surfaces elsewhere in *Uncanny Stories*' (16). For Sinclair's engagement with German Idealism and Idealistic Monism see *A Defence of Idealism: Some Questions and Conclusions* (London and New York: Macmillan, 1917) and *The New Idealism* (London and New York: Macmillan, 1922).
33. Sinclair, 'The Finding of the Absolute', 176. See Augustine, *De Civ.*, XII. 23, on the image of God in man. Also *De Trin.*, XIV.4,6.
34. Robert Hugh Benson, 'The Watcher', in *The Light Invisible* (Falls Church VA: Universal Values Media, 2004), 8.

35. Benson, 'The Watcher', 9, 10.
36. Augustine, *De Civ*, XI.9, XII.7. See also Plotinus, *The Enneads*, I. viii. 2–3: 'If evil exist at all, it must be situate in the realm of non-being. By this non-being we are not to understand something that simply does not exist, but only something of an utterly different order from Authentic Being.' And Mark 7.15: 'There is nothing outside a person that by going in can defile, but the things that come out are what defile.'
37. To call the ghost-story demon 'impossible' demonstrates the very tension which a theological reading reveals. The demon is both impossible within the immanent frame of the Enlightened natural order, and lacking possibility, or *telos*. It is this lack of *telos* which so strongly reveals its inhumanity.
38. Karl Barth, *The Epistle to the Romans*, trans. Edwyn C. Hoskyns (Oxford: Oxford University Press, 1968), 253.
39. Søren Kierkegaard, *The Concept of Dread*, trans. Walter Lowrie (Princeton: Princeton University Press, 1946), 110. Original emphasis.
40. Kierkegaard, *The Concept of Dread*, 106.
41. Robert Louis Stevenson, Letter to J.A. Symonds, 1886, reprinted in *The Strange Case of Dr Jekyll and Mr Hyde*, ed. Martin A. Danahay (Plymouth: Broadview, 2005), 126.
42. S. L. Varnado, *Haunted Presence: The Numinous in Gothic Fiction* (Tuscaloosa AL: University of Alabama Press, 1987), 6.
43. Rudolf Otto, *The Idea of the Holy: An Inquiry into the Non-Rational Factor in the Idea of the Divine and its Relation to the Rational*, trans. John W. Harvey (London: Oxford University Press, 1950), 5.
44. Rudolf Otto, *The Philosophy of Religion*, trans. E. B. Dicker (New York: Richard R. Smith, 1931), 100–101.
45. Otto, *The Idea of the Holy*, 194.
46. See Mircea Eliade, *The Sacred and the Profane: The Nature of Religion*, trans. Willard R. Trask (New York: Harvest, 1968), pp. 9–10. Eliade, starting with Otto's premise, sets out to 'illustrate and define this opposition'. Notably for my discussion here, however, his study does not challenge this antipode.
47. Matthew Lewis, *The Monk: A Romance in Three Volumes, vol. 2* (London: J. Bell, 1796), vol. 3, 296.
48. Lewis, *The Monk, vol. 2*, 266–7.
49. Otto, *The Idea of the Holy*, 29.
50. The Editors, 'Introduction', in *Radical Orthodoxy: A New Theology*, ed. John Milbank, Graham Ward and Catherine Pickstock (London: Routledge, 1999), 3.
51. Owen Chadwick, *The Mind of the Oxford Movement* (Stanford, CA: Stanford University Press, 1960), 12.
52. John Henry Newman, *The Via Media of the Anglican Church: Illustrated in Lectures, Letters and Tracts Written between 1830 and 1841*, Vol. I (London, New York, Bombay: Longman, Greens & Co., 1901), 158.

CHAPTER 3

'Strangely mistaking death for life': Arthur Machen

Most efforts at critical scholarship of Arthur Machen's corpus of fiction are directed at biography, or heavily embedded in it. These show Machen to have been a man whose religious outlook was consistently Anglo-Catholic, and who sought, and later proclaimed, the mystery of human experience within the framework of Christian orthodoxy. Having produced weird tales in the 1890s which stylistically placed him among the Decadent writers of the period, his twentieth-century writing demonstrated an increasingly confident exposition of a sense of the world through Christian mysticism. Such a bibliography leads to a strange dichotomy in the critical scholarship of Machen's work. His philosophical and religious themes are seen as unchanging, indeed becoming repetitive. (Machen's most prolific critic S. T. Joshi, claims, not without reason, that *Hieroglyphics* provides us with all the background we need to understand Machen's work.[1]) Machen's weird tales of the 1890s, however, are nearly always read independently of his later works, seen as the product of a typical *fin de siècle* writer. Most readings claim that the stories reveal an authorial agnosticism which was only many years later replaced by orthodox belief.[2]

This chapter examines Machen's horror fiction with respect to his Anglo-Catholic orthodoxy, claiming that such a reading reveals these stories to be examinations of man's experience of the world which are theologically consistent with Machen's later work. Rather than simply bohemian, these stories adopt the tropes of Decadence in order to expose the spiritual nihilism of late-nineteenth-century materialist aesthetics.

The pervading sense of 'evil' in Machen's stories is one of absence—an absence of soul, an absence of teleological direction. The question which thus arises is: What is the nature of this absence? We shall see that Machen's mystical orthodoxy sheds light on this question by recognising evil as a privation of good, in which characters have lost a Christian understanding of human ontology. Machen admired Thomas Aquinas, and a Thomist understanding of natural and eternal law will reveal the consequences of this absence within Machen's weird tales. A reading of 'The White People' will examine *gifted* glimpses behind the veil and the corruptive influence on such glimpses by imperfect human nature. An examination of 'The Great God Pan' will resituate the 'evil' within the tale not in the figure of Pan, commonly read as a devil figure, but as something brought into existence by the characters through their experience of mystery with*out* an orthodox Christian framework. While Pan may not be the devil, the character of Helen is read here as representing a human being without humanity as understood in a Christological sense, and is thus shown to be an 'anti'-Christ. Finally, a reading of the stories and vignettes which make up *The Three Impostors* will explore Machen's use of Decadent motifs.

In his 1902 essay cum novella *Hieroglyphics*, Machen expounds his theory of true literature as an account of 'ecstasy'. Aesthetic achievement without this ecstatic sense of mystery has, to Machen, no intrinsic literary value. Turning again to Aquinas, *The Three Impostors* is shown to be an example of this theory when given moral consequence. The *absolute* aestheticism portrayed in *The Three Impostors* is the cauldron for evil because it is an aesthetic construct of mystery without a theist understanding of the self in respect to that mystery. Without a Christian humanist framework, Machen's characters participate and create in a way absent of a supernatural teleology. Instead, then, of participating in the 'great sacrament of nature', they partake, in one form or another, of symbolic *Vinum Sabbati*. Machen describes this as the wine used in an ancient evil rite, in which men and women were seduced by 'beings well qualified to assume, as they did assume, the part of devils' to partake of a witches' Sabbath:

> By the power of that Sabbath wine, [...] the house of life was risen asunder and the human trinity dissolved, and the worm which never dies, that which lies sleeping within us all, was made tangible and an external thing, and clothed with a garment of flesh.[3]

This chapter will examine the ways in which Machen's characters are drawn to drink this *Vinum Sabbati*, and what such a process reveals about the paradoxical nature of fallen man.

ANGLO-CATHOLICISM AND ARTHUR MACHEN'S SENSE OF MYSTERY

Arthur Machen's corpus of both fiction and non-fiction is a portrait of his lifelong attempt to give voice to a feeling of communion with the natural world; a feeling which gives man his sense of himself as created being:

> I look back to the time when the mountain and the tiny shining stone, the flower, and the brook were all alike signs and evidences of an ineffable mystery and beauty. I see myself all alone in the valley, under hanging woods, of a still summer evening, entranced, wondering what the secret was that was here almost told, and then, I am persuaded, I came near to the spirit of St. Thomas Aquinas: *Adoro te devote latens Deitas*.[4]

An Anglo-Catholic, Machen remained suspicious of the Roman Church, and never converted (as the like-minded Chesterton did), but his catholic outlook goes to the crux of Machen's view of the world as one great sacrament, in which we know God as he is seen in the mirror of his creatures.[5] Machen's attention to the sacramental universe is indicative of a revival of interest in natural revelation in late Victorian Catholic theology. Following Vatican I and later Pope Leo XIII's appeal to the works of Aquinas in his *Aeterni Patris* of 1879, writers and artists also turned to such sacramentalism to affirm the presence of the incarnation in nature.[6] Gerard Manley Hopkins, for instance, sought in his poetry to reinstate an experience of nature which was specifically Christian. For Hopkins, such sacramentalism was more than simply the divine reflected in nature, but the incarnation renewed. Such an incarnation is seen in the nun's experience of a storm at sea in 'The Wreck of the Deutschland', in which Christ becomes present to her in the storm:

> But how shall I ... make me room there:
> Reach me a ... Fancy, come faster—
> Strike you the sight of it? look at it loom there,
> Thing that she ... there then! the Master,
> Ipse, the only one, Christ, King, Head.[7]

This sacramental understanding stands in contrast to the established views of Broad-Church Anglicans, who were ambivalent or even hostile towards the idea of external 'evidence' of God's hand.[8] Machen followed St Augustine's description of the miracle of God's mystery as visible through the everyday, even amongst the hustle and bustle of the streets of London. Machen writes: 'It is the attitude of primitive man, of the real man, of the child, always and everywhere; it may be briefly summed up in the phrase: things are because they are wonderful.'[9] For Machen, Christianity had the power to reveal to man, or rather remind him of, his communion and participation in this sacrament through forms of ritual which reflected this sense of magic and mystery.

Machen expresses this nicely in a later short story from 1927, 'The Gift of Tongues', in which a supposed miracle occurs in a small Welsh chapel, where the preacher speaks in tongues, and believes himself to have 'been in Heaven before the Throne'. It turns out that the preacher is unknowingly performing the Latin Mass, but in Machen's story the sense of miracle is not diminished: 'Who is to say that the old preacher had not strayed long before into some Roman Catholic Church at Newport or Cardiff on a Christmas Day, and there heard Mass with an exterior horror but interior love?'[10] In contrast, however, religion also has the power to reduce mystery to something mundane. Such was the danger of reformed Christian practice which attempted to make worship more recognisable as part of everyday life. In a letter to A. E. Waite, Machen writes: 'The most holy and interior Truths or Mysteries, being uttered or formulated, *ipso facto*, become foolish and soul-poisoning Heresies.'[11]

What many Victorians saw as the progress of mankind, both in enlightenment philosophy and empirical science, was for Machen in many ways an extension of this religious reductionism. The modern world signified a wall between man and the created world, and this was true both of life and art. Just as the minutiae of modern life could draw a veil across the mystery of the world, so too did writing which sought realist interpretation, serving to destroy any sense of wonder. To Machen, this was the crucial difference between art and artifice, and nothing represented this more than Modernism:

> As to Modernism, I abhor and abjure it utterly: to me it is not only heterodox but silly. I think if you were to look through my *Academy* articles you would collect a very strong insistence on the necessity of orthodox belief. I believe I once defined Modernism as atheism in a chasuble.[12]

Modernist theology, represented in Catholicism by the likes of Loisy, Tyrrell and Blondel, stressed the principle of immanence, an internal 'antenna' which placed human experience as the basis for recognition of the divine. This was a challenge to Catholic apologetics in that it suggested the possibility of divine revelation through reason alone. This, at least, is how Pope Pius X saw it in *Pascendi Domini Gregis*, in which he accused the Modernists of agnosticism and moral relativism. To Modernists, however, the internal experience revitalised thinking about God and reconciled it with contemporary intellectual and scientific pursuit.[13] To Machen such a philosophy, by employing a Kantian view of human reason, resituates at the centre not Christ, but mankind.

It is important to understand exactly what Modernism meant to Machen, and the features which led him to see Modernist thinking as something essentially heretical. To Machen, beyond the societal trends of empiricism, scepticism and 'rationalism', Modernism as he understood it was a mode of thinking in which revelation was something closer akin to personal development than something numinous. Machen writes: 'there are, speaking very generally, two solutions of existence; one is the materialistic or rationalistic, the other, the spiritual or mystic'.[14] As Machen understood the rational or 'Modernist' philosophy, it reduced all religion and art to 'a vast conjuring trick'. 'This is called the scientific standpoint' writes Machen, 'and it owes its name, no doubt, to its utter lack of *scientia*, properly so called.' This Modernist philosophy had two sets of implications. The first was to the practice of Christianity itself, in which, by distancing itself from ritual as symbol, Protestant Christianity and Anglicanism in particular was at risk of becoming meaningless. The 'Modernist' movement within Catholicism was first branded by Pope Pius X in 1907, and it is from Pius that Machen most probably derived his use of the term in his 1908 article 'Modernism', in which he warns of its dangers:

> I am not surprised to find that Modernism has been defined as 'the heresy which contains all the heresies and errors of the past;' indeed, one could find no better definition than this; no better phrase to summarise that impulse in men which continually surges up, declaring in very various idioms that there is no world of vision and wonder, that there is but earth and humanity, and that we have got to make the best of both. This is, indeed, the heresy of all heresies, masquerading sometimes under the most curious disguises, putting on now and again the vestments of the 'occult' sciences, but always constant to the one idea, that man is the master and measure of all things. 'Ye shall be as gods, knowing good and evil;' as in the Garden, so in the modern world, in the world of Modernism.[15]

While the terminology may be early twentieth century, however, this concern—the fear of a principle which places man, not God, at its centre—is prevalent throughout Machen's 1890s weird fiction, no more so than in *The Three Impostors*, as shall be seen.

Machen laid out his philosophy of ecstasy in *Hieroglyphics* in 1902, and here he intertwines the spiritual experience with artistic pursuit, defining art as a gateway, if an inadequate one, to the numinous. When art extends beyond mere artifice, 'then no mere making of likeness of the external shape will be our art, [...] but to us, initiated, the Symbol will be offered, and we shall take the Sign and adore [...] the very Presence and eternal indwelling of God'.[16] Here Machen follows Coleridge's concept of symbol as artistic expression which is not simply metaphor or allegory, but as something which *participates* in that which it (re)presents. It is in this way that Machen distinguishes 'art' from 'artifice', art being an expression of truth through symbol, and thus inextricably Christian.[17]

If writing as an art is an attempt (if not complete) to express the ecstatic experience of the world as sacrament, then modern realist writing, the attempt to reproduce a recognisable version of the world in artistic form, in Machen's view, does the opposite. 'The artificer seldom or never understands the ends and designs and spirit of the artist.'[18] This distinction between art and artifice will be shown to be of vital significance in the reading of *The Three Impostors* below. Here, the consequences of artifice are shown to be more than simply artistic failure. In this collection of tales, artifice becomes a means through which man's creative power is so corrupted as to become the arbiter of evil.

This distinction between art and artifice is shown by Machen to be symptomatic of a precarious line which runs between 'ecstasy' and evil. Machen's weird tales show the numinous to run a troubled path between these, in which the world so easily is tipped from 'a great ceremony' to 'the black and shadowy valley', and the Fall is repeated. Sometimes Machen's characters fall as a result of taking the forbidden fruit of knowledge, but sometimes it seems almost an accident, a misguided step. This perilous line walked by Machen's characters is a line designated by human nature, in which 'man is subject to the fascination of destruction'.[19] Machen makes the analogy of a moth to a flame, rejecting the claim that the moth mistakes the flame for daylight:

> The only light which attracts the moth is one of destruction and death; it does not desire the star or the sun, but only the candle-flame. [...] The moth

and the candle are to me a mystery, since the creature seems to be acting in direct opposition to the whole course of Nature. [...] Whatever the solution of the enigma may be, it is interesting to note the parallel between the moth and the man. Both the one and the other suffer from the fascination of death and destruction. [...] Is it not within the bounds of possibility that it [the moth] and the other creatures who seek their own destruction in such (apparently) aimless fashion are in reality displaying one of the greatest of all human qualities in its rude and primitive condition, in its inchoate state?[20]

Here Machen sets down his view of human nature as something incomplete, lacking. As shall be seen, this incomplete state, or rather fallen state, becomes the door through which Machen's characters pass through into evil.

Machen's 'mystic' writing is sometimes argued to be that of a man whose Christian apologetics is convinced to the point of banality.[21] This is a woefully simplistic understanding of Machen's writing, in which his numinous account of the mystic experience is anything but simple, as evidenced in Lucian's spiritual confusion in *The Hill of Dreams* or the enigmatic conclusion to 'A Fragment of Life'. Rather, the mystic experience is something moulded and framed by the complexities of human nature. As something at once holy and fallen, man's nature is paradoxical, and so too becomes the supernatural experience. It is Machen's horror fiction which most clearly reveals this paradox.

Despite Machen's repeated exploration of the mystic experience in his writing, he saw it as something ultimately ineffable. Throughout Machen's fiction, his characters experience non-verbal communion with the natural world, which we as readers understand has been something transcendental, but which they are later unable to verbally express. Ultimately, only Christian orthodoxy provides a framework through which man's experience and his need to express it can be reconciled, a version of Christianity untempered by protestant puritanism or the 'elaborate blasphemy' of low-Church Anglicanism.[22] In *Dr Stiggins* (1906), Machen's exasperation with non-conformism comes out in a scathing caricature of a non-conformist preacher. While it may be an illuminating example of Machen's outlook, however, *Dr Stiggins* is clumsy as a text, with little or no theological engagement. Machen's horror fiction of the 1890s, by contrast, provides a subtle and much darker expression of the demonic consequences of the *mysterium tremendum* when not experienced through the clarifying lens of orthodoxy. In these stories, the characters have become divorced from God; their Victorian materialism and Enlightenment philosophy have created a hermeneutical vacuum which becomes a catalyst for evil. For Machen's characters lost in a materialist aesthetic, 'the primal fall was repeated and re-presented, and the awful thing veiled in the mythos of the Tree in the garden was done anew'.[23] In his horror fiction, Machen grotesquely dramatises the seminal apologetics of Augustine and Aquinas with a complexity which he himself struggled to express in his later apologetic works. The three textual analyses below of 'The White People', 'The Great God Pan' and *The Three Impostors* look for the apologetics of Augustine and Aquinas reflected in Machen's horror fiction in an attempt to demonstrate a theological consistency which spans Machen's writing career.[24]

Machen's Thomist Anthropology

By using Thomist concepts of virtue and law to describe Machen's weird tales, they are shown to be rooted in a theological anthropology. Aquinas lived from around 1225 to 1274, and is referred to as 'St Thomas' or 'Aquinas', giving rise to the term 'Thomist' for theologians and schools of thought which follow Aquinas. In his *Summa Theologicae*, a multi-volume tome designed as an introduction to theology, Aquinas considers virtue as 'good habit', which once in place necessarily leads us to act towards the good. He writes: 'Virtue is a good quality of the mind, by which we live righteously, of which no one can make bad use, which God works in us, without us.'[25] The more our good habit, or *habitus*, is ingrained or developed, the closer to God we are, as God need make no effort to be good, God and goodness being one and the same. Aquinas follows St Augustine in seeing the Fall as the reason for human moral struggles. Because of the Fall, we have choice to do good or bad, rather than simply 'inhabiting' good, and acting as a result of that habit.

Aquinas deals with eternal, natural and human law in *Summa* 1a2ae q.90-97, although the use of the term 'law' can be deceptive, suggesting something judicial. Rather, Aquinas' laws are concerned with creation and God's conception of it. Aquinas' 'eternal law' is essentially the plan of God in creation:

> Just as in every artificer there pre-exists a type of the things that are made by his art, so too in every governor there must pre-exist the type of the order of those things that are to be done by those who are subject to his government. And just as the type of the things yet to be made by an art is called the art or

exemplar of the products of that art, so too the type in him who governs the acts of his subjects, bears the character of a law, provided the other conditions be present which we have mentioned above.[26]

God is the exemplary 'template' of all things in creation, and the more a thing 'participates' in this template, the more complete it is. Natural law, then, is a way of being which participates in this eternal law.

To modern Thomists, the modern language of moral reason and practice as objective has led us to forget the *context* of morality which makes moral concepts understandable.[27] These concepts were once understood within the context of the community of the Church, and were mediated through the Christian story. The consequence of this is that ethics is not concerned simply with what to do in a 'moral quandary', but in understanding the type of character behind the action. The Church is the community through which we are taught the habits and practices which Aquinas describes as 'virtue'.[28]

As is seen in Machen's three stories 'The White People', 'The Great God Pan' and *The Three Impostors*, Aquinas' descriptions of natural and eternal law not only reinforce the fallen state of human beings, but give us the context through which the 'evil' of Machen's characters is given meaning. Central to Machen's anxiety is the modern Thomist concern for a society divorced from the Church as the fundamental nurturer of human character.

'THE WHITE PEOPLE'

Having finished *Hieroglyphics* in 1899, Machen started work on a tale which would continue the ideas found in *Hieroglyphics*.[29] This work would later be published as three separate pieces: 'The White People', 'A Fragment of Life' and *The Secret Glory*. 'The White People' tells the story of a young girl, presented in the form of her own journal entries. The story is framed by a prologue and epilogue, in which a character, Ambrose, presents the journal of the young girl, 'the green book', as a manuscript, in which she records her experiences of a seemingly supernatural world in the woods and hills surrounding her house. The girl describes trips made into the woods which involve allusions to seemingly pagan activities. Her experiences of the rocks and trees are described in distinctly psychedelic terms. These accounts are intertwined with folklore and stories of witchcraft told to the girl by her nurse, and the accounts become increasingly confused as the journal progresses.

Machen's biographers Reynolds and Charlton see a discordance in both the style and content of 'The White People' with the other two pieces, so much so that 'it is hard to believe that the background to all three was the same period of [Machen's] life. [...] Their disparity is a good index to their author's shattered state of mind'.[30] Although the reading offered in this chapter argues instead for a theological consistency with both *A Fragment of Life* and *The Secret Glory*, 'The White People' is perhaps the most paradoxical and theologically complicated of Machen's weird tales. It is telling that 'The White People' utilises a narrative which places it as an early example of stream of consciousness writing. The use of a heterodox style here is perhaps a reflection of the fractured nature of the narrative. The girl adopts a 'faulty' narrative style as she attempts her 'faulty' reconstructive recollections.

The contradictory nature of 'The White People' shows the numinous to be something paradoxical. Ambrose's prologue contextualises the journal in terms recognisable as natural law as described by Aquinas. It is crucial to Ambrose's conception of sin that it is not so much the description of an action, but of *who one is*. Actions need to be judged in respect of their accordance with the nature of the actor:

> What would your feelings be, seriously, if your cat or your dog began to talk to you, and to dispute with you in human accents? You would be overwhelmed with horror. I am sure of it. And if the roses in your garden sang a weird song, you would go mad.[31]

As human beings, Ambrose argues, our actions become sinful when we fail to keep to the limits of our given nature, our nature being 'the essence of a thing insofar as it is ordered to the thing's proper activity'.[32] By extension, Ambrose is suggesting that the girl's narrative is sinful. This suggestion sits uneasily with the journal narrative that follows it, which, while disturbing, is also suffused with a sense of innocence, as well as a sense of mysticism. Ambrose goes on to describe the 'sinner' and the 'saint', and while his purpose is to cleave a sharp distinction between the two, it in fact goes some way towards describing the paradox within the girl's narrative:

> 'There is something profoundly unnatural about Sin? Is that what you mean?'
> 'Exactly. Holiness requires as great, or almost as great, an effort; but holiness works on lines that were natural once; it is an effort to recover the ecstasy that was before the Fall. But sin is an effort to gain the ecstasy and

the knowledge that pertain alone to angels and in making this effort man becomes a demon.'[33]

A close reading of the girl's journal entries reveal them to have something of each of these. In her rambling account of her trips to the hills, the girl's record of her experiences seems often to be describing something entirely natural (in the Thomist sense), using classic mystic motifs. Other times (and often these are interfused in the narrative) her response seems to suggest something very dark, indeed her response itself contains a dark quality which is uncanny in a childish narrative. The girl seems to find it difficult herself to reconcile her experiences, if not during them, then afterwards, as she attempts to recollect and recount them:

> And all alone on the hill I wondered what was true. I had seen something very amazing and very lovely, and I knew a story, and if I had really seen it, and not made it up out of the dark, and the black bough, and the bright shining that was mounting up to the sky from over the great round hill, but had really seen it in truth, then there were all kinds of wonderful and lovely and terrible things to think of, so I longed and trembled, and I burned and got cold. And I looked down on the town, so quiet and still, like a little white picture, and I thought over and over if it could be true.[34]

Amongst this confusion, nonetheless, many of the girl's accounts could be read as classic mystical experiences. She writes of a 'truth'; of something unchanged and unchanging which has nonetheless changed her. It is only afterwards, as the girl absorbs folk tales and memories of darker magic into her recollections that these experiences take on the tone of something more sinister. Indeed, it could be said that it is a much more 'human' influence (in particular her nurse) which has this corruptive effect. The theological implications of this relationship between childish innocence and corruption will be further explored below.

Firstly, however, it is worth returning to Ambrose's prologue, and the incongruity of his sharp distinction between sin and sinner, and saint, against the confused and paradoxical narrative of the girl. The answer, arguably, is that Ambrose presents a deliberate (on Machen's part) misreading of Aquinas which serves ultimately to highlight and frame the much more complex theological basis of the story itself. Two aspects of Aquinas' work are important here: his Aristotelian concept of potency and act, and his arguments on the knowledge of humans and angels, more specifically knowledge from the senses and knowledge from the intellect. Aquinas' system is based fundamentally upon his conception of the soul as being on a scale which runs from 'potency' to 'act'. God, being perfect and complete, is pure act. As human beings, we are on a teleological journey on which we develop the potential of what is *within our nature* towards act, ergo, towards God. While Ambrose talks of 'the knowledge of angels' as something forbidden to man, for Aquinas human knowledge can be understood in terms of this scale. Aquinas does differentiate between 'types' of knowledge, describing the knowledge of the senses, which is earthy, primitive and fitting that of animals, and intellectual knowledge, which unlike the passive senses, actively abstracts knowledge by building mental images. Through the intellect, the mind can thus understand immaterial things. These intelligences, however, differ from one another primarily by where they are on the grade of potency and act. While the angels, according to Aquinas, have pure intellect, the knowledge of the human soul is at the lowest end of potency, being partly through the senses and partly through the intellect.[35]

The teleological striving towards an intellect closer to that of the angels is thus *natural* to the human soul, and it is difficult to see at which point this would, as Ambrose suggests, become sinful. It may be that the problem lies in the way in which knowledge is sought. If the purpose of action is not to develop the human intellect, but to attain a different *nature* of intellect, then that action would no longer be in keeping with a Thomist understanding of natural law as he describes it in *Summa*:

> Experience can be attributed to the angels through a likeness of things known, not by a likeness of the knowing power. [...] Similarly it should be said that evil phantasy is attributed to the demons because they have a false practical estimate of the true good, and deception in us is properly due to phantasms thanks to which we sometimes adhere to the likeness of things as if they were the things themselves.[36]

Perhaps this is what Ambrose means when he claims that the sinner repeats the Fall, the serpent having promised Eve that she would become like God having eaten from the tree of knowledge. The natural orientation of the soul is towards God, but the line between moving towards God and overstepping one's nature is a fine one. The acceptance of and subjection to the fact that man, being a mixture of potency and act, cannot become pure act, and thus 'become like' God is, paradoxically, that which leads in the mystical tradition to flashes of exactly this knowledge, namely, through grace. The true mystical experience is one not sought, but given. This differentiation is crucial to Machen's portrayal of the attainment of spiritual knowledge, and nowhere is this more subtly envisaged than in 'The White People'.[37]

An understanding of knowledge in Thomist terms allows us to see 'The White People' as an exploration of knowledge as grace, and of knowledge corrupted. Machen's stories are full of scientists and aesthetic materialists who ignore or break natural law in their pursuit of knowledge, but 'The White People' is the story of a child, of whom Machen claims 'that in the world of imagination the child is indeed father of the man'.[38] It is for this reason that 'The White People' offers such a nuanced and complex exploration of mystical or supernatural experience. The narrator of the green book describes her experiences in two ways. The first type are primary and immediate, and these experiences demonstrate many of the modes and much of the symbolism of Christian mystic experience. The girl's communion with the natural world is very much an expression of what Machen calls 'the great sacrament of nature'.[39] An example of this is seen when the girl drinks from a brook, which while the scene is imbued with Romantic tropes (she imagines the touch of the water as the kiss of a nymph), the symbolism is not simply pagan, as some readings have suggested, but deeply Christian. The water seems in some way blessed, and the girl is inspired to think of the phrase 'for ever and ever, world without end, Amen'. The girl likewise expresses the sense of awe and terror not in terms of horror, but in terms of the *mysterium tremendum*: 'And there I saw the most wonderful sight I have ever seen, but it was only for a minute, as I ran away directly, […] because I was afraid, what I had seen was so wonderful and so strange and beautiful.'[40]

That the narrative is that of a child goes a long way in confirming Machen's complex intentions behind this story. In his autobiography he expands his position on childhood:

> I believe that as a child, I realised something of the spirit of the mystic injunction. Everywhere, through the darkness and the mists of the childish understanding, and yet by the light of the child's illumination, I saw *latens deitas*; the whole earth, down to the very pebbles, was but the veil of a quickening and adorable mystery.[41]

It is worth further exploring the theological implications of the girl's childishness in order to reveal the point at which the mysticism of 'The White People' tips over into horror.

In his article 'Fictioning Things', John Milbank explores the significance of childhood within a Christian narrative, a tradition in which 'there is a privileging [...] of the innocent eye'. Milbank does not equate childish innocence with Adamic innocence, but nonetheless argues that 'there is a real powerful echo of Eden' in the beginning of childhood wonder.[42] This echo can be heard in many of the girl's experiences, even in her consciousness of the Christian narrative as something immediate and unreflexive, an absorption of knowledge which she recognises as 'Truth':

> I had remembered the story I had quite forgotten before, and in the story the two figures are called Adam and Eve, and only those who know the story understand what they mean.[43]

How then, does the green book come to be a tale of horror? What is the nature of evil in the tale, or as Ambrose calls it, sin? The answer lies in just this childish innocence and the very human distortion of her experience into something corrupted. This concept of corruption fits the Augustinian (and Thomist) view of original sin as a habitual tendency, and evil as a deviation from good, from man's natural inclination towards God.

This corruptive process comes not only through the girl's own habitual tendency, however (although this is certainly suggested), but rather by the intrusion of human practice and a very 'human' interpretative lens. In terms of human practice, this intrusion is most obviously seen in the shadowy character of the nurse, who introduces to the girl's narrative a more concrete and worldly sense of 'sin'. As the girl recollects an event from early childhood in which she visits the woods with her nurse and is briefly left alone under the shade of a tree, the memory becomes entwined with dreams of two 'wonderful white people'.[44] To the reader, however, it is clear that the nurse has come to meet a lover. I am hesitant to place too much significance on this act as an example of 'sin', as Machen describes sexual acts elsewhere in his corpus, and rarely are they presented as sinful. Other than the obvious sexual 'sin', it is important that the nurse uses 'supernatural' and quasi-religious concepts with which to secure the child's silence, threatening that if she tells anybody of the meeting, she will 'be thrown into the black pit'.[45] The narrative immediately jumps from this scene to the girl's 'adventures' at the age of thirteen onwards, and from this point, a pattern emerges in which the girl initially describes experiences in classic mystical terms, but these experiences become corrupted and tainted as she attempts to recollect them. This corruption is nearly always due to the fact that the girl is recollecting her experiences through the interpretive lens of folk tales and quasi-religious ideas told to her by the nurse:

> I wanted to think of what I had seen but I couldn't, and I began to think of all the tales that nurse had told me so long ago that I thought I had forgotten, but they all came back, and mixed up with the thickets and the grey rocks and the hollows in the earth and the secret wood, till I hardly knew what was new and what was old, or whether it was not all dreaming.[46]

In this way the contrast is established between the innocent communion with 'the great sacrament' and the distortion of quasi-religious (both pagan and Christian) legend, in which quasi-mystical figures are punished and 'taken away', and grace seems very much absent. To the girl, her own experiences become irrevocably confused with the nurse's tales, until she believes that 'Nurse must have been a prophet like those we read of in the Bible.'[47]

The nurse also shows the girl what seem to be pagan rituals, in which knowledge of these rituals is used as power, or rather to create or harness power. Some of these rituals are told by the nurse as folk-legends, such as 'an old game' involving dancing and weaving of grass, 'and when one had danced [...] whatever you are told to do you feel you have to do it'. Others are practised and taught to the girl, such as the making of dolls out of clay. It is notable that the girl later goes on to make these dolls on her own, although she does 'much more than [the nurse] did, because it was the likeness of something far better'.[48] Set alongside the girl's passive and subjugative experiences while alone, these scenes become notable in their spiritual emptiness. For instance, the girl remembers the nurse showing her how to move objects, and the narrative recalls this in language more suited to the description of a Victorian parlour trick:

> Nurse said she would show me something funny that would make me laugh, and then she showed me, as she said, how one could turn a whole house upside down, without anybody being able to find out, and the pots and pans would jump about, and the china would be broken, and the chairs would tumble over of themselves. I tried it one day in the kitchen, and I found I could do it quite well, and a whole row of plates on the dresser fell off it,

and cook's little work-table tilted up and turned right over 'before her eyes,' as she said, but she was so frightened and turned so white that I didn't do it again, as I liked her. And afterwards, in the hazel copse, when she had shown me how to make things tumble about, she showed me how to make rapping noises, and I learnt how to do that, too.[49]

Nonetheless the influence of these events embed themselves into the girl's interpretative process of her own experiences: 'And these were all the things I was thinking about in those days after the strange walk when I thought I had seen a great secret.' As the girl's recollections become increasingly indistinguishable from each other, her childish mysticism and resulting glimpses of 'Truth' are lost amongst black magic and quasi-religion. The girl has no orthodox Christian framework through which to interpret and narrate her experiences, and thus as the story concludes 'she had poisoned herself', and, perhaps inevitably, is found dead.

In Machen's other weird tales, the horror is mostly wrought by a complete teleological nihilism in his characters. In 'The White People', however, Machen demonstrates the complex and paradoxical nature of the human condition. In the childish innocence of the girl we see in human beings the natural inclination towards God, and in the corruption of her experiences we are reminded of man as nevertheless fallen, and of how easily that inclination is misguided by the imperfection of the soul. Ambrose describes real evil (as opposed to a 'bad' act) as something 'wholly positive—only it is on the wrong side'.[50] To him, this Kantian view of evil as radical is demonstrated by the 'unnatural' account of the girl. The visions and experiences recorded in the green book are for Ambrose *wrong*, not in a practical moral sense, but ontologically wrong: 'One might say, perhaps, that the picture in her mind which she succeeded in a measure in putting into words, was the scene as it would have appeared to an imaginative artist. But it is a strange, desolate land.'[51] While the 'desolate land' described by Ambrose is seen below to be more than fitting for the imaginations of many of Machen's characters, its place in the epilogue to 'The White People' is strangely uncomfortable. Rather than commit a crime against natural law, 'the taking of heaven by storm', the green book reveals the breadth and depth of human nature in its place as a created being. Intellectual knowledge of God and communion with nature as sacrament are shown to be *potentially* natural, and possible through moments of gifted vision, but the paradoxical nature of man as both innocent and fallen is shown in the corruption of these experiences. Machen's Thomist understanding of human ontology seeks ultimately to demonstrate not only the need for a childlike innocence with which to encounter the 'great sacrament', but an orthodox Christian narrative through which to recollect and interpret it. Without this, such experiences must inevitably be distorted and corrupted to the point of spiritual destruction.

MAN WITHOUT CHRIST IN 'THE GREAT GOD PAN'

In the opening chapter of 'The Great God Pan', Dr Raymond, a self-proclaimed practitioner of 'transcendental medicine', performs an operation on the brain of a young woman which will supposedly allow her to see 'the great god pan'.[52] Raymond claims to have discovered a part of the brain in which he can potentially bridge the 'unthinkable gulf that yawns profound between two worlds, the world of matter and the world of spirit'. For the woman (or rather girl; she is only 17), Mary, any vision of the 'other side' is short lived: a brief look of 'great wonder' on her face is rapidly replaced by one of 'the most awful terror', and she is left a 'vacant idiot' (to use Raymond's words).[53] In creating this bridge, however, Raymond opens something of a Pandora's box, and in the offspring of this event (a child, Helen, born nine months later to the woman), an evil is unleashed on the world in human form. The character of Helen and the subsequent destruction which follows her suggests Helen as a 'spawn of the devil' (Pan), or a demonic Lillith figure. Such a reading is fairly easily reached, and follows a common motif in horror fiction. The bumbling scientist naively opens a gateway to hell, and the devil in his various guises proceeds through it, wreaking havoc and horror. Such a reading, however, misses an opportunity to unpack the complex Augustinian and Thomist examination of the nature of evil which Machen offers in 'The Great God Pan' (henceforth 'Pan'). A reading which accepts the god Pan as an autonomous devil figure shifts the locus of Helen's very existence to a self-propagating, autonomous evil.[54] This approach, however, detracts from the real significance of Helen as an *embodiment* of evil. The reading offered here relocates the *causal* understanding of evil in 'Pan' in Thomist terms of negation and privation, thus revealing Helen to be paradoxically something embodied, something which has effect, and at once representative of negation. Helen is not an Antichrist, but 'anti'-Christ; an absence; a nothingness.

This absence, however, has power. The result of Helen's influence in London society is a string of suicides by men who have come into contact with her. Helen is not simply a shadowy sense of unease. As Machen's 'detectives', Clarke and Villiers, slowly piece together Helen's story, her evil is revealed to be very real and very dangerous. As Villiers declares: 'Those who are wise know that all symbols are symbols of something, not of nothing.'[55] An examination of Helen which understands her evil embodiment in a Thomist sense, must then tackle this seeming discrepancy of evil as something both negative and positive.

An important distinction in such an examination is that between evil of action and evil of being, a distinction which Machen explores in 'The White People' as discussed above. 'Pan' explicitly focuses on evil as being, as evidenced in the 'creation' of Helen in chapter 2. This first chapter was originally published in 1890 as a self-contained short story, and it is worthwhile examining the chapter in detail here. Although Helen's provenance is only revealed at the end of the story, the experiment in which she is 'conceived' by her mother Mary and apparently, Pan, takes place in this first chapter. After this perverse recreation of the Virgin Birth, the evil acts which Helen goes on to perpetrate, while *positive*, in that they have palpable effect (suicide), are *negative* in that they are the antithesis of Christ's gifts of grace and healing. Helen's effect is one of removal, or privation. The men who come into contact with her are shocking to others in their spiritual desolation. Herbert (a victim) tells Villiers that Helen has 'corrupted [his] soul', and when Villiers comes across Crashaw (another victim), 'I knew I had looked into the eyes of a lost soul, Austin, the man's outward form remained, but all hell was within it'.[56]

This reversal can be traced back to the experiment in chapter 2. Helen is created through the god-mimicking behaviour of Raymond, but this conception is absent of the grace of divine-creation. In *On the Trinity*, Augustine describes God's creative process in terms of 'seminal reasons', in which everything comes about according to its nature:

> For it is one thing to make and administer the creature from the innermost and highest turning-point of causation, which He alone does who is God the Creator; but quite another thing to apply some operation from without in proportion to the strength and faculties assigned to each by Him, so that what is created may come forth into being at this time or at that, and in this or that way. For all these things in the way of original and beginning have already been created in a kind of texture of the elements, but they come forth when they get the opportunity.[57]

Through his experiment, Raymond has inadvertently corrupted the natural laws of creation. He has positioned himself as god-creator, evidenced in his attitude to the experiment, such as his view of Mary: 'I think her life is mine, to use as I see fit', and his failure to understand insights passed down from his mentors: 'You see that parchment Oswald Crollius? He was one of the first to show me the way, though I don't think he ever found it himself. That is a strange saying of his: "In every grain of wheat there lies hidden the soul of a star."'[58] Raymond refuses to acknowledge that God as creator is to be found, or more importantly sought, in everything. Thus Helen's conception becomes a paradox of creation and absence. Helen has human form, but without *humanity*. The Thomist theologian Jacques Maritain could almost have had Raymond's experiment in mind when he examines the Gospel words: 'Without Me you can do nothing.' (John 15.5) Maritain turns this phrase around to elucidate the paradoxical nature of evil as both negative and positive. He explains:

> 'Without Me you can do nothing,' means: Without Me you can not commit the slightest act in which there is being or goodness,—so much for the line of good; but if it concerns the line of evil, then the text should be otherwise interpreted, doing violence to the grammar: '*sine Me potenstis facere nihil,*' without Me you can do nothingness, without Me you can introduce into action and being the nothingness which wounds them and constitutes evil.[59]

Without God's divine creative imput, nothingness has been given form, 'unspeakable elements enthroned, as it were, and triumphant in human flesh'.[60] It is this absence of Christological humanity which Machen's characters interpret as demonic, Clarke ending his account of Helen with: 'ET DIABULUS INCARNATUS EST. ET HOMO FACTUS EST.'[61] Helen is form without Life, as understood Christologically, Jesus having said 'I am the way, and the truth, and the life' (John 14.6). This juxtaposition of being and non-being comes full circle at Helen's death by her own suicide, as recorded amongst the papers of Robert Mattheson, a doctor who appears to have been present. Mattheson at first describes the physical mutations of Helen's body as it begins to melt and dissolve in a way which contradicts his medical understanding of the human body:

> Then I saw the body descend to the beasts whence it ascended, and that which was on the heights go down to the depths, even to the abyss of all being. The principle of life, which makes organism, always remained, while the outward form changed.

This 'principle of life', however, is swiftly overshadowed by Mattheson's awareness of absence or negation in the scene:

> The light within the room had turned to blackness, not the darkness of night, in which objects are seen dimly, for I could see clearly and without difficulty. But it was the negation of light; objects were presented to my eyes, if I may say so, without any medium, in such a manner that if there had been a prism in the room I should have seen no colours represented in it.[62]

Machen's orthodox Christian humanism is important in understanding the significance of Helen's negation, as it means that in Helen there is an absence *of something*, something which is central to a Christian understanding of humanity. Revisiting an orthodox view of humanity through, again, Aquinas (less so Augustine this time), reveals Helen's inhumanity in two important respects, that of *Imago Dei* and *Imago Christi*. The first chapter of 'Pan' has established that Helen is not a divinely created being, and Aquinas writes that human beings are the image of God in as much as we contain the *essence* of God the creator.[63] Having located the *Imago Dei* in this essence, Aquinas can then establish the journey of humanity (from potential to act) as one which moves towards the *Imago Christi*. In Christ, humanity becomes *Imago Dei* in its perfect, actual form. As John Milbank explains: 'Christ is *most* man'.[64] Within this construct of humanity, Christology thus becomes central to what it means to be human.

It is Clarke and Villiers' naiveté that they search for, and seem to find in Helen, the Antichrist, but the Christological truth about Helen is far more complicated, and indeed horrific enough to be beyond the comprehension of Clarke and Villiers. Clarke, who 'prides himself in a certain literary ability', is busy compiling his 'Memoirs to prove the Existence of the Devil', but after the experiment, we are told that for many years 'he clung bravely to the commonplace, and rejected all occasions of occult investigation'. Villiers is likewise warned on several occasions against indulging in the most detailed accounts of Helen's story, for 'you would never know a happy day again. You would pass the rest of your life, as I pass mine, a haunted man, a man who has seen hell.'[65] For Helen is not simply a symbolic Antichrist, she is anti-Christ. In creating Helen as Christologically inhuman, Machen reveals the extraneous, autonomous concept of 'The Devil' to be but a cosy symbol in comparison to the real embodiment of an anti-Christ—a human being without humanity.

By reaffirming an orthodox understanding of humanity, Machen is also aligning the dangers of Helen's emptiness with the metaphysical positivism which he saw reflected in Modernist modes. Such a mode follows Kant in believing that the moral significance of humanity is a priori, capable of being understood through reason alone (i.e. without the necessity of divine revelation).[66] With this in mind, Helen becomes an embodiment of the fear which Machen expressed elsewhere of a world in which humanity is no longer anchored in a redemptive Christian understanding of itself. It is indeed this fear which Villiers and Clarke repeatedly express in their occasional commentaries:

> 'My God!' he had exclaimed, 'think, think what you are saying. It is too incredible, too monstrous; such things can never be in this quiet world, where men and women live and die, and struggle, and conquer, or maybe fail, and fall down under sorrow, and grieve and suffer strange fortunes for many a year; but not this, [...] not such a thing as this. There must be some explanation, some way out of the terror. Why, man, if such a case were possible, our earth would be a nightmare.'[67]

This vision of a world in which humanity in Christ has been replaced by materialist aestheticism comes into full fruition in the nihilistic characters of our next story, *The Three Impostors*.

Aesthetic Nihilism in *The Three Impostors*

The Three Impostors is an episodic novella which was published as part of John Lane's Keynote Series in 1895.[68] The tales presented within it, although connected by the larger story of the characters who tell them, are self-contained, and have often been printed as separate short stories in anthologies. Several of these tales and episodes will be considered in isolation here, along with the running narrative which links them. *The Three Impostors* (henceforth *Impostors*) follows Machen's detective pair Dyson and Phillipps as they go about London looking for adventure. Dyson and Phillipps also appear in Machen's stories 'The Red Hand' and 'Inmost Light', Dyson being a self-styled writer and Phillipps an ardent rationalist and sceptic. *Impostors* opens with an ambiguous scene as two men and a woman leave a house within which something obviously sinister has taken place. The group appear to have left some sort of victim inside the house, as the woman reveals that she has taken an amputated hand as a souvenir. The scene reads more like an epilogue than an opening, the woman declaring: 'Farewell to all occult adventure; the farce is played'.[69]

After this intriguing opening, the reader follows Dyson into 'The Adventure of the Gold Tiberius', in which Dyson has retrieved an object dropped on the street by a fleeing man, which turns out to be a rare Roman artefact. Over the following episodes, Dyson and Phillipps come into contact with several characters, each of whom has a weird tale to tell. It eventually becomes apparent that all of these characters are searching for the same man, 'the young man with spectacles', although they describe him in a variety of guises. They each try to elicit the help of either Dyson or Phillipps in finding him by telling them fantastical tales designed to gain their sympathy. In one of the final episodes, 'The Strange Occurrence in Clerkenwell', Dyson finally encounters the bespectacled man himself, and his story is revealed. Joseph Walters, as he is called, has been embroiled in an occult group who have been searching for him since he stole from them the 'gold tiberius'. The novella eventually comes full circle as Dyson and Phillipps find themselves back at the house from the opening scene, wherein they find the tortured, mutilated body of the man with the spectacles. The result of the final episodes, in which Joseph Walter's story and fate are revealed, is that the reader becomes aware that each of the encounters have been tricks, the identities of the storytellers no more than a made-up character, and the stories themselves fantasies designed to draw in not only Dyson and Phillipps but Machen's readers themselves. This disconcerting feeling that the stories have been at once emotive and 'empty' will be shown to be central to the significance of the work.

The weird tales are presented as embedded narratives which Machen calls 'novels', and these will be worth examining in detail below, but of special interest here is the *form* of these novels, as stories told by the three 'impostors', the telling of these stories and the gullible way in which they are received by Dyson and Phillipps. In the fabrications by the three impostors is shown the ultimate triumph of artifice over art. *Impostors* takes Machen's definition of art and artifice beyond aesthetics, presenting artifice as a morally corruptive and dehumanising force. This is done by a process in which human and theological 'truth' is dismantled. The insult to truth by the three imposters lies not only in that their tales are apparently fabrications, but that the tales which they tell ironically contain fundamental truths about human ontology. It is worth noting that to Aquinas, truth is an ontological state: 'The true is the undividedness of the act of existence from that which is.'[70] The dehumanising force of these stories lies in the processes of distortion and manipulation to which these truths are subjected.

Revisiting this art/artifice dichotomy, it is the *relationship* of man with his environment which is crucial to the distinction, in that it reflects the paradox of human nature as understood in Thomist terms; that man is at once natural, but with a supernatural end integral to his being. Machen examines the role of art and artifice as a mirror to this paradox in *Hieroglyphics*:

> We read the 'Odyssey' because we are supernatural, because we hear in it the echoes of the eternal song, because it symbolises for us certain amazing and beautiful things, because it is music; we read Miss Austen and Thackeray because we like to recognise the faces of our friends aptly reproduced, to see the external face of humanity so deftly mimicked, because we are natural.[71]

Art, then, or our participation in it, reveals to us our supernatural teleology. Here, Machen's concept of art follows Coleridge's description of symbol (as opposed to fancy) as something *participatory*, 'characterised [...] above all by the translucence of the eternal through and in the temporal. It always partakes of the reality which it renders intelligible; and while it enunciates the whole, abides itself as a living part of that unity of which it is representative.'[72] In both the art described in *Hieroglyphics* and Coleridge's symbol, artifice (or fancy) is a comparative failure, absent of this participatory and revealing element and thus an empty gesture. In *Impostors*, however, this absence becomes nihilism.

While Nietzsche's work may not be a source to which Machen himself may have leapt (an assumption based also on publication dates), it will prove useful in helping to unpack the concept of nihilism in moral or Christian terms, if only to understand the ways in which *Impostors* shows the secular consolations within the Nietzschean model of nihilism to be inadequate to a Christological understanding of humanity.

The concept of nihilism can be used in order to reflect a form of Modernist thinking in which the position of human beings as participatory in divine mystery has been replaced with the human being as subject; the radical dependence of all things on the will of God instead becoming a dependence on the human subject. To Machen, this Cartesian assertion of human 'truth' repositions creative power and thus removes mystery. The three impostors create without grace, the ultimate artifice, and in doing so are not only inhuman in their actions, but *destroy* humanity. The young man in spectacles, seemingly so ubiquitous a character in *Impostors*, only appears *as himself* right at the end, when it is already too late for him to escape his pursuers. His bodily destruction at the hands of the impostors is a symbolic ending to a more prolonged destruction which has occurred as the impostors create and recreate him in versions with which to serve their own ends. Moreover, these creations are successful in that they are believed by Dyson and Phillipps, who fail to rescue the bespectacled man, using the stories instead as inspiration with which to indulge in their own creative endeavours. By 'participating' in this artifice, the moral humanity of Dyson and Phillipps is undermined and ultimately corrupted. Ironically, through their investment in the artifice of the impostors, Dyson and Phillipps fail to recognise the most important elements of the fantastical 'novels', which in themselves *do* describe the paradox of human nature and warn of its vulnerabilities. Only when Dyson suddenly realises the artifice does the opportunity arise for the 'true' story to be revealed:

> Dyson saw at once that by a succession of hazards he had unawares hit upon the scent of some desperate conspiracy, wavering as the track of a loathsome snake in and out of the highways and byways of the London cosmos; [...] For him in an instant the jargoning of voices, the garish splendour, and all the vulgar tumult of the public-house became part of magic; for here before his eyes a scene in this grim mystery play had been enacted, and he had seen human flesh grow grey with a palsy of fear; the very hell of cowardice and terror had gaped wide within an arm's-breadth.[73]

Only now (too late) is Dyson prompted to read the 'History of the Young Man in Spectacles'.

The power of the 'novels' to corrupt is dependent on Dyson and Phillipps' willingness to collude in the artifice. The three impostors are able to construct their stories in such a way as to appeal to the individual vanities of the two detective characters. Dyson seems particularly willing to indulge in the 'romance' of the stories, ignoring inconsistencies in order to maintain the enjoyment. This is most clearly seen in the episode of 'The Decadent Imagination', a conversation between Dyson and Mr Burton (an impostor) which serves as a prologue to the 'Novel of the Iron Maid', a short, gruesome and seemingly pointless tale containing nearly all the tropes of the Decadent story, in which a collector of instruments of torture is accidently strangled by his own iron maid. An excerpt sums up Dyson's combination of vanity and credulity:

His visits at once terrified and delighted Dyson, who could no longer seat himself at his bureau secure from interruption while he embarked on literary undertakings, each one of which was to be a masterpiece. On the other hand, it was a vivid pleasure to be confronted with views so highly original; and if here and there Mr Burton's reasonings seemed tinged with fallacy, yet Dyson freely yielded to the joy of strangeness, and never failed to give his visitor a frank and hearty welcome.[74]

Miss Lally/Leicester (the female impostor) proves particularly skilled in manipulating the particular vanities of Phillipps. While she flatters Dyson's artistic pretensions in 'The Recluse of Bayswater', she introduces herself to Phillipps as a maiden in distress who has lost her beloved brother, and weaves a tale for Phillipps which appeals to his self-claimed rationality and materialism, while at once undermining them. In 'The Adventure of the Missing Brother' Phillipps meets a woman in a London park who is clearly in distress. Machen tells us that: 'Flattering himself with the title of materialist, [Phillipps] was in truth one of the most credulous of men, but he required a marvel to be neatly draped in the robes of Science before he would give it any credit'.[75] As Phillipps enters the park, he is reflecting on the way in which stories should be received, and has 'delivered himself of some serious talk on the necessity of accurate observation, and the folly, as he put it, of using a kaleidoscope instead of a telescope to view things'.[76] Unaware that he is equally credulous, Dyson has warned him that 'while you fancy yourself in the golden land of new philosophies, you are in reality a dweller in a metaphorical Clapham; your scepticism has defeated itself and become a monstrous credulity'.[77] It is from these thoughts that Phillipps is drawn by a Miss Lally, who explains that her beloved brother has failed to come to their weekly meeting. Instead, she caught a brief glimpse of him walking past guided by a skeletal, ghoulish figure, at which point he communicated 'I cannot stay', seemingly telepathically. Miss Lally appeals to Phillipps for an explanation, having admitted that she is still recovering from 'a sensation of bristling fear, the fear of a child in the dark, unreasonable and unreasoning'.[78] Phillipps duly replies with a comforting and rational explanation (a hallucination theory), to which Miss Lally responds with 'almost a twinkling as of mirth about her eyes, but her face clouded sadly at the dogmatic conclusions to which the scientist was led so irresistibly'.[79] Having flattered Phillipps into a seeming position of paternal advisor, Miss Lally is now ready to tell him the 'Novel of the Black Seal'.

The 'Novel of the Black Seal' goes on systematically to undermine Phillipps' materialist values. Miss Lally tells of moving to Wales with a Professor Gregg (an acquaintance of Phillipps), ostensibly as a governess, but increasingly as a sort of research assistant. Her position is also the result of a chance meeting in London, when Professor Gregg took the distraught and destitute Miss Lally under his patronage. As a result of many years of research, Gregg is convinced of ancient secrets held in the surrounding Welsh hills, and employs an 'idiot' local boy as his guide. Miss Lally, as she tells it, 'in vain [strives] to summon scepticism to my aid',[80] but is increasingly drawn into Gregg's secret research. Eventually comes the reconnaissance into the hills from which Gregg never returns, and Miss Lally is left with a written explanation, 'the Statement of William Gregg, F.R.S. etc.'.

In Professor Gregg the reader (and Phillipps) is most explicitly presented with Machen's own voice, and Gregg's 'statement' is used to explicate Machen's theories of nature as sacrament, and mystery as essential to life. Confronting Phillipps with this theory of life, Gregg's tale also contains direct warnings to the folly of Phillipps' materialism. Gregg tells Miss Lally:

> Believe me, we stand amidst sacraments and mysteries full of awe, and it doth not yet appear what we shall be. Life, believe me, is no simple thing, no mass of grey matter and congeries of veins and muscles to be laid naked by the surgeon's knife; man is the secret which I am about to explore, and before I can discover him I must cross over weltering seas indeed, and oceans and the mists of many thousand years.[81]

Gregg's joy at this realisation, however, is dampened as he mistakenly takes his theories to his scientific colleagues (men like Phillipps): 'I found I was grossly mistaken; my friends looked blankly at me and at one another, and I could see something of pity, and something also of insolent contempt, in the glances they exchanged.'[82] Gregg's final statement even seems to confer a direct warning on the guises which evil can take in the face of the credulous rationalist:

> Then, again, there were myths darker still; the dread of witch and wizard, the lurid evil of the Sabbath, and the hint of demons who mingled with the daughters of men. And just as we have turned the terrible 'fair folk' into a company of benignant, if freakish elves, so we have hidden from us the black

foulness of the witch and her companions under a popular *diablerie* of old women and broomsticks, and a comic cat with tail on end. So the Greeks called the hideous furies benevolent ladies, and thus the northern nations have followed their example.[83]

Such warnings seem to escape Phillipps, however, and his response to the tale remains embedded in the response of his vanity to his role as rationalist advisor. Utterly convinced of Miss Lally's 'good faith', his approval of the story lies in his claim that is 'in perfect harmony with the very latest scientific theories'.[84]

By exposing Phillipps' 'failed' response to the tale, Machen exposes the inadequacies of Modernist thinking, as he saw it. While Phillipps represents the empiricist in his secular extreme ('I myself am free from [Christian] delusions'), in the later half of the nineteenth century the influence of Enlightenment philosophy was permeating even Roman-Catholic and High-Anglican theological discourse. For Machen, this Modernism was 'always constant to the one idea, that man is the master and measure of all things. "Ye shall be as gods, knowing good and evil;"'.[85] As in the character of Helen Vaughan in 'The Great God Pan', without a distinctly Christological referential, humanity becomes inhuman. Phillipps' rationalist response to Miss Leicester's tale is not only a failure, but is *un*-human. Phillipps' reliance on empirical reason has created the situation in which the artifice can be effective.

In the 'Novel of the White Powder' Machen revisits themes of death through bodily decomposition and degeneration in order to explicate this Christian humanism. Dyson is told the 'Novel of the White Powder' by a Miss Leicester, who claims to be telling the story of her brother. Seeing her brother become drawn and anxious through dedicating himself exclusively to work, Miss Leicester sends him to the doctor who prescribes a tonic which comes in the form of a white powder. After only a few days, Miss Leicester sees a transformation in her brother as he goes from academic hermit to near Epicurean 'lover of pleasure'. Eventually, his sister begins to worry equally about this version of her brother, though she can't quite specify what the problem must be, until:

One morning as we sat at breakfast together I looked suddenly into his eyes and saw a stranger before me.
'Oh Francis!' I cried. 'Oh Francis, Francis, what have you done?' and rending sobs cut the words short. I went weeping out of the room; for I knew nothing, yet I knew all.[86]

Note that despite Miss Leicester's 'What have you done?', nothing is said of the brother's activities as being particularly immoral or criminal; this is an *internal* change. The brother has changed in *who he is*.

One evening at dinner, Miss Leicester notices a mark on her brother's hand, which she knows at once to be a brand. Despite assurance from the doctor that things are fine, it is downhill from here on in, and the brother becomes increasingly unrecognisable. Indeed, Miss Leicester describes a man who is less and less *human*. Finally, Miss Leicester and the doctor make a trip to the chemist who made up the original prescription, where they discover that the powder has turned, having sat too long in its jar. There follow two more sightings of the brother, who has kept himself locked in his room, and these shall be examined in detail below. The second and final sighting is made by the doctor, who breaks into his room to discover nothing left of the brother but a disintegrating mass. Overcome with horror, the doctor attacks the writhing mass with an iron bar: 'He drove in the weapon, and struck again and again in the fury of loathing.'[87]

A few weeks later, chemical analysis is returned on the white powder, and it is claimed to be a powder used many hundreds of years before as part of the ritual for creating *Vinum Sabbati*. The letter from a Dr Chambers also serves as a form of epilogue to the story, Chambers taking the opportunity to write in very Machen-like terms on the sacrament of nature and corruptive power.[88] We are reminded that this corruptive power is not limited to those who absorb it, such as the brother, but also those who encounter it. Dr Haberdeen, for instance, whose instinctive reaction to the physical mass was so violent, finds that the experience 'has tempted me to doubt the Eternal Goodness which can permit nature to offer such hideous possibilities'.[89]

The two sightings of the brother (seen from a window by Miss Leicester and then discovered by Dr Haberdeen) are important, as between them they describe two aspects of the brother's degeneration. The first describes a symbolic absence or nothingness, while the second, the discovery of the writhing mass, illustrates physically the base nature of the human form without humanity. Walking home one day, after her brother has long kept himself to his room, Miss Leicester glances up at his window:

> I happened to look up at the windows, and instantly there was the rush and swirl of deep cold waters in my ears, my heart leapt up and fell down, down as into a deep hollow, and I was amazed with a dread and terror without form or shape. I stretched out a hand blindly through the folds of thick darkness,

from the black and shadowy valley, and held myself from falling, while the stones beneath my feet rocked and swayed and tilted, and the sense of solid things seemed to sink away from under me. I had glanced up at the window of my brother's study, and at that moment the blind was drawn aside, and something that had life stared out into the world. Nay, I cannot say I saw a face or any human likeness; a living thing, two eyes of burning flame glared at me, and they were in the midst of something as formless as my fear, the symbol and presence of all evil and all hideous corruption.[90]

Noticeable here is Miss Leicester's inability to find positive words with which to describe what she sees. It is *not* a face, nor human, and she ultimately describes its formlessness in terms *symbolic* of evil. Moreover, the fear which the vision inspires is negative and negating. The reassurance of the surrounding world is in an instance removed, and Miss Leicester feels that she herself is falling into nothingness. As if in confirmation, when she knocks on the bedroom door a voice tells her 'There is nothing here'. This is the positive 'nothing' described by Maritain. As in 'The Great God Pan', 'nothing' has taken form.

Machen gives this nothingness physical as well as symbolic form when it is seen again by Miss Leicester, having been discovered by Dr Haberdeen:

There upon the floor was a dark and putrid mass, seething with corruption and hideous rottenness, neither liquid nor solid, but melting and changing before our eyes, and bubbling with unctuous oily bubbles like boiling pitch. And out of the midst of it shone two burning points like eyes, and I saw a writhing and stirring as of limbs, and something moved and lifted up what might have been an arm.[91]

Again following motifs from 'The Great God Pan', this form is alive, but does not have Life, as understood by Christian doctrine. In the removal of humanity, human life has been reduced to its most base nature; that shared with the lowest and most primal in existence. Despite allusions to the Pandora's box of Victorian science in the use of the white powder as the instrument for this transformation, Miss Leicester's brother is more like the child protagonist of 'The White People' than Stevenson's Mr Jekyll. His corruption is accidental, and does not introduce a change to his person, but rather draws out that which is base and fallen within him, enveloping and absorbing his higher 'supernatural' being. When humanity is stripped away, what is left is *nothing*. In his depictions of grotesque deaths, Machen is attempting to give form to this negation, and in the

'Novel of the White Powder', an apparently fabricated story has nonetheless revealed truths about human nature.

The structure of *Impostors*, with its 'novels' within a larger series of episodes, creates an unnerving paradox in which the reader is aware of the novels as central and significant, but also that each tale is undermined by both their narrators (the three impostors) and their recipients (Dyson and Phillipps). In situating the novels in this way, Machen creates a larger narrative in which the use of artifice causes the 'truths' of art to be themselves corrupted. The characters of *Impostors* do not participate in the Created world, rather they set themselves up as creators, the centre and subject of their own created worlds. This absence of participation in *Impostors* ultimately becomes nihilistic.

Nietzsche's nihilistic proclamation 'God is dead' is useful in unpacking my claims of nihilism in *Impostors*.[92] Such a proclamation goes to the heart of a world in which the centre of creation has shifted from God to man, along with creative power. To Aquinas, God is known by knowing him not as a being, but as *being*. Aquinas differentiates between existence (*esse*) and essence (*essentia*), explaining that a thing's existence must be caused by either its essence or an external power. God's existence and essence, however, are the same, God having no 'cause', and existing fully in full actuality:

> Just as that which has fire, but is not itself fire, is on fire by participation; so that which has existence but is not existence, is a being by participation. But God is His own essence, as shown above (Article 3) if, therefore, He is not His own existence He will be not essential, but participated being. He will not therefore be the first being—which is absurd. Therefore God is His own existence, and not merely His own essence.[93]

Here, just as God's existence is independent, our existence *is* by participation in God. To exist is to exist *in* God. Likewise God's being is bound up in our participation of Him. In terms evocative of Machen's 'base' beings, Meister Eckhart also describes this reflexive relationship of man and God:

> God *becomes* when all creatures say 'God' then God comes to be.
> When I subsisted in the ground, in the bottom, in the river and font of Godhead, no one asked me where I was going or what I was doing; there was no one to ask me. When I flowed forth, all creatures said 'God'.[94]

God becomes God (to us) as we become ourselves:

> While I yet stood in my first cause I *had* no God and was my own cause [...] I was free of God and all things. But when I left my free will behind and received my created being, *then* I had a God. For before there were creatures, God was not 'God': He was That which He was. But when creatures came into existence and received their *created* being, then God was not 'God' in Himself. He was 'God' in creatures.[95]

When Nietzsche declares that 'God is dead' it is in as far as man has stopped participating as beings in God. The God that is dead is the 'God in creatures'. Nietzsche's madman cries not only that 'God is dead', but that '*We have killed him*—you and I! We are all his murderers.' Man's will to power is a will to creator, in which God becomes an object, not 'being', but *a* being.[96]

If God is dead, however, then so is man, if we follow Aquinas (and Augustine) in seeing that in God we find ourselves. To Nietzsche, the solution is art. Having failed to (re)create God, we must become creators and artificers ourselves:

> *Only as creators!*—This has caused me the greatest trouble and still does always cause me the greatest trouble: to realise that *What things are called* is unspeakably more important than what they are. [...] What started as appearance in the end nearly always becomes essence and *effectively acts* as its essence! Only as creators can we destroy!—But let us also not forget that in the long run it is enough to create new names and valuations and appearances of truth in order to create new 'things'.[97]

Such a solution is inadequate to Machen's nihilist description, however, not only in that it ignores the Christian humanist *necessity* of God to being, but in that it does not account for Machen's distinction of art and artifice. For Nietzsche, the creative power of art and artifice are the same, while Machen sees one only as the 'empty echo' of the other. By not participating in man's Christian teleology, man ceases to exist as being in God, just as God is not present in His creation.

It is this empty creative power which haunts *Impostors*. Each 'novel', as a vehicle for 'truth', is absorbed into the artifice of The Three Impostors, and their creation of nothingness becomes not only empty, but destructive. The young man with spectacles is reduced to a non-being by those that pursue him, as they (re)create him in each story. The 'real' Joseph

Walters is arguably the ghost of these weird tales and episodes, of which only glimpses are caught. When his body is discovered by Dyson and Phillipps, he has both physically and symbolically been reduced to nothing; 'a shameful ruin of the human shape'.[98] Moreover, this power of negation is infectious, tempting Dyson and Phillipps to indulge in their own vanities of artifice. By wilfully ignoring the moral imperatives contained within the 'novels', they become collusive in the unfolding of the bespectacled man's fate. Far from becoming supermen, Dyson and Phillipps are left impotent, imagining romantic fancies in the very house in which a body is burning to nothing.

Conclusion

Arthur Machen's weird tales reinforce his Christian humanism by exploring the spiritual nihil.[99] Establishing evil as negation or privation, Machen's stories force us to look into the empty space, and examine the nature of that emptiness. Far from an apologetics which came to Machen only in the twentieth century, understanding man's relationship with the 'great sacrament' is as crucial to the significance of these weird tales as to 'A Fragment of Life' or *The Secret Glory*.

Man's teleology is one of participation. Machen writes:

> If we, being wondrous, journey through a wonderful world, if all our joys are from above, from the other world where the Shadowy Companion walks, then no mere making of the likeness of the external shape will be our art, no veracious document will be our truth; but to us, initiated, the Symbol will be offered, and we shall take the Sign and adore, beneath the outward and perhaps unlovely accidents, the very Presence and eternal indwelling of God.[100]

As we have seen in Aquinas, through this participation in God's creative miracle, we become *more* ourselves, *more* human. Machen's stories reinforce that man's journey from potency to actuality is in fact a journey into being. Human ontology is here inextricably a theological anthropology.

Machen's weird tales are important to his orthodox apologetics, however, because they recognise the paradoxical nature of human being. Machen's tales show us both the Christological human being, and humanity in its basest form; *inhuman* beings in which the nihil is paradoxically given form. Through these forms Machen attempts to warn against the Enlightenment and Modernist thinking which 'sees nothing in history but the gradual and triumphant Rise of Man'.[101] In 'The Red Hand' Dyson (of *Impostors*) says to a sceptical Phillipps:

> The troglodyte and the lake-dweller, perhaps representatives of yet darker races, may very probably be lurking in our midst, rubbing shoulders with frock-coated and finely-draped humanity, ravening like wolves at heart and boiling with the foul passions of the swamp and the black cave.[102]

Machen's twentieth-century apologetic tales seek to demonstrate the role of grace in drawing man from this primitive form to his 'ultimate end', reminding us 'that man is made a mystery for mysteries and visions, for the realisation in his consciousness of ineffable bliss, for a great joy that transmutes the whole world, for a joy that surpasses all joys and overcomes all sorrows'.[103] His weird tales reinforce that Christian orthodoxy is the *only* framework which provides the clarifying lens for grace, giving man to himself, as it were.

In 'The White People', Machen writes not a wilfully perverse or nefarious protagonist, but an innocent child, whose mystical encounters are corrupted as they lack a Christian narrative through which they can be interpreted and reconstructed. Helen Vaughan of 'The Great God Pan' reinforces the Christological *necessity* to humanity yet further, by presenting us with inhumanity in human form. Finally, *The Three Impostors* describes the inevitable nihilism that comes from man forgetting that his being is a being of participation, instead becoming 'certain of himself as the being that thus founds itself on itself'.[104]

What then, do Machen's weird tales have to tell us about the theology of the supernatural tale? The real ghost in these stories, arguably, is inextricably theological. The ghost which haunts each of these stories is the Christological human being. The humanity which can only be realised through grace haunts the empty and negative spaces which provide the very horror to these tales.

NOTES

1. S. T. Joshi, *The Weird Tale: Arthur Machen, Lord Dunsany, Algernon Blackwood, M.R. James, Ambrose Bierce, H.P. Lovecraft* (Austin: University of Texas Press, 1990), 14.

2. Aidan Reynolds and William Charlton argue that while writing 'The White People' and *The Three Impostors*, Machen was in danger of 'plunging blindly and completely' into 'the *diablerie* of the end of the nineteenth century' (*Arthur Machen: A Short Account of His Life and Work*, London: Published by J. Baker for Richards Press, 1963, 73). Vincent Starrett writes of this period as 'the pinnacle of his tormented genius' (*Arthur Machen: A Novelist of Ecstasy and Sin* Horam: Tartarus Press, 1996, 18), and Fr Brocard Sewell describes Machen as a 'consistent upholder of Catholic doctrine', but then excludes his early works from the claim, suggesting a briefly 'unsettled mind' ('Arthur Machen: His Ideas and Beliefs', *Avallaunius: The Journal of the Arthur Machen Society*. 17, 1997, 3, 4).
3. Arthur Machen, *The Three Impostors or the Transmutations* (London: John Lane, 1895), 177.
4. Machen, *Far off Things*, p. 28 (Hidden God, devoutly I adore Thee. This Eucharistic hymn written by Aquinas continues: *Quæ sub his figuris vere latitas*; Truly present underneath these veils.) Title quotation: Machen uses this phrase several times, and in 'The Novel of the White Powder' Dr Chambers explains this to mean 'that every branch of human knowledge if traced up to its source and final principles vanishes into mystery' (*The Three Impostors and Other Stories*, ed. S. T. Joshi, USA: Chaosium, 2007, 208). A simpler translation would be 'all things pass into mystery'.
5. See Aquinas, *Summa Theologicae*, I, q56, a3.
6. Leo XIII, Pope. *Aeterni Patris*. 1879. www.papalencyclycals.net/Leo13/l13cph.htm.
7. Gerard Manley Hopkins, 'The Wreck of the Deutschland', in *Poems*, ed. by Robert Bridges (London: Humphrey Milford, 1918), 20. For a detailed account of Hopkins' epistemology see Hilary Fraser, *Beauty and Belief: Aesthetics and Religion in Victorian Literature* (Cambridge: Cambridge University Press, 1986), 67–106, and for nature and sacramentalism in the arts, see Mark Knight and Emma Mason, *Nineteenth-Century Religion and Literature* (Oxford: Oxford University Press, 2006), 199–206.
8. See J. B. Mozeley, *Eight Lectures on Miracles* (London: Rivington, 1865); Baden Powell, 'On the Study of the Evidences of Christianity', in *Essays and Reviews* (London: J. W. Parker, 1860), 94–144. In his famous chapter on miracles, Augustine writes that 'whatever miracle happens in this world, it is certainly a lesser marvel than the whole world, that is to say, the heavens and the earth and all that is in them, which God undoubtedly made. [...] And so although the miracles of the visible world of nature have lost their value for us because we see them continually, still, if we

observe them wisely they will be found to be greater miracles than the most extraordinary and unusual events.' *De Civ.* X.12.
9. Arthur Machen, *Hieroglyphics* (London: Grant Richards, 1902), 176.
10. Arthur Machen, 'The Gift of Tongues', in *Ritual and Other Stories* (Lewes: Tartarus, 1997; 1992), 214.
11. Reprinted in Arthur Machen, *Selected Letters: The Private Writings of the Master of the Macabre*. Ed. Godfrey Brangham, Roger Dobson and R. A. Gilbert (Wellingborough: Aquarian, 1988), 41.
12. Machen in a letter to P. D. Ellis, 1912. Quoted in Sewell, 'Ideas and Beliefs', 8. See also Machen, 'Modernism', *The Academy* Vol. LXXIV, April 18, 1908, 686–689, 'Realism and Symbol', *The Academy* Vol. LXXV, August 1, 1908, 109–110. Nicholas Freeman discusses Modernist understandings of 'epiphany' at length in 'Arthur Machen: Ecstasy and Epiphany' (*Literature and Theology*, 24.3, 2010, 242–255), in which he contrasts Machen's description of ecstasy with Modernist writers such as Woolf, Joyce and Lawrence. Freeman writes that in contrast to Machen, 'Lawrence and his contemporaries were as suspicious of the Victorian pieties as they were of their omniscient narrators' (242). While Freeman's comparison is insightful, I am anxious to avoid equating 'Modernism' here with current definitions of Modernism as a literary mode, which would inevitably lead to an underestimation of the breadth of Machen's philosophical arguments against 'Modernist thinking'.
13. For an in-depth discussion of the Protestant and Catholic varieties of Modernist theology, see, Gabriel Daly, 'Theological and Philosophical Modernism.' In *Catholicism Contending with Modernity: Roman Catholic Modernism and Anti-Modernism in Historical Context*. Ed. Darrell Jodock (Cambridge: Cambridge University Press, 2000) 88–112 and Anthony J. Carroll, 'The Philosophical Foundations of Catholic Modernism', *In George Tyrrell and Catholic Modernism*, 38–55.
14. Machen, *Hieroglyphics*, 71.
15. Machen, 'Modernism', 687.
16. Machen, *Hieroglyphics*, 169–70.
17. See Samuel Taylor Coleridge, *The Statesman's Manual; Or, the Bible the Best Guide to Political Skill and Foresight, a Lay Sermon. with an Appendix* (London: Gale and Fenner, 1816), 'On Poesy or Art', in *The Complete Works of Samuel Taylor Coleridge Vol. IV*. Ed. Professor Shedd. (New York: Harper and Brothers, 1853). IV, 328–36.
18. Machen, *Hieroglyphics*, 130.
19. Arthur Machen, *Notes and Queries*. (London: Spurr & Swift, 1926), 115. See also Edgar Allan Poe, 'The Imp of the Perverse', in *The Works of the Late Edgar Allan Poe*, ed. Rufus Wilmot Griswald (New York: Redfield, 1857), 353–359.

20. Machen, *Notes and Queries*, 115.
21. S. T. Joshi describes Machen's notions of ecstasy and symbolism as narrow, ultimately limiting the scope of his writing. He goes on to argue that 'the sole goal of Machen's philosophy was to restore the sense of wonder and mystery into our perception of the world; everything that tended to foster such a goal—mysticism, occultism, Catholicism, symbolism—was to be encouraged, and everything that hindered it [...] was to be furiously combated' (Joshi, *The Weird Tale*, 16).
22. Machen, 'Fragment of Life', 22. Machen's life-long interest in grail legends, and later in the primitive Celtic Church, are surely indicators of this desire to find appropriate expression for mysterious experience.
23. Machen, 'The White People', in *The House of Souls* (London: E. Grant Richards, 1906), 438.
24. In his autobiography, Machen writes: 'I had been thinking at the old century end of the work that I had done in the fifteen years or so before, and it suddenly dawned upon me that this work, [...] had all been the expression of one formula, one endeavour. What I had been doing was this: I had been inventing tales in which and by which I had tried to realise my boyish impressions of that wonderful magic Gwent. [...] I wrote "The Great God Pan," an endeavour to pass on the vague, indefinable sense of awe and mystery and terror that I had received' (*Far Off Things*, London: M. Secker, 1922; 1915, 19–20).
25. Aquinas, *Summa* 1a2ae q.55 a.4.
26. Aquinas, *Summa* 1a2ae q.93 a.1.
27. For a detailed discussion of virtue ethics, see Alasdair C. MacIntyre, *After Virtue: A Study in Moral Theory* (London: Duckworth, 1981). *After Virtue* traces the disintegration of this 'narrative' of morality in modernity.
28. See Stanley Hauerwas, "The Church in a Divided World. The Interpretative Power of the Christian Story." *The Journal of Religious Ethics* 8.1 (1980): 21. For a contemporary interpretation of Aquinas' model of *habitus*, see *The Peaceable Kingdom: A Primer in Christian Ethics*. (Notre Dame, Ind.: University of Notre Dame Press, 1983) and *A Community of Character: Toward a Constructive Christian Social Ethic* (Notre Dame, Ind.: University of Notre Dame Press, 1981).
29. Although not published until 1902, *Hieroglyphics* was written in 1899. Title quotation: Dante, *The Divine Comedy*, Purgatorio XVI, 91. 'The White People' is in many ways reminiscent of Dante's description of 'the simple little soul' (88) who innocently reaches out, but without the guides and curbs of law goes 'off course' (82).
30. Reynolds and Charlton, *Arthur Machen*, 70. The quotation makes reference to the recent death of Machen's first wife.

31. Machen, 'The White People', 116.
32. Aquinas, *On Being and Essence*, ch. 1.
33. Machen, 'The White People', 117.
34. Machen, 'The White People', 155-6. This distinction between the mystic experience and its later recollection is a common theme in Machen's stories, and reflects St. Augustine's conviction in the inaccessibility of God to human comprehension, and the inadequacy of language to speak about Him. See Augustine, *De Trin*, V.1.1-2, VII.4.7, VIII.2.3.
35. Aquinas, *On Being and Essence*, ch.1. *Summa*, I, q54, a3.
36. Aquinas, *Summa*, I, q54, a5.
37. Gen 3.4-6: 'But the serpent said to the woman, "You will not die; for God knows that when you eat of it your eyes will be opened, and you *will be like God*, knowing good and evil." So when the woman saw that the tree was good for food, and that it was a delight to the eyes, and that *the tree was to be desired to make one wise*, she took of its fruit and ate.' My emphasis. This and all further biblical references are from the New Revised Standard Version (NRSV).
38. Machen, *Far Off Things*, 20.
39. Machen, *The House of Souls* (New York: Ayer Company, 1922), Introduction, p. xii, and elsewhere.
40. Machen, 'The White People', 132, 137.
41. Machen, *Far Off Things*, 26.
42. John Milbank, 'Fictioning Things: Gift and Narrative.' In *Theology and Literature after Postmodernity*, ed. by Zoë Lehmann Imfeld, Alison Milbank and Peter Hampson (London and New York: Bloomsbury T&T Clark, 2015), 218.
43. Machen, 'The White People', 160.
44. Machen, 'The White People', 120. There are clearly also psychoanalytical connections to be made between the figures in the girl's dream and the trysting couple. It could well be that the figures are in fact a distorted memory of watching the couple: 'She said I had been dreaming, but I knew I hadn't', 120.
45. Machen, 'The White People', 145.
46. Machen, 'The White People', 139.
47. Machen, 'The White People', 161.
48. Machen, 'The White People', 159.
49. Machen, 'The White People', 157.
50. Machen, 'The White People', 115.
51. Machen, 'The White People', 165.
52. Arthur Machen, 'The Great God Pan' in, *The House of Souls* (London: E. Grant Richards, 1906), 169. 'The Great God Pan' could reasonably be described as a 'novella', although I treat it as a short story here. The story

is about 60 pages long, and although divided into chapters, none are more than a few pages in length. Title quotation: John Milton, *Paradise Lost*, Bk. 1 (63).
53. Machen, 'Pan', 172, 178.
54. There are several compelling arguments against accepting Machen's Pan as a devil figure. Certainly the nineteenth-century perception of Pan was in no way unanimously negative, as many adopted this symbol in an attempt to reconcile spirituality with the natural world. (An obvious example is the Romantic use of Pan, such as Keats' *Endymion*. For an in-depth discussion of the Victorian symbol of Pan, see Patricia Merivale's *Pan, the Goat-God, His Myth in Modern Times* (Cambridge, Mass: Harvard University Press, 1969, Ch. III). Likewise Machen's own approach to Paganism and Pagan symbols was surprisingly inclusive. Rather than a religion in opposition to Christianity, Machen shares Chesterton's approach in looking to Paganism to elucidate the preternatural and ritualistic roots of Christianity. Chesterton writes: 'All that genuinely remains of the ancient hymns or the ancient dances of Europe, all that has honestly come to us from the festivals of Phoebus or Pan, is to be found in the festivals of the Christian Church' (*Heretics*, London: Bodley Head 1905, 156). This ambiguity in the Pan symbol is not in itself an argument against W. R. Irwin's assertion that Machen's Pan is 'irresistible and indescribably evil' ("The Survival of Pan." PMLA 76.3, 1961, 161). However, that Machen chooses such a complex symbol warns against the assumption that Pan is anti-Christian, and therefore the/an Antichrist.
55. Machen, 'Pan', 178.
56. Machen, 'Pan', 192, 224–5. Later Villiers reports that 'he would only say that she had destroyed him, body and soul' (207).
57. Augustine, *De Trin.*, III, 9. 16. See also *De Gen.* IX. 17. 32.
58. Machen, 'Pan', 173–4.
59. Jacques Maritain, *Saint Thomas and the Problem of Evil (the Aquinas Lecture 1942)*, trans. Mabelle Louise Cunningham Andison (Milwaukee: Marquette University Press, 1942), 36.
60. Machen, 'Pan', 188. Later, as Villiers attempts to come to terms with his encounter with Helen, he acknowledges the horror induced by this paradox of being and non-being: 'But you and I, at all events, have known something of the terror that may dwell in the secret place of life, manifested under human flesh; that which is without form taking to itself a form. Oh Austin, how can it be? How is it that the very sunlight does not turn to blackness before this thing, the hard earth melt and boil beneath such a burden?' (232)

61. Machen, 'Pan', 188. 'And the devil was made incarnate. And was made flesh.' This first phrase inverts the Christian *Credo*, where it is used in reference to Christ.
62. Machen, 'Pan', 236–7.
63. Aquinas, *Summa*, I, q.93, a.1.
64. John Milbank, quoted in John Milbank, Simon Oliver, Zoë Lehmann Imfeld, Peter Hampson, 'Interview and Conversation with John Milbank and Simon Oliver: Radical Orthodoxy and Christian Psychology I—Theological Underpinnings', *Edification*, 6.1 (2003), 43.
65. Machen, 'Pan', 179–181, 193.
66. See Immanuel Kant, *Religion within the Limits of Reason Alone*, trans. Theodore Meyer Greene, Hoyt H. Hudson and John R. Silber (New York: Harper & Brothers, 1960). For a more detailed description of Modernist humanism as positivist, naturalist and progressive, see John P. Bequette, *Christian Humanism: Creation, Redemption and Reintegration* (USA: University Press of America, 2004).
67. Machen, 'Pan', 187–8.
68. Machen's title is taken from *Moses, Christ and Mahomet: The Treatise of the Three Impostors*, a legendary book denouncing these three religious figures, and attributed to various medieval European writers. It is referred to in Thomas Browne's *Religio Medici*, of which Arthur Machen makes use in *Far Off Things* (24 & 38). Publication in the Keynote series placed *The Three Impostors* firmly in the Decadent camp in the view of the general public.
69. Machen, *The Three Impostors*, 8.
70. Aquinas, *De Veritate*, Ia q.1 a.1.
71. Machen, *Hieroglyphics*, 51.
72. Samuel Taylor Coleridge, *The Statesman's Manual*, 40. My use of Coleridge here involves something of a misuse of his construct of imagination. While I take Machen's description of 'art' to closely reflect Coleridge's 'symbol', I have chosen to align 'artifice' with 'fancy', rather than 'allegory', believing that this more closely reflects Machen's emphasis on the process and genesis of 'artifice' (or lack thereof).
73. Machen, *Impostors*, 188.
74. Machen, *Impostors*, 137.
75. Machen, *Impostors*, 53.
76. Machen, *Impostors*, 54.
77. Machen, *Impostors*, 54.
78. Machen, *Impostors*, 59.
79. Machen, *Impostors*, 63.
80. Machen, *Impostors*, 100.
81. Machen, *Impostors*, 73.

82. Machen, *Impostors*, 79.
83. Machen, *Impostors*, 106.
84. Machen, *Impostors*, 120.
85. Machen, 'Modernism', 687. Machen's quotation is taken from A. Leslie Lilley, *What We Want: An Open Letter to Pius X from a Group of Priests*. (London: John Murray, 1907), 53. See also Pius X, *Pascendi Dominici Gregis*. Web. For a discussion of Pius' treatment of Modernism, see Oliver P. Rafferty, 'Introduction', in *George Tyrell and Catholic Modernism* (Dublin: Four Courts Press, 2010), 10.
86. Machen, *Impostors*, 159.
87. Machen, *Impostors*, 172.
88. By using a Stevensonian pseudo-scientific plot structure to introduce the white powder, Machen creates an uncomfortable launching point for his theories of sacrament and corruption, and it is arguable that this juxtaposition is not altogether successful.
89. Machen, *Impostors*, 178.
90. Machen, *Impostors*, 167–8.
91. Machen, *Impostors*, 171–2.
92. Friedrich Nietzsche, *The Gay Science*, trans. Josefine Nauckhoff, ed. Bernard Williams. (Cambridge: Cambridge University Press, 2001), Section 125 (119). Also repeated in *Thus Spoke Zarathustra*.
93. Aquinas, *Summa*, I, q3, a4.
94. Meister Eckhart, *The Complete Mystical Works of Meister Eckhart*, trans. Maurice O'Connell Walshe, ed. Maurice O'Connell Walshe, (USA: Crossroad, 2009), 81 (Sermon 26). Original emphasis.
95. Eckhart, *The Complete Mystical Works*, 271 (Sermon 52).
96. Nietzche, *Gay Science*, section 125 (120). Original emphasis. See also Martin Heidegger, *Schelling's Treatise on the Essence of Human Freedom*, trans. Joan Stambough, (USA: Ohio University Press, 1985), 50sq.
97. Nietzche, *Gay Science*, section 58 (60, 70). Original emphasis.
98. Machen, *Impostors*, 214.
99. Title quotation: Edwin Muir, 'The Incarnate One' (8), *Collected Poems 1921–1958*. (Eastbourne: Faber & Faber, 1960). 228.
100. Machen, *Hieroglyphics*, 169.
101. Machen, 'Celtic Magic' in *Notes and Queries*, 61.
102. Machen, 'The Red Hand', in *The House of Souls* (London: E. Grant Richards, 1906), 476.
103. Machen, 'A Fragment of Life', 86.
104. Martin Heidegger, *Nietzsche, Vol. IV*, trans. Frank A. Capuzzi, ed. David Farrell Krell (USA: Harper and Row, 1982), 97.

CHAPTER 4

'What is this that I have done?': M. R. James

There seems to be something paradoxical about M. R. James the scholar and M. R. James (henceforth MRJ) the ghost-story writer.[1] While the ghost stories may be infused with MRJ's vast knowledge of biblical studies and medievalism, he shies away from any grandiose claims for his tales, prefacing nearly every collection with the reminder that they were written merely to be read for the entertainment of friends at Cambridge (or indeed schoolboys at Eton). In his first collection *Ghost Stories of an Antiquary* (1904) he writes that:

> The stories themselves do not make any very exalted claim. If any of them succeed in causing their readers to feel pleasantly uncomfortable when walking along a solitary road at nightfall, or sitting over a dying fire in the small hours, my purpose in writing them will have been attained.[2]

Inevitably, scholars have tended to accept this apparent juxtaposition, following Julia Briggs in her claim that 'his ghost stories seem almost to parody his scholarly investigations into Holy Writ, for they frequently adduce biblical or literary references to prove the existence of spiritual forces, yet these appear to be introduced in the spirit of an academic joke'.[3] However, this chapter will argue that such readings arise from a false situation of the terror in the tales. Reading MRJ's stories without reference to his otherwise orthodox moral scheme is a missed opportunity.[4] As in Machen's tales, it is ultimately not the ghosts and demons which haunt MRJ's stories, but the human being as fallen man. MRJ's Christian orthodoxy means that the haunted characters of the plot are at once those who haunt the piece. Certainly MRJ's comments on the art of ghost-story writing lend little to an understanding of his theological outlook, unlike Machen's lengthy treatises on the moral and spiritual value of fantastic tales. In the absence of such writings, this chapter will argue that rather than accepting MRJ's ghost stories as a frivolous side-line to his serious academic work it is his scholarship which provides the key to the depth and meaning of his stories. His work on the Apocrypha in particular, which he began as an undergraduate in the 1880s, demonstrates a mind committed to the value of texts and stories as religious and spiritual truths. The text itself, its provenance and authority, reveal that truth to be either revelatory or distorted. In compiling *The Apocryphal New Testament*, which was eventually published in 1924, MRJ comes to the conclusion that the Apocrypha described within it, through their ultimate failure in 'the instilling of true religion and the conveyance of true history', reinforce in him 'an added respect for the sense of the Church Catholic, and for the wisdom of the scholars of Alexandria, Antioch, and Rome'.[5] It will be argued here that MRJ the Cambridge scholar, with his fascination with religious texts and 'Truth' through careful tradition, is inextricable from MRJ the ghost-story writer. Rather, the voice of religious authority permeates the stories, and the outcome for protagonists becomes intertwined with how well that voice is heard. Just as in Machen's weird tales, human weakness and human desire are a distorting lens through which religious and moral truth is perceived, and the result is a set of disturbing and terrifying tales.

M. R. James, Anglican Dogma and the Moral Authority of Text

MRJ spent nearly all his adult career as a scholar at King's College, Cambridge (eventually returning to Eton as provost at the age of 56). MRJ was the son of a conservative evangelical-Anglican rector, and his childhood moulded the adult man.[6] I will argue in this chapter that MRJ's ghost stories are rooted firmly in an appeal to dogmatic orthodoxy, and the seeds for this conservatism are reflected in the writings of his father. In the 1880s, for instance, Herbert James warned against a departure from dogmatic theology. The 'ill-regulated' theologian, he claimed, would be like a kite cut loose from its string. He might have a certain liberty, and soar to a certain height. But he soars only to fall, and the higher the height, the more damaging the descent.

Independence of Theology may be purchased at too dear a price. Dislike of dogmatic truth is apt to degenerate into the barest, narrowest, shallowest Positivism.[7]

Although MRJ never took priestly orders, it is clear from his personal correspondence that this was a prospect which he took seriously, and this was even expected by some.[8] MRJ discussed this with his friend St Clair Donaldson, who wrote in 1883:

It is in your power, if you choose, to do work both for science and the Church, such as has not been done for years. In Archaeology you are to teach Cambridge. In Theology you can bring to bear what is sorely needed—great knowledge (which you know how to use) and a wide grasp of universal history.[9]

Rather than the priesthood, MRJ took his religious commitment into his career as biblical historian and textual archaeologist, eventually compiling descriptive catalogues for the Cambridge college libraries, but maintaining throughout his interest in the sources of apocryphal writings and apocalypses. This interest was not simply one of cataloguing fragments, but of theological assessment within Church tradition. For MRJ, historical truth and religious authority were inextricable.

By contrast, MRJ scholar Rosemary Pardoe makes the claim that while clearly informed by Christian scholarship, MRJ's ghost stories 'most definitely do not conform to these required rules of morality'. Instead she sees a group of tales which are governed by an 'unreasonable, irrational universe'.[10] Pardoe's precise and comprehensive scholarship on MRJ's writings is invaluable in the field. However, I would argue that in the case of reading the theology of MRJ's ghost stories, Pardoe succumbs to a binary over-simplification of Victorian Christianity which is unequal to MRJ's insight. She writes:

He was troubled because he was never quite able to come to terms with the dichotomy between the comfortable Christian world view of his upbringing, which he wanted to accept but couldn't, and the darkly amoral version of pantheism which, try as he might to deny it to himself, he felt truly reflected the state of the world.[11]

I will argue that in fact, far from some parochial Anglicanism, the theology of MRJ's supernatural tales reveals all the moral complexities of the fallen human condition when no longer anchored in Christian orthodoxy. If we accept MRJ's ghost stories as inherently theological, and moreover theologically complex, then we begin to see them as fascinating discussions of theological anthropology, in which, like Machen's weird tales, the frailty of the human condition is exposed as providing the real terror to the tales.

MRJ's supernatural tales provide a reflection of nineteenth-century post-Enlightenment thinking set against the background of Church tradition. MRJ's approach to apocryphal writing was ultimately one suspicious of departures from orthodoxy. Of the Clementine Literature, for instance, he writes: 'The body of doctrine thus set forth is not orthodox. It is, in fact, eccentric.'[12] This suspicion is entrenched in the misfortunes of his ghost-story protagonists. While some may wilfully pervert Christian morality, such as Mr Abney in the story 'Lost Hearts', for most their misfortune is due rather to an unwitting disregard for the ancient authoritative voices that echo through the stories. Scholars harbour 'cherished dreams of finding priceless manuscripts' and revel in the antiquities to be found in churches, but pay little heed to the content of local oral tradition or to the warnings of obscure writings discovered along the way.[13] MRJ's scholarly protagonists, while in many ways clearly modelled on their author, are more importantly the product of post-Kantian empiricism. They have forgotten all but the material value of the writings and voices of these treasures, and thus approach artefacts of religious tradition with the secularism which MRJ found so unacceptable.[14]

In his essay on MRJ and the magical tradition, Ron Weighall notes that MRJ's first collection of ghost stories followed the growth of the Decadent movement, 'with its call for a reappraisal of good and evil, its obsession with diabolism and the nature of the Holy'.[15] While not, perhaps, Decadent, certainly MRJ's characters have situated themselves in a position which no longer looks to patristic theology as the lens through which to examine 'good' or 'evil'. Theologian Catherine Pickstock's description of post-Christian thinking applies neatly to MRJ's characters, in which the pre-modern ethical discernment of truth as sacred or profane has been replaced by the Cartesian *cogito*, and truth 'need no longer make any such act of discernment. For the *cogito*, and the truths derived from it, are declared to remain true even if we are the victim of demonic deceit.'[16] Unaware that he is about to disturb a spirit, for instance, Mr Wraxall of 'Count Magnus' imagines the count in the following terms:

It could not be denied that this [an excerpt from Magnus' papers referring to a black pilgrimage] threw a rather lurid light upon the tastes and beliefs of the Count; but to Mr. Wraxall, separated from him by nearly three centuries, the thought that he might have added to his general forcefulness alchemy, and to alchemy something like magic, only made him a more picturesque figure.[17]

MRJ's protagonists enact an indictment against orthodox religion which Charles Taylor claims is posited by the modern condition, namely the claim that orthodoxy offends against reason by harbouring a role for mystery and proposing paradoxical notions.[18] Thus they do not encounter the world with the expectation that it will reveal something outside their understanding. There is nothing of a revelatory nature to be found in the stories and traditions which they come across in their historical research. Mr Wraxall, searching among the papers of a Swedish alchemist, does not seek understanding, but information with which to illustrate *his own* world-view.

The Greek word αποκαλυψις (Apocalypse), the biblical motifs of which MRJ so often used, means revelation. MRJ's characters, however, are neither seeking nor expecting revelation, and thus when faced with their own individual apocalypses are not equipped to encounter the experience as anything other than the late-modern apocalypse of horrific and complete destruction. This claim reinforces the argument that MRJ's ghost-story themes are to be found *within* the theological tradition. MRJ's protagonists, whether wilfully abandoning Christian morality, or unwittingly opening their own Pandora's box, all face the universal condition of man as fallen, but lack the tools with which to encounter it.

With this in mind, a brief return to Pardoe's 'darkly amoral version of pantheism' is warranted. Certainly, MRJ invokes panic fear, and many stories have echoes of Machen in their depictions of primordial nature encroaching into modern civilisation. An obvious example is 'Oh Whistle and I'll Come to You, my Lad', with its juxtaposition of a golf course against the rugged terrain in which Parkins digs up the Pan-like whistle, and summons a terrifying vision on an extraordinary wind.[19] However, just as in Machen's weird tales, it is ultimately not *what* lies outside the Christian concept of the world which provides the terror of MRJ's tales, but the way in which man encounters that world when he views it without the clarifying and redemptive lens of Christian orthodoxy.

MRJ's Theological Anthropology

Two important factors highlight the theological anthropology which informs MRJ's ghost stories. The first is the place of the universal nature of sin and redemption, and the second man's relationship with spiritual knowledge. A distinction between the pre-modern concepts of original sin and universal sin is relevant to an understanding of MRJ's 'innocent' protagonists. The following will use the writings of Saint Irenaeus and Augustine to tease out this distinction with regard to MRJ's characters. Moreover, in a discussion of 'Mr Humphrey's Inheritance' it will be argued that MRJ's orthodoxy demonstrates a thematic repetition of Irenaeus' writings against Gnosticism by challenging the validity of esoteric religion and reinforcing the necessity of patristic guidance.

The notion of universal sin is important here in answering the puzzle of MRJ's apparently innocent but hapless protagonists. These characters have led several scholars to argue that the stories depict a world entirely without a moral scheme.[20] By resituating these characters from individual guilt or innocence into the Christian concept of corporate guilt, however, the stories are shown to correspond with a Christian schematic in which the condition of man as fallen is reinforced, and thus the necessity of man as a communal being. This is crucial, as the theological importance of universal sin is ultimately not guilt, but redemption—if guilt is universal, so redemption is universal.

Augustine is an obvious authority to whom to turn, as he makes a useful distinction between the *event* of original sin (*peccatum originale originans*), in which Adam and Eve took the forbidden fruit, and the *condition* of original sin (*peccatum originale originatum*), in which all of humankind partake.[21] It is this condition of sinfulness which necessitates redemption through Christ. A lengthy discussion over the theological controversies of this distinction would be impractical to attempt here, but the recognition of the notion of a *condition* of sinfulness is valuable if we are to draw MRJ's characters out of those readings which evaluate only their individual actions. The writings of Irenaeus also become useful here as their focus is not on the cause of universal sin (Adam), so much as its universality. For Irenaeus, writing two centuries before Augustine, the connection between universal sin and salvation was a social and communal one. *Everybody* is in a condition of sinfulness, thus *everybody* requires the redemptive salvation of Christ, and can be guided to that salvation through the communal body of the Church. Moreover, just as St. Paul roots the redemption of Gentiles in the covenant community of Israel, Irenaeus stresses the *communal* universality of Christ's redemption:

> For it was not merely for those who believed in Him in the time of Tiberius Caesar that Christ came, nor did the Father exercise His providence for the men who are now alive, but for all men altogether, who from the beginning, according to their capacity, in their generation have both feared and loved God.[22]

Solidarity in grace means that the role of the religious community, the Church, becomes fundamental. The *togetherness* of grace is here not just incidental but *necessary*. Through a discussion of 'Canon Alberic's Scrapbook' and 'Count Magnus', this chapter will seek to demonstrate that far from being the victims of a capricious universe, the protagonists' experiences are inextricably linked to their relationships with, or isolation from, the humanity which surrounds them.

The real significance of Irenaeus for this chapter, however, is in his writings in response to Gnosticism. Irenaeus' major work, *Against Heresies*, is a vigorous defence of Christian orthodoxy in reply to the challenges of the Gnostics. This Gnostic movement, which became influential in the late Roman period, appeared to offer a new and esoteric reading of Scripture and the Apocrypha which privileged transcendental, internal knowledge. In keeping with the insistence that the Christological being is communal rather than individual, *Against Heresies* is an apologetic for the patristic tradition and the primacy of Scripture against the 'secrets' of Gnosticism, for 'such spirits as are commanded by these men, and speak when they desire it, are earthly and weak, audacious and impudent, sent forth by Satan for the seduction and perdition of those who do not hold fast that well-compacted faith which they received at first through the Church'.[23]

Such a debate might be likened to the shift from pre-modern to modern thinking in theology, in which the theocentric tradition of human nature and revelation was replaced with a Cartesian anthropocentric approach. By appealing to textual authority and the patristic tradition in his treatment of apocryphal texts, MRJ ultimately repeats the apologetics laid out by Irenaeus. In his scholarship, MRJ demonstrates an attempt to rediscover the line at which religious writing becomes heresy. MRJ's Irenaean apologetic also becomes the driving force behind his ghost stories, and the voice of Christian orthodoxy whispers through their pages, appealing to, but not always heard by MRJ's 'modern' protagonists.

Of course, MRJ's apologetic cannot be seen to simply mirror Irenaeus' clear recognition of a linear Scriptural and Church authority. However, the spiritual insecurities which are so often identified by MRJ's commentators are revealed by the ghost stories to be instead an apologetic which is explorative.[24] The moral complexity of the stories lies in the fact that they do not simply reinforce a univocal orthodoxy, but rather that they explore dangers and pitfalls faced by man as he attempts to distinguish that orthodoxy from among many voices as he navigates the worlds in which he finds himself.

'CANON ALBERIC'S SCRAPBOOK' AND 'COUNT MAGNUS'

An exploration of the fallen human condition in MRJ's stories will begin by examining the protagonists of 'Canon Alberic's Scrapbook' and 'Count Magnus', both included in *Ghost Stories of an Antiquary* (1904).[25] These stories give us Mr Dennistoun, whose search for European biblical manuscripts leads him to a demonic scrapbook, and Mr Wraxall, who inadvertently releases supernatural powers after coming across the story of the first Count Magnus in a small town in Sweden. Both, on immediate inspection, are prime examples of the victims of capricious fortune. However, it is through these two characters that I will seek to demonstrate the incompatibility of such a construct with MRJ's orthodoxy. Rather, the *perception* of such an arbitrary condition will be shown to be integral to man's flawed understanding of himself.

In 'Count Magnus', we are told the story of Mr Wraxall, pieced together from a diary kept while visiting Sweden with the intention of publishing a travel guide. While it appears that little is known about Wraxall, the narrator (who has come across the writings while researching his own travel book) does provide an opinion on the man's character.

> He must have been an intelligent and cultivated man. It seems that he was near being a Fellow of his college at Oxford—Brasenose, as I judge from the Calendar. His besetting fault was pretty clearly that of overinquisitiveness, possibly a good fault in the traveller, certainly a fault for which this traveller paid dearly enough in the end.[26]

On arriving in a small rural town, Wraxall becomes interested in legends of a count who lived there many years before, a tyrannical landowner who is said to have made a 'black pilgrimage', amongst other occult and alchemist activities. Count Magnus is said to have 'brought something or someone back with him from this pilgrimage, and the subsequent oral tradition of the town seems to involve stories almost exclusively of men fleeing from some terrifying force. Wraxall's landlord, for instance, tells him of some hunters who, with the Count long dead and buried, go poaching in his wood. The villagers find the men the next day, one of them still alive:

> Hans Thobjorn was standing with his back against a tree, and all the time he was pushing with his hands—pushing something away from him which was not there. So he was not dead. And they led him away, and took him to the house at Nykjoping, and he died before the winter; but he went on pushing with his hands.[27]

This image of flight is repeated in the scenes which Wraxall finds engraved on Count Magnus' sarcophagus, one of which shows a man 'running at full speed, with flying hair and outstretched hands' from a strange form. 'It would be hard to say whether the artist had intended it for a man, and was unable to give the requisite similitude, or whether it was intentionally made as monstrous as it looked.'[28] Wraxall decides that this apparently allegorical representation of a fiend pursuing a hunted soul must be the origin of the stories surrounding Count Magnus.

To Augustine, this sense of movement is integral to the human condition. Crucially, however, man flees from nothingness, *towards* God. In this flight from the nihil, we move towards our Christian *telos*. This teleology is one of being or non-being, following Plotinus: 'We exist more as we turn to him, less as we turn away.'[29] To Augustine, however, our fallen condition means that on this teleological journey we are constantly pursued by our fallen aspect, the dark and ungodly part of ourselves which is inexplicably drawn to the nihil. Just as Arthur Machen's *The Three Impostors* establishes the nihil as the antithesis of human 'being', 'Count Magnus' also demonstrates this nothingness through the removal of what makes its victims recognisably human. The hunters in the wood, chased by the form depicted in the engraving so uncannily like but not like a man, are literally rendered faceless: 'he was once a beautiful man, but now his face was not there, because the flesh of it was sucked away of the bones. You understand that?' Wraxall, however, recognises no such teleology in himself, and rather calls *for* the Count. Wraxall it seems, has a habit of talking to himself aloud, but, perhaps acknowledging the analogy to prayer, he is careful to note that 'unlike some of the Greek and Latin particles, I do not expect an answer'.[30] It might better be said that he does not acknowledge that he *wants* an answer, and in this way Wraxall summons the Count, each time unlocking a padlock from the Count's sarcophagus.

The role of oral tradition is worth noting here, as, if this orthodox reading of MRJ is to be accepted, oral tradition creates a potential tension between authoritative and communal 'truth'. However, if one also accepts the orthodox argument that the self is inherently communal, then the role of oral tradition can itself ease this tension. On writing about recorded history and fiction, for instance, Pickstock acknowledges our need for 'recounted life', arguing that humanity understands itself in terms of an 'oral' memory of the past.[31] In this way they are extra-temporal and extra individual histories, and can inform the Thomist *esse*.

If oral tradition reinforces the communal nature of man, Wraxall's failure to *hear* it is emphasised in the crippling sense of isolation which saturates the climax of the story. After the opening of the sarcophagus (it is not clear what exactly comes out), the narrator notes that Wraxall's writings become disjointed and confused as he makes his way back to England. The sense of pursuit, however, is constant, and strongest of all a sense of isolation. Two men in dark cloaks appear to be following Mr Wraxall, and while he makes 'no less than six painful attempts' to describe his other fellow passengers on the journey, the result is always a description of one of these two men. In his last despairing writings, Wraxall seems to have realised his condition, turned, as it were, away from God and towards the nihil:

> He is expecting a visit from his pursuers—how or when he knows not—and his constant cry is 'What has he done?' and 'Is there no hope?' Doctors, he knows, would call him mad, policemen would laugh at him. The parson is away. What can he do but lock his door and cry to God?[32]

In his examination of the scapegoat figure in MRJ, Scott Connors identifies Northrop Frye's description of the scapegoat as *pharmakos* in the victims of MRJ's supernatural tales.[33] It is worth unpacking this idea further, as while Frye's *pharmakos* reinforces the Aristotelian pathos for Connors, it in fact gives the lie to the arbitrary tragedy of MRJ's victimhood; that the 'inevitable irony of human life' is in fact not inevitable, but that the *perception* of the human condition as such is in fact yet another distorting voice drowning out the voice of man's orthodox *telos*. Frye writes that:

The central principle of tragic irony is that whatever exceptional happens to the hero should be causally out of line with his character. Tragedy is intelligible, not in the sense of having any pat moral to go with it, but in the sense that Aristotle had in mind when he spoke of discovery or recognition as essential to the tragic plot. [...] Irony isolates from the tragic situation in the sense of arbitrariness, of the victim's having been unlucky, selected at random or by lot.[34]

The archetype of the inevitably ironic, according to Frye's model, is Adam, human nature under sentence of death, and the archetype of the incongruously ironic is Christ, the perfectly innocent victim. A Christological understanding of the human condition, however, might universalise Adam's sentence of death, but it offers a redemptive *telos* through the *Imago Christi*. While MRJ's characters may present themselves as Frye's *pharmakos*, then, their victimhood is neither inevitable nor incongruous. The tragic irony for Wraxall or Dennistoun is not that they are the *pharmakos*, but that they perceive themselves as such.[35]

Dennistoun faces his ἀποκαλυψις when he discovers the scrapbook of Canon Alberic while on the hunt for biblical manuscripts in France. After an uncomfortable visit to the church of a small town, in which he is accompanied by a sacristan with a 'curious furtive, or rather hunted air', he falls into conversation with the man, and discovers that he holds some old papers at home. The scrapbook which Dennistoun is then shown is a tremendous find in terms of antique manuscripts, and he promptly buys it from the sacristan (for much less than its value), who seems at once eager to be rid of it and hesitant to let Dennistoun have it. On one of the pages of the scrapbook, Dennistoun has noticed a ghastly illustration which depicts a terrible and seemingly demonic beast in front of King Solomon:

> At first, you saw only a mass of black matted hair: presently it was seen that this covered a body of fearful thinness—almost a skeleton, but with the muscles standing out like wires. The hands were of a dusk pallor, covered like the body with long coarse hairs, and hideously taloned. The eyes, touched in with a burning yellow, had intensely black pupils, and were fixed upon the throned king with a look of beast-like hate.[36]

From that moment on, Dennistoun is severely troubled, with the conviction that he is being followed. Dennistoun has been given a crucifix to wear by the daughter of the sacristan, but he removes it on returning to his hotel room, and as he lays it down on the table, catches sight of a hand lying just to the left of his elbow. The hand is unmistakably that of the beast in the picture, and Dennistoun turns to see the beast behind him, 'and the exulting hate and thirst to destroy life which shone [in its eyes] were the most horrifying features in the whole vision'.

Hearing his screams, two serving men rush in, and feel a presence rushing past them out the door. Dennistoun returns to England with the scrapbook, but without the drawing, which he photographs and then burns before leaving the town.

Dennistoun, like Wraxall, is clearly a man of no malice, nor has he committed any apparent 'crime' for which he must be punished. (As Canon Alberic's own story emerges, it must be said, he clearly does have his own sins to answer for, as will be discussed below.) In the drawing of the beast, however, and in the reasons for its effect on those who see it, MRJ gives some of his clearest allusions to man as a universal sinner. These come in the form of the writings on the back of the drawing, and the mention of certain biblical passages to which Dennistoun refers when thinking of his experiences. For instance, on one occasion he recalls the Book of Isaiah: 'Isaiah was a very sensible man; doesn't he say something about night-monsters living in the ruins of Babylon? These things are rather beyond us at present.'[37] This refers to Isaiah 34, in which the city of Edom is razed by God in his anger against all men, all nations. In these biblical verses, the ruins of Edom are to become overrun with wild beasts, the domesticated animals having been smitten with their owners: 'They will possess it forever, and dwell there from generation to generation' (34:19–20). This passage from Isaiah provides a fitting metaphor for the human spirit which, cut-off from God, allows its primordial, beastly nature to emerge.

In this way MRJ echoes Machen in his depiction of a being without Life, in the Christological sense. The beast of the scrapbook is at once human-like and inhuman:

> Imagine one of the awful bird-catching spiders of South America translated into human form and endowed with intelligence just less than human, and you will have some faint conception of the terror inspired by this appalling effigy.[38]

Compare this to Machen's description of Helen's death in 'The Great God Pan':

Then I saw the body descend to the beasts whence it ascended, and that which was on the heights go down to the depths, even to the abyss of all being. The principle of life, which makes organism, always remained, while the outward form changed.[39]

This sense of the beast as human but not human is crucial. In the previous chapter on Machen's stories, I established his beasts as 'least man', a primordial form of life without the potential for grace and the fulfilment of a Christological teleology. Machen's beasts are therefore characterised by *absence*, in which the Christological human has become the ghost figure. MRJ's beast complicates this by being at once a continuation of this nihilistic absence, and an *intrinsic* presence. MRJ's characters are chased and followed by these beasts, and the ghost figure is again revealed to be haunting the human 'being'. In a certain extraction of the gothic doppelgänger, the human being is haunted by the un-human, or in-human, being. A tension thus develops between 'least human' and 'un-human', the difference residing in the potential to become more human. The teleological move from Machen's stories to MRJ's reflects this, from Machen's nihilistic presences who are only masked as human, to MRJ's semi-anthropomorphic demons.

As in Machen's story, however, this beast is a creature furthest from the *Imago Christi*, thus furthest from what it means to be human, and it is in this sense that the context of the drawing in which the beast appears reveals its significance. The beast is depicted before King Solomon, who, while 'his face expressed horror and disgust, yet there was in it also the mark of imperious command and confident power'.[40] MRJ's story is ostensibly one of attempted power over a demonic beast, but as shall be seen, by infusing that beast with anthropomorphic qualities, MRJ also reveals Thomist and Augustinian associations of the lower being *within* man, and the struggle for control over that being. Michel Foucault vividly describes this internal animalistic struggle in *Madness and Civilisation*:

> The beast is set free; it escapes the world of legend and moral illustration to acquire a fantastic nature of its own. And by an astonishing reversal, it is now the animal that will stalk man, capture him, and reveal him to his own truth. Impossible animals, issuing from a demented imagination, become the secret nature of man; and when on the Last Day sinful man appears in his hideous nakedness, we see that he has the monstrous shape of a delirious animal.[41]

Just as the horror of Machen's primordial beasts is that they are revealed as beings without humanity, so too can MRJ's beast be read as such. Moreover, MRJ's depiction of the beast as standing before Solomon thus becomes crucial to this argument as understanding man's being as *guided* towards God.

MRJ included 'Solomon and the Demons' from *The Testament of Solomon* in his volume *Old Testament Legends* in 1913, and MRJ's approach to the authority of the biblical text is useful in interpreting the symbolism of both the biblical Solomon and that of the testament. The biblical King Solomon is associated most strongly with his wisdom, but this wisdom is inherently one of submission. As he becomes king, Solomon immediately establishes his reign as one guided by the word of God, asking: 'Give your servant therefore an understanding mind to govern your people, able to discern between good and evil'.[42] Over time, however, Solomon is persuaded by his many wives to worship at the altar of other gods, and for this he is punished with the loss of his sovereignty.

The 'Testament of Solomon', a text which MRJ describes ultimately as 'without doubt very foolish, and superstitious, and corrupt, and bad', expands on this distancing of Solomon from God as he becomes seduced by his own power over demons.[43] After several anecdotes in which Solomon is shown to force demons into subservience, Solomon declares that 'when I became mighty my heart was lifted up, and I committed foolishness'. As in the Bible, Solomon then turns to worship false gods in order to win a certain bride. 'And forthwith my glory departed from me, and I forgot my wisdom, and became weak and foolish in my mind'.[44] MRJ concludes his translation of this text (or rather collection of texts) with Solomon's warning to others: 'Therefore I have written this testament, that men might remember me, and think of their latter end as well as of their beginning.' Solomon's wisdom brings him power over the demonic and beastly, both within and without himself, but that wisdom is destroyed as soon as he forgets his submission to God's guidance.

This explicit need for the guidance of the authoritative word of God for man to 'think of their latter end as well as their beginning' is very clearly mirrored in 'The Scrapbook of Canon Alberic'. In the pages of the scrapbook Dennistoun finds a plan of the church and a legend which makes it clear that the Canon attempted to harness the power of the demon for his own ends, in order to find some treasure:

> It was asked: Shall I find it? Answer: Thou shalt. Shall I become rich? Thou wilt. Shall I live an object of envy? Thou wilt. Shall I die in my bed? Thou wilt.[45]

After Dennistoun's experiences in his hotel room, the footnoted information that the Canon died 'in bed, of a sudden seizure'[46] takes on a certain irony. In this way the 'haunting' image of the drawing becomes not only the beast, but Solomon, distracted by his own will to power from the guiding voice of Christianity. The ease with which the beast 'follows' both the sacristan and Dennistoun demonstrates the universal *tendency* of man to turn away from God and towards his baser self. In this way MRJ reinforces the Augustinian claim that the Fall manifests itself in man as a forgetfulness of God, and a volitional turn towards the nihil. Augustine writes: 'This alone I know: without you it is evil for me, not only in external things but within my being'.[47] Once again, a 'ghost' story is seen to be haunted not by an unknown demon, but by man as fallen. The narrator of 'Scrapbook' retains the photograph of the drawing, and why he has not been visited by the beast is not made clear. However, the universality indicated by this reading suggests a latency to the photograph through which this narrative detail becomes chilling.

That this universality of the human spirit is also potentially positive and certainly communal, as suggested by Irenaeus, is further indicated by Dennistoun's isolation from those around him. Just as Wraxall failed to absorb and respond to the oral traditions of the Swedish community, Dennistoun's Modernist world-view isolates him from the members of the French village. This spiritual isolation is subtly symbolised in the crucifix given to Dennistoun by the sacristan's daughter.

Having purchased the scrapbook and left the sacristan's house (only, notably, after reassuring the sacristan that he will be shortly joined by friends), Dennistoun is chased by the daughter, who wishes to give him a crucifix for protection. Dennistoun's immediate response is one of mistrust and suspicion; that she wishes to sell him the crucifix and 'perhaps, like Gehazi, to "take somewhat" from the foreigner whom her father had spared'.[48] Dennistoun has left the sacristan and daughter eagerly, preferring to be alone with his find. Once in his room, he removes the crucifix, and it is at this moment that the beast appears. I would argue, however, that MRJ is not suggesting that the crucifix provides some sort of supernatural protection as an object. Rather, that the care which is *gifted* to Dennistoun by the daughter has offered protection to Dennistoun as a *communal* being. Dennistoun's mistake lies not in a failure to adopt the daughter's superstition, but in his failure to respond to the invitation to communal care.

I have attempted here to demonstrate, through the examples of Wraxall and Denninstoun (I could have chosen from a host of others), that if understood through the lens of an orthodox theological anthropology, the capricious nature of MRJ's ghost stories is revealed instead to be a telling reflection of fallen man's isolation from his own *telos*. MRJ's protagonists are estranged from their sense of self as at once fallen and the *Imago Dei*. As they encounter man in his fallen and basest form, they have no recourse to the redemptive potential of that universal state. The tales are thus haunted by the *potential* man, and it is through the characters' isolation from this Christian *telos* that the horror of the tales is played.

'Mr Humphreys and His Inheritance'

In 'Mr Humphreys and His Inheritance' (henceforth 'Inheritance'), MRJ takes the notion of man's *telos* as guided and brings it to the fore.[49] The Gnostic instinct to turn inwards in search of spiritual revelation is shown to distort and corrupt, leading 'into a land of darkness and the shadow of death, without any order and where the light is as darkness'.[50] In 'Inheritance' we meet John Humphreys as he arrives on the train from London to embark upon his new life as landed gentry. A recognisable M.R. Jamesian protagonist, academic and sensible, Humphreys has inherited his estate from an estranged uncle, including the curiosity of an overgrown and shut-up topiary maze within the grounds. A combination of library research and a project to clear and restore the maze reveals that it was built by a James Wilson as an act of esoteric religious fervour. The story tells of Humphreys' experiences as the secrets of the maze are unleashed.

Martin Hughes has noted that through this story 'the reader encounters another kind of maze, created by the allusions and symbols which James uses'.[51] The richness of this symbolism (such as the motifs inscribed on the metal globe at the centre of the maze) has not gone unnoticed by scholars, several of whom have explored the potential messages of these symbols.[52] I will not attempt a further detailed examination of these symbols here, not only because much light has already been shed by Hughes and Pardoe, but moreover as it is my claim that it is the maze itself which is the most potent symbol of this story. James Wilson's maze is the most prominent example of MRJ's orthodox apologetic, acting as it does as a metaphor for the progress of the human soul towards God, no less so than the floor labyrinths of Christian Cathedrals.

The maze is represented in three ways in 'Inheritance'. Firstly, it stands as a physical object in the gardens of the estate, and secondly it is represented on paper as John Humphreys attempts to make sense of it by mapping its path. We also come across a third maze, as part of *A Parable of this Unhappy Condition*, a passage which Humphreys comes across in a small book in the library. This parable describes a 'Labyrinth or Maze [...] as was not laid out in the Fashion of our *Topiary* artists of this Age, but of a wide compass, in which moreover such unknown pitfalls and Snares, nay, such ill omened Inhabitants encountered at the Hazard of one's very life'.[53] The parable goes on to tell the story of a man who, despite warnings against it from the community, is lured into a maze which promises a precious jewel at its centre. After a day and a night, the community decides the man must have perished in the maze, as one more of 'those unfortunates that had suffer'd shipwreck on that Voyage', but they find him at the gate of the maze in a swoon. Although he has retrieved the jewel, he has also been pursued by some darker prize. He tells the others: "tis here in my Breast: I cannot flee from it, do what I may'. He goes on to tell of how he reached the centre of the maze easily, but as he tried to find his way out as night fell, he became conscious of some creature keeping pace with him. The rest of the night was spent in terrified flight through the maze, along with 'the constant Fear of falling into some Pit or Trap'. The parable ends with an exposition of the intended parallel:

> For is not this Jewel a just Emblem of the Satisfaction which a Man may bring back with him from a Course of this World's Pleasures? and will not the *Labyrinth* serve for an Image of the World itself wherein such a Treasure (if we may believe the common Voice) is stored up?[54]

Despite ending with a passage so rich in MRJ's theological themes, John Humphreys' response to the parable is to lay it aside in favour of a game of patience. This is particularly surprising as so much of the parable mirrors Humphreys' own experiences of the maze. Like the man in the parable, Humphreys (twice) finds his way almost without thought to the centre of the maze, but finds it hard to get back out, his exit accompanied by an increasing sense that he is being followed, and is not alone.[55]

Labyrinths and mazes have an ancient history as symbols for man's journey, a tradition of which MRJ makes full use in 'Inheritance'.

Although a pre-Christian symbol, the labyrinth as adopted by Christianity becomes a potent metaphor for man's spiritual teleology. The symmetry of the Christian labyrinth stands in contrast to the 'irrational' pagan maze. The symmetry and structure of the church maze is dictated by the presence of the cross, which imposes not only symmetry, but a double-retrograde, in which the walker journeys *nearly* to the centre several times, each time returning outwards in a mirror to their steps inward. Crucially for this metaphor, this symmetry is not at all apparent to the walker of the labyrinth, but only by standing *outside* the labyrinth; a clear symbol for man's limited perception in contrast to God's omnipotent eye.[56]

As shall be seen, Humphreys struggles to overcome this limit in 'Inheritance', as he attempts to bring the topiary into order and draw a map of the maze. The Christian interpretation to such a metaphor, however, responds in two very different ways, and I would argue that it is this conflict which MRJ explores in 'Inheritance'. The crux of this conflict lies in the motto cut over the entrance to the maze: *Secretum meum mihi et filiis domus meae*, a motto which has repeatedly challenged scholars of the story.[57] This phrase translates as 'My secret is for me and the sons of my house', although I would suggest that the emphasis of the possessive meum/mihi construction also makes plausible the translation 'I have a secret for me and the sons of my house alone.' Martin Hughes describes the inscription as both a warning and an invitation, and notes that Humphreys appreciates neither the warning nor the promise, and thus 'neither thinks how to protect himself nor considers whether the promise is really attractive'.[58] In this way Humphreys joins Wraxall and Dennistoun in their inability to perceive the voices which populate their path. Hughes' observations lead him to the conclusion that the exclusivity of the secret, for the 'sons of the house', is a clear indication that the motto declares the triumph of 'secret morality' (symbolised by the maze) over conventional morality. However, while the story's maze clearly symbolises esotericism, the moral complexity of the statement is much more subtle.

In his history of the symbolic maze, Craig Wright explains that the Gnostics were one of the first branches of Christianity to adopt the labyrinth symbol, seeing it as representative of the spiritual life filled with sin and error, through which Christ descends to bring special wisdom (Gnosis) which leads the soul from the labyrinth.[59] The motto above the entrance, along with the heavily inscribed globe at the centre of the maze makes it clear that this maze was laid by James Wilson as some form of esoteric religious expression. Humphreys is slowly drawn into this invitation to secret wisdom, albeit unwittingly, as he attempts to 'master' the maze, by plotting it and decoding the symbols on the globe at its centre.

Meanwhile, however, he is also surrounded by more orthodox voices; the parable, for instance, or the uneducated but insightful commentary of Mr Cooper, tasked with introducing Humphreys to his new position.

While Humphreys has seemed until this point oblivious to any of these voices, while unconsciously drawn to the promise of the secrets held by the maze, his attempts at mastering it eventually reach their terrifying conclusion as he sits one evening tracing a plan of the maze for Lady Wardrop, a maze enthusiast to whom he has given an unsuccessful tour. In a repetition of the feeling of being pursued out of the maze, Humphreys has the feeling that something is in the room with him: 'not a bat, but something more considerable—that had a mind to join him. How unpleasant it would be if someone had slipped noiselessly over the sill, and was crouching on the floor!'[60] As he draws, he notices a black spot in the middle of the original, resembling a hole. The hole seems to go not only through the paper, but the table beneath, 'yes, and through the floor below that, down and still down, even into infinite depths'. As Humphreys stares in horror into the hole, something starts to move towards him from its depths:

> Nearer and nearer it came, and it was of a blackish-grey colour with more than one dark hole. It took shape as a face—a human face—a *burnt* human face: and with the odious writhings of a wasp creeping out of a rotten apple there clambered forth an appearance of a form, waving black arms prepared to clasp the head that was bending over them.[61]

In his horror, Humphreys throws himself backwards hitting his head. While disoriented and recovering, Humphreys demands that the globe in the maze be opened, revealing, of course, the ashes of a cremation.

MRJ has clearly established the Gnostic path through the labyrinth as one which leads to damnation. The Roman Christian poet Prudentius provides a useful model for this metaphor, by contrasting the single-path of the labyrinth with the multi-cursal maze. The single path represents one guided by God, as portrayed later in the cross formation (see above), while in the maze, one follows Satan:

> On the manifold way the guide is the devil, who on the left hand splits it into the confusion of a hundred paths. [...] You have no fellowship in the way with the people of God. Depart ye afar, and enter into your own darkness, whither that guide calls you, who goes before you over tangled ways from the road, in the night of hell![62]

However, in keeping MRJ's gentle, explorative apologetic, it is important that the story is not simply a condemnation of esotericism. Where Gnosticism is here secret, introspective and isolated, MRJ infuses the story with voices of Christian orthodoxy and in this way repeats Irenaeus' response to the Gnostics.

There are two aspects to this response within the maze metaphor. The first is that the path through the Christian labyrinth is *guided*, and the second that this path is *communal*.[63] These two aspects are inextricable, in that the voice of authority is at once communal and exemplary. Irenaeus writes: 'The apostles, like a rich man depositing his money in a bank, lodged in her [the Church] hands most copiously all things pertaining to the truth: so that every man, whomsoever will, can draw from her the water of life.'[64] All are entitled to this truth, but it is the authoritative tradition which ensures continuing access to that truth: The Christian *telos* of man is one guided by truth, and that guidance is there for those who recognise themselves as fallen but guided, and submit to that guidance. Again, it is in this way that the Christian mode of being is necessarily a communal one. It is through the faithful community that this tradition is nurtured and the guidance given voice.

MRJ gives voice to this communal tradition through the community of estate workers and the range of texts in the library. Humphreys has a choice of voices to which to listen, but is unable to do so without recognising his own Christological position; his own *need* of guidance. Although he expects to find treasures in the library, for instance, he is struck by 'the extreme unreadableness' of a great portion of the collection. 'Editions of classics and Fathers, and Picart's *Religious Ceremonies*, and the *Harleian Miscellany*, I suppose are all very well, but who is ever going to read Tostatus Abulensis, or Pineda on Job?'[65] Likewise Mr Cooper serves as a constant companion to Humphreys' encounter with the maze, supplying commentary which although ostensibly simplistic, shows a distinct wisdom in light of this orthodox apologetic. On Humphreys' first and suspiciously easy exploration into the centre of the maze, for instance, he observes:

> 'You've penetrated into the heart of the mystery *unaided* and unannealed, as the saying goes. Well! I suppose it's a matter of thirty to forty years since any human foot has trod these precincts. Certain it is that I've never set foot in them before. Well, well, what's the old proverb about angels fearing to tread? It's proved once again in this case.'[66]

Cooper then heads back out of the maze with Humphreys, and despite Cooper's claims to have never trodden the maze, this is the only time that Humphreys retraces his steps with ease. Cooper thus symbolises the necessary guide, essentially a Christ figure. The metaphor closely mirrors Gregory of Nyssa's claim that Christ enters the metaphorical maze in order to lead man out: 'They would not have escaped had they not followed their guide step by step.'[67]

Ultimately, however, MRJ shows the redemptive power of this guiding voice most clearly in his story draft 'John Humphreys', in which a protagonist of the same name has also inherited an estate, and while walking through it finds that the path has changed as to become unrecognisable, at which point he is overcome with an inexplicable sense of terror and despair. The draft may not have the brilliant complexity of 'Inheritance', but its climax is one of the clearest of MRJ's orthodox apologetic.[68] With this in mind, it is worth quoting the passage in full:

> Of two things he felt convinced all the while: one was that this deadly fever came from someone outside himself, someone who was near to him then; the other that there was something which he ought to remember and could remember if the pressure [of dreadful images] on his brain would only relax for an instant! The only words he could summon were words of fear, that he had read that morning. They droned through his head incessantly, 'ubi umbra mortis et nullus ordo sed sempiternus horror inhabitat'.[69] Over and over again they came back and he felt himself being sucked away from the world of men, and indeed he does not see how he could have helped yielding to the strain that was on him, and giving up hope and reason if not life itself, had he not paused on the words *umbra mortis*. They brought to his mind in a moment the image of some lettering in a brass on a tomb—this is how he puts it—that he had been taken to see years before. '*Umbra mortis*,' he seemed to say to himself, 'to be sure, that was it—*etsi ambulavero*.'[70] He raised his head and drew breath. 'Absurd,' he said again. 'Of course that was what I wanted. Dear me. Why couldn't I think of that before?' The strain was relaxed. He rose to his feet and looked about him: the field was its own familiar self again and the sun bright in the sky. An exaltation of spirit came upon him which he could hardly repress, and he does not know what surprises of laughter and singing he may have inflicted on casual hearers as he went home. [Upon his graver feelings there is no need to dwell]
>
> The satisfaction he felt was complete and permanent: he [was sure now that even the bare unhoused spirit has nothing to fear] had a talisman now which could always [dispel the darkness] rout the influence that had been deliberately trying to kill his physical life and blind his mental eye. And soon he began to think what that influence could be. He had felt when he rose from the ground as if someone had hastily moved away, and that in anger. What more he thought, I do not think it necessary to set forth now.[71]

In this scene Humphreys is in direct battle against being dragged into the nihil. The 'someone who was near to him' has, so he feels, been following him at a distance for several days, echoing again the motif of the soul pursued. And again, as with Dennistoun and Wraxall, the effect of this pursuit is to create isolation: 'he felt himself being drawn away from the world of men'. In this story draft MRJ's protagonist is redeemed by turning directly to Scripture.[72] Moreover, this redemption is 'complete and permanent'. By knowingly turning to this voice, the threat to Humphreys is removed entirely and replaced with 'an exultation of spirit'. In this draft at least, the voice of orthodoxy has triumphed.

Conclusion

In many ways, MRJ's ghost stories have something of the Doppelgänger tradition.[73] As discussed in chapter 3, Arthur Machen's weird tales turn to orthodoxy to combat the *absence* of Christological humanity, but for MRJ, it is the constant presence of man's blinded self, thrashing about in the abyss, which haunts. Charles Taylor describes the modern self as 'bounded', and this description fits perfectly MRJ's protagonists. The pre-modern self by contrast was continuous with external things, in constant exchange with them. In this way the external world (both natural and otherwise) can affect the self, impose meaning on the self. For the modern bounded self, by contrast, 'the possibility exists of taking a distance from, disengaging from everything outside the mind. 'My ultimate purposes are those which arise within me, the crucial meanings of things are those defined in my responses to them.'[74] For MRJ's protagonists, they see their experiences as having value in so far as those experiences reinforce or assimilate to their own world-view. It is of no little significance that Catherine Pickstock, drawing on Taylor's 'bounded' self, describes the modern process of secularisation as 'less the loss of a sense of God than of a sense of the demonic'.[75] Crucial to MRJ's stories is that this claim refers not to the disappearance of the demonic, but to the *sense* of the demonic. These demons, these least (Christologically) human versions of ourselves, are still there, waiting for us in the spiritual labyrinth.

It is this 'sense' of the demonic which orthodoxy offers MRJ's characters, providing a lens through which they can (potentially) interpret these meetings with themselves. The world which MRJ depicts, however, is not that of Irenaeus' clear Church lineage and Patristic clarity, but a world flooded with many voices, both instructive and deceptive. MRJ's maze is the modern world itself, and the threat to MRJ's protagonists lies as much in their failure to hear or heed meaning as any of MRJ's beasts and demons.

Despite the horror of the stories, however, MRJ does allow for the voice of guidance to whisper through his stories, invariably through the community in which his protagonists find themselves, community being so intrinsically bound up with orthodoxy.[76] As Mr Cooper, just such a figure, surmises:

> Mr Cooper's view is that, humanly speaking, all these many solemn events have a meaning for us, if our limited intelligence permitted of our disintegrating it.[77]

Notes

1. MRJ, as used by M. R. James himself in personal letters and book inscriptions. In other chapters, the moniker 'James' is used to refer to the author Henry James.
2. M. R. James, 'Preface', in *Ghost Stories of an Antiquary* (London: Edward Arnold, 1905), viii.
3. Julia Briggs, *Night Visitors: The Rise and Fall of the English Ghost Story*. (Bristol: Faber and Faber, 1977), 125.
4. Michael Cox, while remarking on the ingenuity and 'sheer artistic accomplishment' of MRJ's tales (142), goes so far as to suggest that 'though James' stories are amongst the very best of their kind it is easy to claim too much for them, and even easier to impose on them a weight of critical analysis and speculation that they can hardly bear' (*M.R. James: An Informal Portrait* London: Oxford University Press, 1983, 149). Victor Sage is one of the few scholars to view MRJ's ghost stories as extensions of his theological scholarship, placing them as responses to the Protestant Establishment, and writing that 'the two sides of his character sum up perfectly the connection [Sage has] been trying to make between the apparently secure daylight centre of Anglican culture and its concomitant twilight of political and theological unease' (*Horror Fiction in the Protestant Tradition*, New York: St Martin's Press, 1988, 61). This chapter departs from Sage in so far as it reads the tales as ultimately reinforcing Protestant orthodoxy.

5. M. R. James, *The Apocryphal New Testament: Being the Apocryphal Gospels, Acts, Epistles, and Apocalypses* (Trowbridge: Oxford University Press, 1980), xii.
6. See Pfaff, 7–8; Cox, *M.R. James*, 71–4; Cox, *Casting the Runes*, xi.
7. Herbert James, *The Country Clergyman and his Work: Six Lectures on Pastoral Theology Delivered in The Divinity School, Cambridge, May Term, 1889* (London and New York: Macmillan and Co., 1890), 46.
8. For a more detailed discussion of MRJ's relationship with organised religion, see Cox, *An Informal Portrait*, p. 72 sq., Richard William Pfaff, *Montague Rhodes James* (Bristol: Scholar Press, 1980), 88sqq.
9. Quoted in Pfaff, 89. Original material held in King's College Archive Centre, Cambridge.
10. Rosemary Pardoe, 'Some Thoughts on M.R. James's World View.' *Ghosts and Scholars*, 18 (1994), 43. Pardoe's journal *Ghosts and Scholars* (also available online) is a marvelous resource for MRJ material held at Kings College Cambridge, as well as publishing research into MRJ.
11. Pardoe, 'Some Thoughts', 44.
12. MRJ, *Apocryphal New Testament*, xxiv. The Clementine Literature is a set of dogmatic homilies said to originate with Pope Clement I.
13. MRJ, 'Canon Alberic's Scrapbook', in *Ghost Stories of an Antiquary* (London: Edward Arnold, 1904), 10.
14. An interesting example of the intensity of MRJ's feelings about secular approaches to religious texts can be seen in his correspondence to *The Classical Review* in 1917, following the publication of an article by Jane Harrison entitled 'The Head of John Baptist'. In a passage by passage dismantling of Harrison's article, MRJ is clearly horrified by what he sees as the carelessness of 'comparative mythology'. 'To speak of the love of Salome for the Baptist is to put the loathsome performances of Flaubert and Oscar Wilde in place of the Gospel Story,' claims MRJ. 'And is this Comparative Mythology? Or is it tolerable by this or any other name?' "Some Remarks on 'the Head of John Baptist'." *The Classical Review*, 31. 1 (1917): 1–4, 4. See also Jane Harrison, "The Head of John Baptist. τίνος πρόσωπον δη τ' ἐν ἀγκάλαις ἔχεις; (Eur. Bacch. 1277)." *The Classical Review*, 30. 8 (1916): 216–219.
15. Ron Weighell, 'Dark Devotions: M.R. James and the Magical Tradition.' In *Warnings to the Curious: A Sheaf of Criticism on M.R. James*, ed. S. T. Joshi and Rosemary Pardoe (New York: Hippocampus Press, 2007), 132.
16. Catherine Pickstock, *Repetition and Identity* (Oxford: Oxford University Press, 2013), 121. See also René Descartes, *Meditations on First Philosophy*, trans. John Cottingham (Cambridge: Cambridge University Press, 1990), 16sqq.
17. MRJ, 'Count Magnus', 163.

18. Charles Taylor, *A Secular Age* (USA: Harvard University Press, 2007), 305.
19. 'Oh Whistle and I'll Come to You, My Lad' is not explored in this chapter as it recalls closely the themes already discussed in Arthur Machen's chapter. However, it is interesting to read 'Oh Whistle' in mind of Machen's theological motifs.
20. See for instance Pardoe, 'Some thoughts'; Michael A. Mason, 'On Not Letting them Lie: Moral Significance in the Ghost Stories of M.R. James.' *Studies in Short Fiction*, 19 (1982): 253–60.
21. See Augustine, *City of God* XIII.13–15. *Against Julian*, V.2,3, VI.3.
22. Irenaeus, *Against Heresies*, IV.22. Cf. Acts 4:27–32, Gal 3:26–29.
23. Irenaeus, *Against Heresies*, I.13, 4.
24. Cf. Pfaff, *Montague Rhodes James*, 90, Cox, *Informal Portrait*, 72, Martin Hughes, 'A Maze of Secrets in a Story by M.R. James.' *In A Warning to the Curious: A Sheaf of Criticism on M.R. James*. (New York: Hippocampus Press, 2007), 261.
25. 'Scrapbook' had been published in magazine form in 1894.
26. MRJ, 'Count Magnus', 153.
27. MRJ, 'Count Magnus', 161, 168. Several suggestions for what exactly MRJ refers to by this 'black pilgrimage' are given by MRJ scholars. See for instance 'The Black Pilgrimage', Rosemary Pardoe and Jane Nicholls, in *A Pleasing Terror*, ed. Christopher Roden and Barbara Roden (British Columbia: Ash-Tree, 2001), 601–608; Michael Cox, *Casting the Runes and Other Ghost Stories*, notes; 'Count Magnus', 310. For the purposes of this reading, an understanding of the 'black pilgrimage' undertaken by Count Magnus as a symbolic journey into occult or demonic territory will be considered sufficient.
28. MRJ, 'Count Magnus', 171.
29. Plotinus, *Enneads*, VI. 6. 6. 12. See also Augustine, *Confessions*, II.x.18, X.xxiv.35. Natale Joseph Torchio offers a good description of Augustine's telos and nihil in *'Creatio Ex Nihilo' and the Theology of St Augustine: The Anti-Machinaean Polemic and Beyond* (New York: Peter Lang, 1999), 116–8, Machen, *Notes and Queries* (London: Spurr & Swift, 1926), 115.
30. MRJ, 'Count Magnus', 169, 164.
31. Pickstock, *Repetition*, 98.
32. MRJ, 'Count Magnus', 179.
33. Scott Connors, '"What Is This That I Have Done?" The Scapegoat Figure in the Stories of M.R. James', in *Warnings to the Curious: A Sheaf of Criticism on M.R. James*, ed. S. T. Joshi and Rosemary Pardoe (USA: Hippocampus Press, 2007), 215–224.
34. Northrop Frye, *Anatomy of Criticism* (USA: Princeton University Press, 1990), 41.

35. René Girard's seminal study of scapegoats as mimetic figures is discussed in relation to Sheridan Le Fanu in chapter 5.
36. MRJ, 'Canon Alberic's Scrapbook', 18.
37. MRJ, 'Scrapbook', 28.
38. MRJ, 'Scrapbook', 18–19. It is perhaps also worth mentioning MRJ's well-known arachnophobia.
39. Arthur Machen, 'The Great God Pan', in *The House of Souls* (London: E. Grant Richards, 1906), 236.
40. MRJ, 'Scrapbook', 17.
41. Michel Foucault, *Madness and Civilisation: A History of Insanity in the Age of Reason*, trans. Richard Howard (New York: Vintage Books, 1988), 21.
42. 1 Kings 3:9. See M.R. James, *Old Testament Legends* (London: Longmans, Green and Co, 1913), 107–119. It should be noted that MRJ does not consider the Testament of Solomon to be in itself an authoritative biblical text, but rather part of the later Apocrypha. Cf. MRJ, 'The Testament of Solomon.' *Guardian Church Newspaper*. 15th March 1899, 67.
43. MRJ, 'The Testament of Solomon', 367.
44. MRJ, *Old Testament Legends* 118, 119.
45. MRJ, 'Scrapbook', 7.
46. MRJ, 'Scrapbook', 12.
47. Augustine, *Confessions*, XIII.viii.9
48. MRJ, 'Scrapbook', 21.
49. First published in *More Ghost Stories of an Antiquary*, 1911.
50. MRJ, 'John Humphreys' (story draft), King's College Cambridge MS MRJ/A/11. Transcribed and annotated by Rosemary Pardoe, *The Ghosts and Scholars M.R. James Newsletter 11* (2007). Web. N. pag. Cf. Job 10.21-22. It should be noted that while sharing several core themes which will be utilised here, as well as the protagonist's name, 'John Humphreys' is not simply a draft of 'Inheritance', and has a substantially different plot.
51. Martin Hughes, 'A Maze of Secrets', 258.
52. See for instance Rosemary Pardoe and Jane Nicholls, "James Wilson's Secrets." *Ghosts and Scholars*, 24 (1997), 45–48, Hughes, 'A Maze of Secrets'.
53. MRJ, 'Inheritance', 185. Compare this to Prudentius, *Apotheiosis*: 'So many crossroads meet us, which have been trodden smooth by the misguided straining of the faithless […] and if, wandering at random, a man follows them, leaving the straight path, he will plunge into the snare of a hidden pitfall.' in *Works, I*, trans. H.J. Thomson (Cambridge MA: Harvard University Press, 1949), 117–119.
54. MRJ, 'Inheritance', 187, 188. Original emphasis.
55. It should be noted that in the company of Cooper, arguably the voice of 'simple wisdom' in the story, Humphreys finds it just as easy to leave the maze. The significance of this is discussed in further detail below.

56. See Craig Wright, *The Maze and the Warrior: Symbols in Architecture, Theology and Music* (Cambridge MA: Harvard University Press, 2001), 69sq.
57. MRJ, 'Inheritance', 180.
58. Hughes, 'A Maze of Secrets', 266.
59. Wright, *Maze and Warrior*, 73.
60. MRJ, 'Inheritance', 196. Several bats are flying around the darkened room.
61. MRJ, 'Inheritance', 85. Note again the semi-anthropomorphism.
62. Prudentius, 'Contra Oratorium Symmachi, Liber II', in *Works II*, 77–79.
63. Saint Jerome transforms Ariadne's thread into Christ's thread: '*et gyrans gyrando vadit spiritus, et in circulos suos revertitur (Eccl. I, 6); Labyrinthios patimur errores, et Christi caeca regimus filo vestigia.*' ('And turning in circles, the spirit goes forth and returns into its own circles; We suffer labyrinthine errors, and guide our blind steps with the thread of Christ.' My translation.) 'Commentariorum in Zachariam Liber Secundus', in *Patrologiae Latinae Cursus Completus XXV* (apud Garnier fratres et J.-P. Migne successores, 1845) 1453.
64. Irenaeus, *Against Heresies*, IV.1.
65. MRJ, 'Inheritance', 184.
66. MRJ, 'Inheritance', 181. My emphasis.
67. Quoted in Wright, *Maze and* Warrior, 75 (Wright's translation).
68. Further notes show that this would not have been the finale to the story had it been completed.
69. Job 10:22, 'the land of gloom and chaos, where light is as darkness'.
70. 'From the Vulgate Psalms xxiii, 4: "sed et si ambulavero in valle umbrae mortis non timebo malum ..." ("though I walk through the valley of the shadow of death, I will fear no evil"). The words "umbra mortis" also appear on an area of the globe in "Mr Humphreys and His Inheritance".' Footnote, Pardoe, 'John Humphreys', N. pag.
71. 'John Humphreys', N. pag. Text in square brackets are from notes on the manuscript by MRJ, included by Rosemary Pardoe.
72. See also Dennistoun's response to the beast in 'Scrapbook': 'He has never been quite certain what words he said, but he knows that he spoke, that he grasped blindly at the silver crucifix' (25).
73. Title quotation from Novalis, *Fichte Studies*, ed. Jane Kneller (Cambridge: Cambridge University Press, 2003), 185.
74. Taylor, *Secular Age*, 38.
75. Pickstock, *Repetition*, 121.
76. See Taylor, *Secular Age*, 43.
77. MRJ, 'Inheritance', 198.

CHAPTER 5

'These devils have made quite a saint of you': Sheridan Le Fanu

The Augustinian orthodoxy of Arthur Machen and M. R. James' stories shows the demonic experience to be inextricably linked to the human condition as fallen being.[1] Following Augustine in depicting evil as the privation of good, Machen's characters bring about evil agency from the nihil. MRJ's characters, meanwhile, are haunted by representations of their fallen selves as demonic beings; confrontations which demand recognition and reconciliation through submission to God. In the stories of Sheridan Le Fanu, whom MRJ called 'one of the best storytellers of the nineteenth century', and to whom all the other authors in this volume expressed a debt, a theological reading reveals even more fractured depictions of the human condition.[2] For Le Fanu, the gothic motif of doubling becomes central to describing a mode of being which, in its fallen state, responds both to the call of grace and demonic destruction.

By reading Le Fanu's stories theologically, it is possible to trace a journey of transformation from the fallen state to salvation. Indeed, it is possible to trace several journeys. The first is the journey taken by Le Fanu's protagonists as they recognise themselves as fallen beings, and accept the conditions necessary for grace and salvation. I will argue that in this journey, Le Fanu depicts a Lutheran 'justification in faith' which is fulfilled by an explicitly Augustinian transformation of being. The stories discussed here show the various stages of this journey, and I will use Kierkegaard's concept of dread as the lens through which to identify a Lutheran/Augustinian *Anfechtung*.

This is a departure from readings by scholars such as Victor Sage and James Walton, who see Le Fanu's depiction of dread as a Protestant anxiety in the face of the supernatural. Sage, for instance, identifies Le Fanu's gothic tales as playing with the tension between testimony to Anglo-Irish Protestant authority and the undermining of that 'sceptic' authority with 'superstition'.[3] Alison Milbank has offered another explanation, that rather than reflect theological conflict, these tales use the grotesque and the carnivalesque to allow Le Fanu's religious hybridity to be celebrated.[4] I will take Milbank's explanation further in this chapter, and describe this hybridity in terms of reconciliation, suggesting that an Augustinian lens allows the freedom of the carnivalesque to facilitate transformation.

The second journey revealed in these stories is one of narrative, a journey in which the reader participates. It is here that theological interpretations of terror bring Le Fanu's narratives into fruition. James Walton explains the Radcliffean distinction between horror and terror by describing horror as 'terror's *un*aesthetic opposite'.[5] The readings performed here will link this aesthetic aspect of horror and terror to theological terror: I will argue that those stories which are aesthetically unsuccessful are also those which are theologically unconvincing.

The concurrent themes of horror and terror are reflected in the ubiquitous appearance of doubles. The agency of Le Fanu's doubles is complicated, and these figures often appear to offer at once the possibility for salvation and the temptation of damnation. While stories such as 'The Mysterious Lodger' attempt to construct a Swedenborgian model of 'tempting demon' and 'saving angel', it will be argued that those stories in which this distinction is disintegrated depict haunting as a more genuine catalyst for spiritual change.[6] In these stories, doubling comes in the form of separation rather than mimesis, analogous to Augustine's double representation of the *Imago Dei* as at once showing our participation in and distance from God.

On this journey towards grace, the doubles of Le Fanu's stories confront their 'counter'-parts both with guiding voices of orthodoxy which anticipate MRJ, and with the demonic voices of man turned away from God, as is so vividly depicted in Machen's tales. The Faustian double certainly has a prominent role in Le Fanu's stories, but this role is complicated by doubles which appear as agents of Pauline resurrection. This agency is explored further in a reading of 'The Haunted Baronet'. Indeed, throughout Le Fanu's stories, the distinction of death, pseudo-death and resurrection is a reoccurring preoccupation. The fullness of death and

Pauline resurrection becomes aligned with the completion of spiritual change through grace, and spiritual stagnancy or entrapment is shown through pseudo-deaths, such as cataplexy or burial alive.

LE FANU AND THE IRISH PROTESTANT ESTABLISHMENT

Joseph Sheridan Le Fanu was born in 1814 in Dublin, the son of a clergyman in the Anglo-Irish Church. W. J. McCormack describes the Le Fanu family as having 'established themselves as comfortably bourgeois; as merchants and amateur bankers operating within the Protestant establishment'.[7] The Le Fanu family position as Huguenot descendants and members of the Protestant middle classes was one of uneasy positioning in the Irish establishment. McCormack describes just such an unease in Le Fanu's father's role as a Dean in the Church of Ireland: 'Church and landed estate provided oases of security for the establishment in the years before Catholic emancipation.' But, he goes on, 'they were dangerously remote oases, remote from each other, from the public opinion in Ireland, and from the realities of British politics'.[8] By the Catholic emancipation of 1829, violence was increasingly directed at the established classes of which the Le Fanu family was part, and both McCormack and Victor Sage see childhood anxiety of threat and isolation erupt in Le Fanu's later works. McCormack points towards representations of isolated houses suddenly disturbed by violence, and Sage sees the threat of the Catholic majority reflected in the resurgence of Catholic superstition in Le Fanu's gothic tales.[9]

Within this unease, however, is the second factor of the Le Fanu Huguenot inheritance, which is of particular interest to the readings which follow here. The Irish Huguenots had been French Calvinists who fled France from Catholic persecution in the seventeenth century. Many from the Huguenot community established themselves within the Anglican Church, although much of the Church's episcopal structure conflicted with Calvinist doctrine. In Ireland the early refugees needed to decide between the difficulties involved in remaining non-conformist (although they were free to practise their religion), and the security and social prospects of joining the established Church.[10] While many Huguenots joined the Anglicans, many even becoming central figures in its ecclesiastical ranks, a background of Calvinist non-conformity remained. Indeed, Raymond Hylton has suggested that nineteenth- and twentieth-century histories of Huguenot assimilation into the Anglican establishment has often ignored or minimised an active non-conformity in the Huguenot community. 'The place occupied by the Huguenots,' writes Hylton, 'as regards religion, in the life of Ireland would revolve around the question of Conformity vs. Dissent.'[11] It is this uneasy inheritance in which the Le Fanu family lived.[12] Where Sage identifies a resurgence of Catholic superstition in Le Fanu's tales, the readings below will suggest that just such a tension is to be found between the doctrines of Irish Protestantism and Calvinist election anxiety.

Sheridan Le Fanu embarked on his writing and journalistic career after graduating from Trinity College, and while critically acclaimed by his literary successors, during his lifetime he remained relatively undistinguished. In searching for the seeds of Le Fanu's supernatural tales in such a biography then, scholarly focus turns inevitably upon the long illnesses and death of his wife Susanna as one of the most striking and influential events in Le Fanu's life. Indeed, McCormack sees the apparent religious doubts of Susanna Le Fanu in the months leading to her death as the model for the wife in 'The Mysterious Lodger', arguably the most obvious religious allegory of Le Fanu's tales, in which the faith of a wife and the scepticism of a husband are each tested when they take in a demonic lodger.[13]

Certainly, Le Fanu's diary fragments from his early bereavement give some insight into the widower's religious frame of mind, suggesting that he sought comfort in the reassurances of pre-election of the soul. He writes:

> In these events there is no such thing as chance, and, over all seeming accidents presides the eternal dominion of our Heavenly Father, a control the most minute, and power immeasurable.[14]

While Le Fanu turns regularly to Luther in his diaries and letters, this notion demonstrates a Protestant conservatism which is distinctly Calvinist in its understanding of predestination. This tension between Calvinist anxiety and Augustinian grace is central to understanding the theology of Le Fanu's tales.

LE FANU'S AUGUSTINIAN JOURNEY—DOUBLING AND TRANSFORMATION

Unlike Luther's *Anfechtung*, in which terror can be the catalyst for grace, within Calvinism a feeling of doubt about one's own salvation can itself be a sign of damnation. Le Fanu's fiction, however, demonstrates something more problematic, or at least complex. The passivity of Calvin's elect is not represented in the supernatural journey depicted in his tales. Perhaps this is because in contrast to a doctrine in which the event of death fulfils spiritual ontology, either in salvation or damnation, Le Fanu's supernatural tales take place almost invariably in a narrative moment in which his protagonists are suspended in a pre-death state. For Feltram in 'The Haunted Baronet' this is a ghost-like resurrection; for Borrhomeo immortality in a cataplectic state. By suspending the transition between life and death, Le Fanu creates a '*super*-natural' space in which spiritual transformation is possible. It is in this suspended moment that the protagonists are confronted with themselves as theological beings. The suspended state introduces potentiality.

To describe this process, however, it is necessary to examine the theological concepts which are at stake. Central to this is grace, and the conditions necessary for grace. Augustine describes grace as partaking in divine life. However, underlying this doctrine is the Fall. Made in the image of God, man nonetheless no longer has communion with God. The Fall is first and foremost a separation from God. (As is discussed in chapter 4, for instance, the stories of M. R. James directly engage with this link between isolation and the human condition.) Grace, the 'intervention' of the divine on the human spirit, thus becomes the bridge through which man can return to God. Faith, and recognition of the self as fallen, provides the conditions for grace, for justification.

The 'justification of faith alone' is central to Lutheran theology, in that it brought a fundamental shift from the 'salvation by grace' described by the Patristic Fathers. For Martin Luther, justification through faith removes the role of the sinner in performing actions through which to attain salvation. Rather, faith alone allows for grace. Indeed, even faith itself is no longer an act, but a gift. God provides everything necessary for salvation. Le Fanu himself affirms this doctrine in his diaries, noting that, 'The wages of sin is death, but the *gift* of God is life everlasting—We all, every day, earn the one, but thou, Oh God of untiring & magnificent beneficience, wilt *give* the other!'[15] A certain doubling already occurs in Luther then, in that man can be at once a sinner and righteous. Luther likens the relationship to a patient and doctor whom the patient trusts to cure him. He writes:

> Can one say that this sick man is healthy? No; but he is at the same time both sick and healthy. He is actually sick, but he is healthy by virtue of the sure prediction of the physician whom he believes. [...] In the same way Christ,

our good Samaritan, brought the man who was half dead, his patient, to an inn and took care of him (Luke 10:30 ff.) and commenced to heal him, having first promised to him that he would give him absolutely perfect health unto eternal life. [...] Now can we say that [the patient] is perfectly righteous? No: but he is at the same time both a sinner and righteous, a sinner in fact but righteous by virtue of the reckoning and the certain promise of God that he will redeem him from sin.[16]

Such a justification leads inevitably to 'predestined' believers, who God can anticipate will receive faith and therefore righteousness. It is important to note for our readings below that this does not include an election for damnation (as in Calvinism). All are invited to respond to grace.

Crucially, not only grace but the conditions for grace are 'alien'. Righteousness (salvation) comes not from anything within us, but as an external gift. For Luther, this fulfils the promise of Christ, in that through faith in Christ, 'Christ's righteousness becomes our righteousness and all that he has becomes ours'.[17] Such an intervention of alien grace is most clearly depicted in 'The Mysterious Lodger', in which emblems of faith and hopelessness take the form of an apparent angel and a demon. This would appear to be radically different from the idea of a gradual transformation towards a state of grace.[18]

However, a specifically Augustinian understanding of justification opens up the possibility for a redemptive journey. For Augustine, this gift occurs *within* our being. Man is *changed* by grace. Augustine sees this change as a healing (also adopting the doctor/patient analogy), and Aquinas, in his exploration and expansion of Augustinian theology, describes this as habitual grace.[19] Here, grace brings about a habitual change in us, coming with the remission of sin. Aquinas writes: 'Not only grace, therefore, but many other of God's gifts pertain to grace. And hence the remission of sins does not take place without *some effect divinely caused in us*.'[20] Understanding a specifically Augustinian version of Luther's justification through faith is crucial to a theological reading of Le Fanu's tales, as by allowing for grace as transformative, it establishes the premise for the human condition as not just seemingly doubled (in that we do not know if we are saved or damned), but doubled in that both are *possible*. Man is at once the image of God and estranged from God, and man's *telos* is a process of sanctification. While on this teleological journey, the double is 'oneself as another', the teleological condition of man as estranged from God but returning to Him.

As Augustine's *Confessions* describe, the transformation of grace is not a momentary event, but a journey. Book 7 of *Confessions* describes a series of seemingly 'failed' attempts at mystical experience. In his book *The Mysticism of Saint Augustine: Rereading the Confessions*, however, John Peter Kenney challenges this reading of failure with the claim that 'the brevity of spiritual recognition is itself significant only when understood in light of the enduring truths revealed, especially the soul's abiding connection to the eternal forms.'[21] Indeed, in these experiences Augustine recognises both the supreme good and unchangeability of God, and the comparative insufficiency of the human soul: 'I was not stable in the enjoyment of my God. I was caught up to you by your beauty and quickly torn away from you by my weight.'[22] For a sustained relationship, Augustine realises the need for grace in the form of a mediator: 'I sought a way to obtain strength enough to enjoy you; but I did not find it until I embraced the mediator between God and man, the man Jesus Christ.'[23] Within this Augustinian description of mystical grace, then, is also a form of doubling, not simply a conflicting doubling of sinner and saved, but a constitutive one. Man is doubled with the man Christ, and it is by this doubling that Pauline resurrection of the soul can be fulfilled.

I have suggested that to read Le Fanu's supernatural tales is to link this theological journey to their aesthetic composition. Ann Radcliffe, in her seminal article on the gothic form, describes the response to supernatural events in terms of terror and horror. 'Terror and horror are so far opposite, that the first expands the soul, and awakens the faculties to the high degree of life; the other contracts, freezes, and nearly annihilates them.'[24] However, if we understand the response to the supernatural as a response to the opportunity for grace, then this distinction becomes not oppositional, but transitional.

Kierkegaard (under the pseudonym Anti-Climacus) describes this transition from horror to terror to grace as the 'corridor of faith', recognising a spiritual journey which must begin with anxiety.[25] Kierkegaard explores this in more detail in *The Concept of Dread*,[26] describing dread as the inevitable consequence of sin in fallen man. Here, in a way that remembers St Irenaeus' treatment of sin described in chapter 4, Kierkegaard emphasises original sin not as an event, but as a universal experience.[27] For Kierkegaard, each act of sin brings more sin into the world, and with it more dread: 'dread comes back again in relation to what was posited and in relation to the future'.[28] Our anxiety then, is towards our freedom to sin: 'However deep the individual has sunk, he may sink still deeper, and this "may" is the object of dread.'[29] This dread, however, can be *transformative*, in that the possibility of freedom can educate. 'Now the dread of possibility holds him as prey, until it can deliver him saved into the hands of faith.'[30] Thus the anxiety of the possibility of sinning becomes the anticipation of infinity.

It is within this process of transformation that Kierkegaard identifies the demonic, and it is worth exploring Kierkegaard's demonic in detail, as again here the double plays a prominent role:

> Generally the phenomenon is described in such a way that one sees clearly that it is a question of bondage to sin, a state which I cannot describe better than by recalling a game men play where two are concealed under a cloak, appearing to be one person, and while one speaks the other gesticulates without any pertinence to what is being said. For it is thus the beast has clothed itself in the form of the man and then caricatures him by gestures and byplay. [...] The individual is in sin, and he is in dread of the evil. This formation, viewed from a higher standpoint, is in the good, and for this reason the individual is in dread of the evil. The other formation is the demoniacal. The individual is in the evil and is in dread of the good. The bondage of sin is an unfree relation to the evil, but the demoniacal is an unfree relation to the good.
>
> The demoniacal becomes thoroughly evident only when it is touched by the good, which now comes to its confines from the outside. It is noteworthy therefore that in the New Testament the demoniacal shows itself only with Christ's coming in contact with it. Whether the demon is legion (cf. Matthew 8:28-34; Mark 5:12; Luke 8:26-39) or is dumb (cf. Luke 11:34) the phenomenon is the same, it is dread of the good; for dread can quite as well express itself by muteness as by loud cries. The good of course signifies to it the reintegration of freedom, redemption, salvation, or whatever name one would give it.[31]

Here Kierkegaard associates the demonic with doubling in two important ways, both of which have already been seen in the chapters discussing Arthur Machen and M. R. James. Firstly, the demonic clothes itself in the guise of man, and in this way traps man in his own fear of evil. The demonic represents man's fear of the worst of himself.[32] Secondly, however, Kierkegaard doubles the demonic with the good, and it is this doubling which facilitates the transformative quality of dread. The demonic appears only to bring with it recognition of the possibility for redemption, for grace (as a name one would give it).

In a lecture entitled 'The Novels and Stories of J.S. Le Fanu', M. R. James finds pictorial analogy of Le Fanu's writing in a woodcut by Thomas Bewick, in which a peddler walks through a wood which is crowded with what MRJ calls 'bird hobgoblins'.[33,34]

MRJ highlights the threat that these creatures pose to the peddler, who will leave the place a raving maniac, if he leaves alive at all.[35] However, I would argue that this pictorial analogy is even more fitting for its sense of dread. The landscape here both conceals and reveals what the peddler already knows is present. The peddler stands poised before the wood, and it is unclear whether he apprehends the figures in the shadows. From here, the peddler must make three steps. The first is to acknowledge the presence of the figures (horror), and the second is to acknowledge that his journey takes him through this wood (terror). The third is to make the journey through the wood (faith). It is this transformative journey which we will discover in Le Fanu's supernatural tales.

MIMETIC CRISIS AS GOTHIC HORROR IN 'SPALATRO' AND 'BORRHOMEO THE ASTROLOGER'

Before beginning Le Fanu's journey, it is worth examining the theological horror from which it emerges.[36] For this I turn to two tales, 'Spalatro: a tale in two parts', published in 1862, and 'Borrhomeo the Astrologer', 1843, in both of which Le Fanu situates scenes of doubling in a firmly gothic setting. Both tales, set in seventeenth-century Rome and Milan respectively, are theologically pessimistic, portraying souls easily and hopelessly tricked by Faustian pacts. These stories, when not indeed clothing demons themselves in monastic cassocks, portray what Jack Sullivan calls 'ineffectual orthodoxies and institutions'.[37]

This pessimism arises from mimetic characters and situations, but with a mimesis in which a creative Aristotelean *telos* is absent. Here, the mimetic double *undermines* the original being—in a reverse mimesis, Spalatro and Borrhomeo become their doubles. 'Borrhomeo', with its less complex plot structure, seems an appropriate text with which to describe what René Girard calls a 'mimetic crisis'.[38] Borrhomeo is a powerful astrologer who has seemingly successfully predicted the pestilence which has come to Milan in the form of the plague. The astrologer is yet more ambitious, however, and is obsessed with uncovering the secrets of alchemy, a pursuit which has already left him isolated and seen as suspicious in the eyes of the community.

One day, the figure of a young man appears to Borrhomeo in his workshop, emerging from the smoke of the furnace, who demonstrates that he can turn lead to gold, and likewise claims to know the recipe for the elixir of immortality. It is important to note, however, that true to Le Fanu's doubling figures, this alchemist repeatedly warns Borrhomeo against the consequences of learning such alchemy. The young man has at once appeared unsolicited to tempt Borrhomeo with his secrets, yet makes him promise never to use them: 'in return for satisfying your curiosity, I ask only your solemn promise to prosecute this dread science no more. Ha! you'll not give it. Take, then, my warning, and remember the wages of this knowledge is sorrow.'[39] As becomes clear, this juxtaposition in fact serves only to heighten the illusion of free will in what will become a pact with the devil. The young man is eventually persuaded to take Borrhomeo to see his master, from whom he learnt his secrets. Again Borrhomeo is warned: 'If you desire it, I will bring you before him: but, once in his presence, you cannot recede, and his conditions you must accept.'[40] They go to a vintner's of disrepute, which Borrhomeo knows well and 'sometimes stole, disguised, by night, to be no longer a necromancer, but a man, and, so, from a man to become a beast'.[41]

Borrhomeo is told to breathe on a piece of human skin, which he then lays over his face. The piece of skin then shrinks to a tiny portrait, just like a miniature of a young lady which the figure had produced when demonstrating his alchemy. The young man explains:

> Every adept has his portrait here [...] so a good likeness is always pleasant; but these have a power beside, and establish a sympathy between their originals and possessor which secures discipline and silence.[42]

Only now does the young man reveal his demonic form, and his pseudo-religious discourse becomes mocking. 'Have I not been your good angel?' he asks, as one of his feet shrinks briefly into a goat-like hoof.[43] 'You must for once resemble a Christian,' he goes on, 'and with us deal truly and honestly.' The sense of Christian morality and guidance in ritual has become parodic. Borrhomeo is duly given drops of a wine which give him one thousand years of life, and is then told to go around the city daubing the Church doors with an S. (The fiends of hell do this to bring pestilence to a house, but they cannot touch the consecrated buildings.) Borrhomeo carries out this task, wrongly believing that he is still invisible, as he seemed to be when accompanied by the young man. 'Therein was shown forth to all the world the craft of the fiend, and the just judgement of heaven', and he is quickly spotted and arrested.[44] He is sentenced to be hanged for a day, then impaled on a gate for three days before burial. Borrhomeo has no fear, however, knowing that he cannot die and must only wait for the chance to escape. Another visit from the young man soon reveals his real and devastating fate, however, as he explains that Borrhomeo will 'appear' dead, and thus suffer the agonies of his execution without the means to escape it.

René Girard, in a series of studies on scapegoating and sacrifice in religious communities, as well as the Gospels' responses, claims that all human relationships can be reduced to mimeticism.[45] In mimetic desire, Girard describes not envy of what the other has, but the other's desire itself. It is the desire which makes the object desirable.[46] Borrhomeo is a good example—his desire is not for gold, but for alchemy itself. Borrhomeo wants to *be* an alchemist. When the visitor reveals that he knows the secrets of the *elixir vitae*, Borrhomeo cries: 'you stand before me an angel of wisdom, in power and immortality like a god!'[47] For Girard such desire brings about a mimetic crisis, which can only be resolved through a sacrificial scapegoat. For Borrhomeo (and Spalatro), however, there is no such scapegoat, and the mimetic crisis turns into a living death. Le Fanu will return to the motif of living death again and again, but its portrayal is most explicit in 'Borrhomeo'.

The young man explains that the shock of an act which would kill a mortal man induces a form of cataplexy in an immortal one, foiling Borrhomeo's plans for escape: 'Escape! why, you *have* escaped. They can't kill you', mocks the young man. Borrhomeo will live powerless through hanging, impalement and burial in a great pit, 'where his stupendous punishment proceeds'.[48] Borrhomeo's immortality has thus become a parody both of eternal life and of the redemptive release of death.

In Le Fanu's later tales, as in those discussed below, the figure of the double will itself play a double role, both potentially destructive and potentially redemptive. The theologically redemptive possibilities of these doublings become more striking, however, when set against the mimetic doubling in Borrhomeo and Spalatro. These doubles, either in the form of mimetic figures or in portraits, are not only paralysing, but absorb and disintegrate the original. The character of Spalatro—not, we are told, the Napoleonic bandit, but 'the celebrated original'[49]—is brought up under the tutelage of a seemingly demonic monk, whose purpose seems to be to entirely retard and undermine the boy's spiritual development. In anticipation of the anti-Gnosticism of M. R. James, the monk overwhelms the boy with 'metaphysical conversation' of such a nature that 'far from acquiring any higher morality, even [his] natural sense of right and wrong became confused and blunted'.[50] As an adult, Spalatro seems without any real purpose, and after an adventure in an inn full of murderous robbers, in which divine intervention seems to save him (in the form of biblical warnings whispered in his ear), Spalatro nonetheless enters into a life of debauchery. He soon finds himself at the carnival in Rome, and in this setting, in which identity is necessarily hidden and obscured, Spalatro finds himself following a harlequin through the streets. The harlequin begins a strange song which has a hypnotic but distressing effect on Spalatro, and which, 'like the most extraordinary ventriloquism', serves further to collapse the distinction between Spalatro and his companion. The song, which calls on the 'Mighty oppressor of earthly kind', seems to be a song *about* Spalatro, but is also enigmatic, suggesting a story which is already underway: 'He has given thee his heart; now master his brain.'[51]

The harlequin soon reveals himself to be Father Anthony, the demonic tutor, and the mimetic power which he holds reaches its climax. Spalatro is forced to imitate demonic grimaces and echo blasphemies, at last culminating by drawing his own knife to his throat in imitation of the demon before him. The spell is broken just in time by a passer by, who thinks he is intervening in a suicide attempt. After this, Spalatro makes a halfhearted attempt at a reformed lifestyle, but is soon back to his old ways, at which point the tale takes a vampiric turn. Spalatro visits the house of an old man, and despite his horror at a strange dinner in which the old man eats nothing but drinks what seems to be blood, and a Dante-esque ball filled with dancers 'bearing upon their lifeless faces the fearful stamp of sin and eternal anguish', Spalatro becomes bewitched by the daughter of the house, and returns again until he realises he is entirely under the power of Satan.[52] Spalatro tells all of this to the narrator, a confessor who meets him in his prison cell, awaiting execution for a multitude of murders and criminal acts. Spalatro has by this point lost not faith in God, but faith in any redemptive possibility through religion or the Church.

In 'Spalatro' as in 'Borrhomeo', portraiture plays a significant role as a mimetic motif, a theme to which Le Fanu would return fully in 'Schalken the Painter'. For Spalatro, it is the portrait of the vampiric daughter, whose beauty tempts him to stay despite his instinctive dread of the house. Here, Spalatro is seduced not by the daughter herself (who will in fact try to warn him away), but by her image: 'Like one lost in a sad and beautiful dream, I stood rapt and moveless. […] Thus gazing and dreaming on, the tears flowed silently down my cheeks. Strange fascination!'[53] The dissolution of the distinction between image and original is reinforced by the old man, who tells Spalatro, 'You shall probably before long have the opportunity of comparing the counterfeit with the original'. This statement can be read in two ways, and it is not clear whether the person who Spalatro is about to meet is the original or the counterfeit. In these stories, imitation through the artistic image is the opposite of the Aristotelean cathartic function.[54] These portraits serve rather as an 'anti-*telos*', absorbing the spirit and nature of the original, and leaving it an empty shell.

In his seminal text on the fantastic in literature, Tzvetan Todorov describes the metamorphoses of the fantastic as the collapse of the distinction between matter and mind. He writes: 'The multiplication of personality, taken literally, is an immediate consequence of the possible transition between matter and mind: we are several persons mentally, we become so physically.'[55] Certainly this description is a fitting one for the collapsing of the self into its double, as seen in 'Spalatro' and 'Borrhomeo'. However, by understanding the self in terms of a theological teleology, this collapse becomes not only 'disruptive', but integral to the spiritual condition of human being. In these two theologically pessimistic tales, this collapse is reductive, and the mimetic destruction is contagious. Spalatro's effect on his confessor, for instance, mimics that of his own tutelage, and the monk finds his 'mind full of doubts and fears'. He laments: 'I have no more certainty, no more *knowledge*, mystery and illusion are above, and below, and around me.'[56]

In these two tales, doubling is fracturing. Both Spalatro and Borrhomeo are trapped by this mimesis, and the fate of each one seems inevitable.

Reminiscent of Calvinist predestination, neither character is able to respond to the voices of Christian orthodoxy which act as warnings, and thus these voices are rendered impotent or even parodic of the institutions which they represent. The 'temptation' of the supernatural and the inability of Catholic ritual to counteract it, reinforces a Lutheran insistence on the reliance of participation in grace. It is ultimately this impotence which places 'Spalatro' and 'Borrhomeo' firmly as exercises in gothic horror. The pessimism of these two tales, however, serves to highlight their contrast with those tales discussed below. Having witnessed horror in these first two tales, the next, 'The Haunted Baronet', moves us to the next step—to the terrified realisation of the possibility of grace.

From Horror to Terror: Incomplete Resurrection in 'The Haunted Baronet'

'The Haunted Baronet' (1871) is a retelling of a Le Fanu story from 1838, 'The Fortunes of Sir Robert Ardagh'.[57] In this earlier version, the tale of Sir Robert Ardagh is told twice, first as a legend, a classic Faustian pact in which Ardagh is accompanied by a devilish companion to the races, where he invariably wins his bets. This companion later comes to claim Ardagh, who is dragged down with him into a gaping chasm. This 'legend' is then retold as a 'true' account, declaring its sources as direct witnesses. This time the devilish companion takes the form of a mysterious and controlling valet. The 'real' Ardagh is again summoned on a night which has been foretold, and is found dead by his wife.

The Faustian doubling of 'Sir Robert Ardagh' is developed and complicated in 'The Haunted Baronet', in the characters of Sir Bale Mardykes and his valet Philip Feltram. I will argue that here Philip Feltram represents less the demonic other than the double as another 'part' of a whole. With both men connected through an ancestral legend of a Feltram wife to the Mardykes family, who was later disowned and drowned in the local lake, the tale becomes one of atonement and reconciliation. Feltram's own drowning and subsequent recovery draws inevitable allegory to the Pauline description of resurrection, but as will be seen, this resurrection brings (at first) no spiritual glory or seeming triumph over death. Rather, Feltram's resurrection is incomplete without the spiritual transformation of Sir Bale also.

Not, at first, the 'despotic' dictator from 'Sir Robert Ardagh', Feltram is a gentle and 'innocent fellow' who acts as valet to the baronet (now transposed from Ireland to England). The histories of the Mardykes and Feltram families are intertwined, however, following a rumour that a Mardykes predecessor married a woman from the Feltram family, only to turn her out with two young children, denying the marriage. The woman is said to have disappeared but to have later returned as a drowned spectre to a group of fishermen on the local lake. Indeed, as this story is first recounted in the local inn, the teller confuses the story with the current Sir Bale, setting the tone for a motif of inherited sin which will permeate 'The Haunted Baronet'. Through this shared history, and apparent claim to the Mardykes land and title, Sir Bale and Feltram are at once counterparts and united.

Certainly as the tale opens, however, these characters are identifiable more for their polarity than any unity, and this polarity is reflected in their responses to their surroundings. In many of Le Fanu's tales, the landscape is portrayed as something constitutive for the characters. Le Fanu's characters live in various degrees of symbiosis with their natural surroundings, and this symbiosis often influences their self-awareness and their story. The landscape of 'The Haunted Baronet' is just such a setting, in which the imposing hills and prominent lake are presented almost entirely through a character's response to it, creating myriad different lakes, and different hills, arising 'as from the stroke of an enchanter's wand'.[58] It is through these phenomenological responses to the landscape that Sir Bale and Feltram are spiritually situated, and situated in relation to each other. Although being troubled by Snakes Island, a presentiment on what will become the location for the supernatural aspect of the tale, Feltram looks to the scenery for comfort, guided by Mrs Julaper, the housekeeper and one of Le Fanu's demonstrably 'porous' characters: 'See how bright and soft everything looks in that pleasant light; *that's* better, child, than the finest picture man's hand ever painted yet, and God gives it us for nothing.'[59] Later, Feltram will seem increasingly attuned to the communication of nature, most notably in the birdsong, as birds come to represent a medium of communication with the natural and supernatural. At this early stage of the tale, however, Feltram's response is one of dread, a horror which Le Fanu describes as 'latent'.[60] This latency which Feltram detects, but which Mrs Julaper does not (being on the 'other side' of dread), is indicative of Feltram's 'story' as latent, something yet to emerge.

At first glance, it seems that Sir Bale's response could not be more different, manifesting not in horror but antipathy. With visitors, he discusses the mountains and lake with resigned distaste: 'But, I suppose, as we can't get rid of them, the next best thing is to admire them. We are pretty well married to them, and there is no use quarrelling.'[61] Even here, however, the sense of *latency* acknowledged by Feltram is glimpsed, as Sir Bale describes the boredom of boating as finding 'we have got down into a pit'. Sir Bale would rather an open horizon, he claims, 'than be suffocated among impassable mountains, or upset in a black lake and drowned like a kitten'. Alone, Sir Bale reflects more openly on his dislike, and Le Fanu imbibes his response with prophetic meaning. In one passage in particular, the themes of ancestry, latent dread, prophecy and theophanic mysticism are all brought together in the motif of the lake:

> There were two things about Mardykes [Sir Bale] specially disliked.
> One was Philip Feltram, who, right or wrong, he fancied knew more than was pleasant of his past life.
> The other was the lake. It was a beautiful piece of water, he, educated at least in the excellence of landscape painting, acknowledged. But although he could pull a good oar, and liked other lakes, to this particular sheet of water there lurked within him an insurmountable antipathy. It was engendered by a variety of associations.
> There is a faculty in man that will acknowledge the unseen. He may scout and scare religion from him; but if he does, superstition perches near. His boding was made-up of omens, dreams, and such stuff as he most affected to despise, and there fluttered at his heart a presentiment and disgust.[62]

This presentiment is brought to fruition as the plot develops, and the volatile Sir Bale, panicking already at his own financial situation, accuses Feltram of stealing a £100 bank note. Leaving Mardykes Hall to return to the old Feltram homestead on the other side of the lake, hoping to return to the 'airy solitude' of 'a pastoral and simple life', Feltram sets off across the lake, but is pulled down into the water. When his drowned body is returned to Mardykes Hall, the fishermen who were bringing him across insist that something like a hand came out of the water and dragged Feltram down. This hand, one supposes, is that of the drowned wife of the ancestral Lord Mardykes, also Feltram's ancestor.

Resurrection and Transformation

Feltram's drowned body having been brought back to the hall, he is confirmed dead by the doctor, and prepared for burial. As the women who have lain him out sit vigil, however, Feltram is suddenly restored, and the women turn to find him sitting up and well. From this moment, the relationship between Feltram and Bale changes dramatically, as does each of their relationships with their surroundings. Notably, Sir Bale's immediate response to Feltram's apparent resurrection is one of loneliness and isolation. He retreats into 'that lonely place, those frightful mountains'[63] on long walks, and it is on one of these walks, shrouded in mist, that Sir Bale is confronted by a ghostly figure. The figure in the mist seems to look in the same direction as Sir Bale, again with the effect of a mirroring, and points at something which Sir Bale cannot make out. Continuing more cautiously, Sir Bale sees the figure again, which this time brings him to a standstill. At last, Sir Bale descends from the mist into the clear air, and sees the figure a third time. This time, he recognises the figure as Feltram.

From this time on, Feltram is dramatically changed, and with a morose and dark manner he acquires an uncanny quality, unnerving those at the hall and seeming to develop a growing influence and control over Sir Bale. One day, as Sir Bale broods over his debts, and fantasises about a large win at the races, he is startled by the appearance of Feltram, who claims to have met a fortune teller who not only has the names of the race winners, but has lent a bag of money for Sir Bale to use for the bets. Sir Bale, having been asked by Feltram what he would give to know the winners, begins to think that the money must be Feltram's own, and challenges him. Feltram's enigmatic answer will later be revealed to show that Feltram's 'self' has become completely absorbed into the supernatural world which will now guide Sir Bale's fate:

> 'And do you mean to say you got all that from a gipsy in Cloostedd Wood?'
> 'A friend, who is—*myself*,' answered Philip Feltram.
> 'Yourself! Then it is yours—*you* lend it?' [...]
> 'Myself, and not myself,' said Feltram oracularly; 'as like a voice and echo, man and shadow.'[64]

The theme of resurrection here clearly has Christological allusions, and Feltram has in some way been transformed. However, set against the Pauline doctrine of resurrection, the symbol becomes problematic.

Feltram's role as Sir Bale's double is morally ambiguous, he seems at once to be the orchestrator of a Faustian pact, but also to have some transcendental knowledge which Sir Bale needs. He embodies at once the possibility for Sir Bale's salvation and his condemnation. As suggested above, Feltram as Sir Bale's double represents not the other, but that part of Sir Bale within which the possibility for transformation is contained. Feltram's resurrection is problematised as it is incomplete. The resurrected Feltram is in turn confronted by his double in Sir Bale, one whose response is still one of horror and incomprehension.

In his first letter to the Corinthians, St Paul describes resurrection as the triumph of eternal life over death. Moreover, it is the triumph of redemption, as 'the sting of death is sin'. In resurrection, however, 'just as we have borne the image of the man of dust, we will also bear the image of the man of heaven'.[65] Resurrection then, is the completion of the transformative process from sin into grace. For neither Feltram nor Sir Bale does resurrection seem a triumph, however. Feltram is spectral in his gloomy presence, and Sir Bale becomes increasingly withdrawn and unwell. Eventually, again in financial trouble, Sir Bale is convinced to visit the mysterious money-lender and seer himself, although he is reluctant to go across and not around the lake. Feltram explains: 'Now you see he compels you to seek him out, and when you do, I think he'll help you through your trouble. He said he would.'[66] As they set off together, it is again unclear whether Feltram is leading Sir Bale to salvation or damnation. On the journey the men are immersed completely in the landscape, and Feltram's connection to it is reinforced, as is Sir Bale's alienation. Likewise the landscape is a reminder of both men's identities as inheritors of a trans-generational history. Once again birds are used as an image for this preternatural communication. Exotic mixes of birds fly around the men as they cross the lake, which baffle Sir Bale, but remind Feltram that they were stocked and nurtured by his ancestors. Only as they reach the shore does Sir Bale begin to respond sensitively to his surroundings, both in the landscape and in his companion: 'The solitude and grandeur of the forest, and the repulsive gloom of his companion's countenance and demeanour, communicated a tone of anxiety to Sir Bale.'[67]

Deep in the forest, Sir Bale meets his mysterious benefactor, along with a woman seer, and after drinking with them some strange wine he returns with another bag of money to bet, 'stuffed with a heavy burden'.[68] Reminded that the man will summon him again, Sir Bale returns to Mardykes Hall with Feltram, and as they cross the lake, Sir Bale is conscious that the fog seems to tug at the boat, Feltram seeming each time to wave it away with his hand, 'and the mist seemed to obey the gesture; but returned again and again, and the same thing always happened'. This is significant not only as an ominous scene, but for Sir Bale's response. The sense of endangerment during Sir Bale's trip seems more pressing here than at any time, and yet Sir Bale no longer recoils in horror or disbelief. Rather, a sense of awe seems to accompany Sir Bale's anxiety, 'akin to the sensation of a man going into battle'. Bale's anxiety has progressed from a recoiling horror to a terrified acknowledgement of 'some unknown reality at the bottom of that which he had affected to treat before as illusion'. Moreover, this change is disintegrating Feltram and Sir Bale's diametric relationship, as Sir Bale's emotions seem to correspond 'with the pale and sombre frown which Feltram wore, and the manifest change which had come over him'.[69]

Despite this indication of transformation, however, things only get worse for Feltram and Sir Bale from here on in, Sir Bale's health suffering a rapid decline, and he becoming ever more subordinate to Feltram. For Feltram himself, 'the change which had taken place in him became more and more pronounced. Dark and stern he always looked, and often malignant. He was like a man possessed of one evil thought which never left him.'

Things seem temporarily to improve for Sir Bale when he marries one of three sisters from a family whose lineage can be traced back to the Feltrams. On their way to visit, however, one of Lady Mardykes' sisters receives a vision of Lady Mardykes in terrible distress, asking them to come more quickly. Arriving, they find that Sir Bale has informed his wife that though quite well, he knows that he will die that night. This comes to pass, and his wife also dies some time later, ending the Mardykes lineage. In Lady Mardykes' will however, the estate and title is passed on to her cousin, married to Feltram's brother. Thus a prediction is fulfilled that the Mardykes estate will be returned to the Feltrams.

As in 'The Fortunes of Sir Robert Ardagh', then, this tale is ultimately situated also as a legend, the fulfilment of a prophecy. The confrontation of the supernatural restores moral order, but not directly to the individuals who experience it. The intervention of the supernatural in both visions and in the seeming resurrection of Feltram enables transformation through the atonement of sin, but that sin is affirmed as universal and inherited, as Feltram and Sir Bale's stories conclude a multi-generational story. Moreover, by establishing a doubling in Feltram and Sir Bale, Le

Fanu situates Pauline resurrection as something communal—the individual resurrection from drowning of Feltram is spiritually incomplete without Sir Bale's atonement. This communal sense of sin and redemption situates Le Fanu's Lutheranism firmly in an Augustinian context, privileging as it does inherent deification over individual righteousness.[70] Other tales explored above have portrayed the gothic role of the double as paralysing or entrapping, but in 'the Haunted Baronet', the double contains within it the momentum for transformation.

Next, our journey takes us to two stories in which this transformation of terror into faith is brought to fulfilment. Here, however, I contrast a tale of 'alien' grace with one of transformative grace through the acknowledgement of sin. In this way an Augustinian reading of grace is shown to be integral to Le Fanu's aesthetic and theological project.

Terror Brought to Actuality in 'The Mysterious Lodger' and 'The Familiar'

> Have pity on me, have pity on me,
> Oh you my friends,
> for the hand of God has touched me![71]

Several of Le Fanu's haunted characters reflect the laments of the eponymous figure of the Book of Job. In this Old Testament Book, Job is a righteous and devout man with good fortune, whom God tests by sending down Satan and allowing him to destroy Job's cattle, servants, and kill his ten children.[72] Eventually, Job breaks down and curses and questions God, attempting to reconcile the realisation that God is both the cause and the means to relief for his suffering. 'The Mysterious Lodger' (1850) uses Swedenborgian ideas of spiritual guidance to answer this lament, to ultimately confirm a Lutheran justification through faith. As will be seen, however, the model constructed in 'The Mysterious Lodger' is problematic, and the resolution to this religious allegory is both aesthetically and theologically unsatisfactory. 'The Familiar' (1872, from 'The Watcher', 1851), the story of a man who is haunted by someone he has wronged, provides a more complex account, and is Augustinian in its recognition of the need for mediation to bring about habitual change. In 'The Familiar', the *immanence* and persistence of a ghostly presence forces the haunted man, Captain Barton, to acknowledge his *actual* situation as a sinner.[73] The very impossibility of the haunting reveals the truth to Barton of himself as a man in need of salvation.

In 'The Mysterious Lodger', a Swedenborgian model of spiritual guidance offers to reconcile the concurrent state of righteousness and sin in a new way. In this story, a happy family take in a lodger, who turns out to be a demonic presence, destroying the family's idyllic dynamic by undermining the religious faith of the wife, before bringing about the death of the two small children. Indeed, the lodger's aim seems not simply to bring grief and calamity to the household, but to alienate the couple from the consolation of Christianity. The wife, finding herself unable to pray, is taunted by the lodger:

> It is perfectly plain your Christian system can't be a true one—faith and *prayer* it everywhere represents as the conditions of grace, acceptance, and salvation; and yet your Creator will not *permit* you either to believe or to pray. The Christian system is, forsooth, a *free* gift, and yet he who formed *you* and *it*, makes it absolutely impossible for you to accept it.[74]

Here, the demon specifically undermines the concept that man can be at once a sinner and saved.

Likewise, Le Fanu's motif of 'false' or 'apparent' death is used here for the lodger to undermine the concept of the reconciliation of death. In a horrible turn of events, the lodger explains that the protagonist's young daughter had not been dead, as she had seemed, and has thus been buried alive. This is confirmed when the body is exhumed, and the father realises that in burying the child, *he* has in fact killed her. In this way, the consolations of the Christian burial ritual are removed. It seems to the protagonist that he is being punished for the 'blasphemous vehemence' of his atheism, and is saved from his despair only by the appearance of another figure, who comes to 'speak comfort and healing to [his] heart'.[75] This figure reveals to the protagonist God's will, and he realises that the 'calamity which bore at first such evil fruit'[76] has been good for him, by turning his mind to God. It is also through this figure that the promise of everlasting life is restored, as the wife recognises the figure from a dream in which he bore her dead son away, promising to care for him and one day return him to her.

In its plot construct, 'The Mysterious Lodger' draws firmly on the complex model of the natural and supernatural world as described by Emmanuel Swedenborg, in whose writings Le Fanu took an interest. In this model, various stages of heaven, earth and various hells exist in parallel, and their inhabitants are discoverable through mystic experience. For Swedenborg moreover, God, having become removed from man, uses the angelic and spiritual inhabitants through which to communicate, claiming that 'because we have separated ourselves from heaven, the Lord has provided that there should be angels and spirits with each of us and that we should be governed by the Lord through them'.[77] However, in Swedenborg's model the influence of hellish spirits is potentially just as strong, their 'malice and craft' being at the level of angel's intelligence.[78] As an additional requirement to Luther's *sola fide*, Swedenborg adds the requirement that the heart is filled with the good. Those whose hearts are good will follow the angels to heaven, and those who are selfish or egotistical will follow their demons into hell.[79] In this way, the progress of Le Fanu's protagonist is also entirely Swedenborgian, in that his faith is awakened as the revelation of God is 'streamed on [his] heart'. Le Fanu's protagonist is not evil of heart, but simply 'in the complacency of [his] wretched ignorance'.[80] The angelic figure's revelations, then, simply articulate the truths which he has craved.

Crucially, these experiences bring about no *ethical* or *habitual* change in the protagonist, and I would argue that it is this which leads to the ultimately unsatisfactory sense of this allegorical tale. Certainly in terms of plot, there is a swiftness to the resolution of the tale which is unlikely to have been more convincing to contemporary readers than today. Only moments after he has re-interred the body of his unfortunate daughter, the protagonist once again meets his angelic friend, who again explains to him the will of God revealed in tribulation. Instantly, 'the wreck and desolation [in his heart], lost their bleak and ghastly character, like ruins illuminated by the mellow beams of a solemn summer sunset'.[81] Soon after, the couple move out of their house, find new prosperity without the need for a rental income, and bear three replacement children. Despite the descriptive change in conviction for the protagonist, the resolution of the story is ultimately circumstantial. Both the demonic lodger and the unhappy couple leave the house in which the tragedies have occurred (the lodger on the instructions of the angelic figure), and the circumstances of their formerly happy life are reinstated. Despite the instances of Swedenborgian mysticism (perhaps because of it), there is no real spiritual *change* in 'The Mysterious Lodger'.

It is clear from this tale, however, that Le Fanu *wants* to explore the function of terror in theological transformation. Note that like the Satan depicted in the Book of Job, the explanations given by the angelic figure, as well as his actions, mean that the demonic lodger has ultimately *contributed* to the protagonist's revelation of God's will. This would seem to confirm Luther's description of *Anfechtung*, in which God himself presents man with situations of absolute despair, in order that he will turn to Christ. Alister McGrath explains:

> Most significantly of all, as we have already noted, God himself must be recognised as the ultimate source of Anfechtung: it is his *opus alienum*, which is intended to destroy a man's self-confidence and complacency, and reduce him to a state of utter despair and humiliation, in order that he may finally turn to God, devoid of all the obstacles to justification which formerly existed [...] It is for this reason that Luther is able to refer to Anfechtung as a 'delicious despair'.[82]

This sense of terror as the catalyst for salvation is fulfilled in 'The Familiar', in which a sea captain is haunted by the ghost of one of his mistreated crew. This tale is far more complex in its treatment of supernatural confrontation, leaving Swedenborgian antinomy for a manifold Augustinian response.[83] In this story I have suggested that the *immanent* presence of the ghost reveals Captain Barton's *actual* condition. I use the term immanent here not in reference to Charles Taylor's secular immanent frame, but in a way which moves closer to William Desmond's immanence as 'in the midst of'. In this I digress slightly from Desmond's own discussion of immanence and transcendence, but focus rather on his recognition that a metaxological metaphor of God (as Le Fanu's doubling has been establishing), is itself something double.[84] Desmond writes: 'from the "midst" of immanent being a passage (poros) is opened, and we may become porous to something communicated of what is "beyond" or "above"'.[85] I would suggest that the immanence of the familiar's presence in Le Fanu's tale reflects this metaphor of 'in the midst of'.

Captain Barton, first described to us by definition of his (social) normality, experiences a haunting which is notably material, or physical in its manifestation.[86] Barton is followed home first by footsteps, then by the appearance of a figure in public whom Barton clearly recognises. Barton's friends also see this figure, and even interact with it as a natural person. Barton alone is truly horrified by the figure, as he recognises it as a member of his crew who died in Naples from injuries sustained under his mistreatment. The *immanence* of the figure is reinforced by the impossibility of his presence. Indeed, Barton turns to one of Le Fanu's own preoccupations to try to process this paradox; that of cataplexy or 'false' death. Under the care of a physician for his apparent hysteria, Barton seems to care little for his own well-being, but instead questions the doctor as to the possibility of mistakenly pronouncing a man dead. As becomes clear when the identity of the figure is revealed later in the tale, Barton has been seeking to rationally explain the presence of a man he knows to be dead.

It is the persistence of this impossible presence though, which strips Barton of his own immanent frame of being (to return to Taylor), which is his socially constructed identity. Through the haunting, Barton will lose his position as a prospective husband, and ultimately be removed from his social circle to a life of total isolation (as a 'cure' for his hysteria). In this process, Barton is forced to confront his *actual* identity as a sinner in need of salvation. By realising his condition, Barton re-examines his being in relationship to God, once again demonstrating the lament of Job:

> 'I am sure—I *know*,' continued Barton, with increasing excitement, 'that there is a God—a dreadful God—and that retribution follows guilt, in ways the most mysterious and stupendous—by agencies the most inexplicable and terrific;—there is a spiritual system—great God, how I have been convinced!—a system malignant, and implacable, and omnipotent, under whose persecutions I am, and have been, suffering the torments of the damned!—yes, sir—yes—the fires and frenzy of hell!'[87]

There is a crucial difference in Barton's revelation to that of the protagonist in 'The Mysterious Lodger', in that it comes with the recognition that in despair lies the possibility of personal redemption from sin: 'I have no hope to cling to but one, and that is, that by some other spiritual agency more potent than that which tortures me, *it* may be combated, and I delivered.'[88] Barton's crisis is essentially an Augustinian one, firstly in his recognition of his own inadequacy in the face of God, and secondly in his recognition of the need for a mediator for grace.

In *Confessions*, St Augustine's own narrative of his conversion and religious experience, he is repeatedly confronted with the impasse of seeking out a supreme God while being himself a flawed being. He writes: 'I a mere man, and a man with profound defects, was trying to think of you the supreme, only and true God.'[89] Augustine repeatedly tries to picture a transcendent and immutable God, but is constrained by his own limits: 'I made an effort to lift my mind's eye out of the abyss, but again plunged back. I tried several times, but again and again sank back.'[90] Without grace, he is unable to contemplate the absoluteness of God, and thus himself in the *Imago Dei*:

> My heart vehemently protested against all the physical images in my mind, and by this single blow I attempted to expel from my mind's eye the swarm of unpurified notions flying about there. Hardly had they been dispersed when in the flash of an eye they had regrouped and were back again. [...] So my heart had become gross, and I had no clear vision even of my own self.[91]

Likewise Captain Barton is trapped by his own perceived distance from a terrible and transcendent God:

> 'Try! [to pray] I *have* tried, and the attempt only fills me with confusion; and, sometimes, terror. [...] The awful, unutterable idea of eternity and infinity oppresses and maddens my brain whenever my mind approaches the contemplation of the Creator, [...] The idea of an eternal Creator is to me intolerable—my mind cannot support it.'[92]

For Augustine, he at last realises the need for a mediator, and finds that mediator in Christ. In this realisation, Augustine relinquishes what he calls his 'arrogance' in his search for God, and turns rather to humble submission. Augustine allows himself to be transformed. Again, Captain Barton's narrative is recognisably Augustinian, when in his appeal to 'some other spiritual agency more potent than that which tortures [him]' he also turns to this submission, and gives himself over to the need for an intervention upon his spiritual condition. He even appeals to a priest for intercession:

> I tell you I cannot help myself; I cannot hope to escape; I am utterly passive. I conjure you, then, to weigh my case well, and if anything may be done for me by vicarious supplication—be the intercession of the good—or by any aid or influence whatsoever, I implore of you, I adjure you in the name of the Most High, give me the benefit of that influence—deliver me from the body of this death.[93]

This need for intercession returns us to the theme of the double role of the haunting figure, both as tormentor and as saviour. Indeed (and with the insistent physicality of a handwritten note), the haunting figure itself seems to recognise his own double role. Early in the tale, shortly after Barton has heard footsteps following him for the first time, he receives two notes from someone who signs himself as 'The Watcher'. The Watcher warns Barton to avoid the street on which he heard the footsteps, or 'he will meet with something unlucky, for he has reason to dread'. Barton himself notices the contrary tone of the note, remarking that 'the object seemed a friendly one, and yet he subscribed himself as one whom he had "reason to dread."'[94] (Barton seems to have immediately recognised The Watcher as the producer of the footsteps the previous night, although this is not stated in the letter.) A week later Barton receives a second note, which this time alludes to a doubling of The Watcher with Barton, and directly links the haunting to Barton's conscience:

> You may well think, Captain Barton, to escape from your own shadow as from me; do what you may, I will see you as often as I please, and you shall see me, for I do not want to hide myself, as you fancy. Do not let it trouble your rest, Captain Barton; for, with a *good conscience*, what need you to fear from the eye of The Watcher.[95]

Notable also is The Watcher's reinforcement of his immanent presence; 'I will see you as often as I please, and you shall see me'. With this persistent haunting, The Watcher forces Barton to examine his *actual* condition, as judged by his conscience, over his socially constructed identity as a rationally moral but religious sceptic. Only once 'that demon' has drawn him 'to the verge of the chasm' through his hauntings, does Barton recognise his own sin against the man who haunts him, and with it has a vision in which his immediate sense of self drops away, and he experiences himself as an eternal being:

> My head was leaning on the lap of a girl, and she was singing a song, that told, I know not how—whether by words or harmonies—of all my life—all that is past, and all that is still to come; and with the song the old feelings that I thought had perished within me came back, and tears flowed from my eyes [...] And then I awoke to this world, as you saw, comforted, for I knew that I was forgiven much.[96]

In this way, a haunting which is immanent by its insistent presence, 'in the midst of', is the very confrontation which dismantles the Taylorean 'immanent frame' of Captain Barton's spiritual condition.

Conclusion

For M. R. James' characters, the confrontation of the supernatural brings them out of what Taylor would call their 'bounded selves', and brings about self-revelation as theological, porous beings.[97] Le Fanu's supernatural is no less a confrontation of the self, and it is by returning to the theme of confrontation that we find the final doubling in Le Fanu's tales. Le Fanu's characters are haunted by the *possibility* that they can be saved. As Kierkegaard notes, 'the demoniacal is the dread of the good'.[98] The supernatural is here transformative because it is alien but at once 'in the midst of'. Its presence is both latent and insistently present. Le Fanu creates a suspended temporality in which latency and immanency can co-exist, by suspending the moment between life and death. Thus, 'the mortal and immortal prematurely make acquaintance'.[99] The significance of that suspension is only apparent, however, as death is understood as the fulfilment of a theological teleology.

In Marlowe's *Doctor Faustus*, Faustus has his own good and bad angels to commentate his journey:

FAUSTUS 'Tis thou hast damned distressed Faustus' soul.
Is't not too late?
[…]
BAD ANGEL Too late.
GOOD ANGEL Never too late, if Faustus will repent.[100]

For Faustus, these *alien* voices cannot ultimately bring about his salvation, and we see his fate repeated in the characters of Spalatro and Borrhomeo. When Le Fanu attempts to give these figures Swedenborgian agency in 'The Mysterious Lodger', the result is unconvincing. However, Le Fanu ultimately brings Marlowe's good angel's claims to fruition, both by suspending the moment of judgement and by recognising the condition of sin (and thus salvation) as communal, as universal.

The journey of doubling in Le Fanu's works shows that for Le Fanu at least, it is not enough to say that man is at once sinful and righteous, nor that he is at once damned and saved, in the Calvinist sense of elective anxiety. The doubling is transformative because characters are *actually* sinful but *potentially* redeemed. The *return* to the *Imago Dei* is signalled by the confrontation of the supernatural double, and the possibility of that return is *realised* by recognising the hobgoblins and choosing to journey, terrified, through the wood.

NOTES

1. Title quotation Sheridan Le Fanu, 'The Familiar', in *In a Glass Darkly* (London: R. Bentley and Son, 1872), 163.
2. M. R. James, 'Introduction' to *Madam Crowl's Ghost and Other Tales of Mystery*, ed. M. R. James (London: G. Bell & Sons, 1923), vii.
3. Victor Sage, *Le Fanu's Gothic*, (New York: Palgrave MacMillan, 2004), 14sq. James Walton, *Vision and Vacancy: The Fictions of J.S. Le Fanu* (Dublin: University College Dublin Press, 2007). It is also intriguing to read Sage's claims in the light of Machen and MRJ's reassertion of orthodox authority to validate 'superstition'.
4. Alison Milbank, 'Joseph Sheridan Le Fanu: Gothic Grotesque and the Huguenot Inheritance', in *A Companion to Irish Literature vol. 1*, ed. by Julia M. Wright (Oxford: Wiley-Blackwell, 2010), 364.
5. James Walton, *Vision and Vacancy*, 84. Original emphasis.
6. For a perspective which examines doubling in the context of Calvinist elective anxiety, see Alison Milbank, 'Sacrificial Exchange and the Gothic Double in *Melmoth the Wanderer* and *A Picture of Dorian Gray*', in *Shaping Belief: Culture, Politics and Religion in Nineteenth Century Writing*, eds. Victoria Morgan and Claire Williams. (Liverpool: Liverpool University Press, 2008), 113–128.
7. W. J. McCormack, *Sheridan Le Fanu* (Oxford: Clarendon Press, 1980), 1.
8. W. J. McCormack, *Sheridan Le Fanu and Victorian Ireland* (Oxford: Clarendon Press, 1980), 12.
9. McCormack, *Le Fanu and Victorian Ireland*, 33; Sage, *Le Fanu's Gothic*, 9, 28–9. In his memoir *Seventy Years of Irish Life*, Le Fanu's brother William writes of local faction fights and later the united Catholic marches during their childhood. (London: Edward Arnold, 1893), 31–35.
10. For a detailed account of Huguenot immigration to Ireland and their relationship with Irish-Protestantism, see Jean-Paul Pittion, 'The Question of Religious Conformity and Non-Conformity in the Irish Refuge', in *The Huguenots and Ireland: Anatomy of an Emigration*, ed. by C. E. J. CAldicott, H. Gough and J-P. Pittion (Dublin: The Glendale Press, 1987), 285–296. Also Raymond Hylton, *Ireland's Huguenots and their Refuge, 1662–1745* (Brighton: Sussex Academic Press, 2005), 175sqq.
11. Hylton, 179.
12. It is notable that this inheritance is also shared by the gothic writer Charles Maturin, another son of an Anglican Dean.

13. See McCormack, *Le Fanu,* 127, 132sq. I would challenge the extent of the similarities which McCormack identifies, mostly as the analogy demands that Le Fanu be seen as a religiously sceptical figure, which is neither supported in Le Fanu's correspondence nor in the religious allegory of the tale.
14. In Jean Lozes, 'Fragment d'Un Journal Intime De J.S. Le Fanu: Document Inédit En Date Du 18 Mai 1858.' *Caliban*, 10.1 (1974), 157.
15. Lozes, 'Fragment', 157. Original emphasis.
16. Martin Luther, *Lectures on Romans,* trans. Wilhelm Pauck (Louisville KY: Westminster John Knoxville Press, 2006), 127.
17. Martin Luther, 'Two Kinds of Righteousness', in *Martin Luther: Selections from his Writings,* ed. John Dillenberger (New York: Anchor, 1961), 87. Note that original sin is likewise alien (88), reflecting the doubleness of the *Imago Dei.*
18. See A. G. Dickens, *Martin Luther and the Reformation* (New York: English Universities Press, 1967), 30sq., Brengt Hägglund, *The Background of Luther's Doctrine of Justification in Late Medieval Theology* (Philadelphia: Fortress Press, 1961), 34.
19. Aquinas, *Summa,* 1a1ae q.55 a.4. See also 'Machen's Thomist Anthropology', chapter 3.
20. Aquinas, *Summa* 1a1ae q.110 a.1. My emphasis.
21. John Peter Kenney, *The Mysticism of Saint Augustine: Rereading the Confessions* (Abingdon: Routledge, 2005), 62.
22. Augustine, *Confessions*, VII.xvii (23).
23. Augustine, *Confessions*, VII.xviii (24).
24. Ann Radcliffe, 'On the Supernatural in Poetry', *New Monthly Magazine,* 16.1 (1826), 149.
25. Søren Kierkegaard, *The Sickness Unto Death,* trans. Alastair Hannay (New York, NY: Penguin, 1989), 98.
26. Under the pseudonym Vigilius Haufniensis.
27. See 'MRJ's Theological Anthropology', 108–12.
28. Søren Kierkegaard, *The Concept of Dread,* trans. Walter Lowrie (Princeton: Princeton University Press, 1946), 99.
29. Kierkegaard, *The Concept of Dread,* 101.
30. Kierkegaard, *The Concept of Dread,* 140.
31. Kierkegaard, *The Concept of Dread,* 106.
32. See also Arthur Machen's reference to Edgar Allan Poe's 'The Imp of the Perverse', discussed in chapter 3.
33. M. R. James, 'The Novels and Stories of J.Sheridan Le Fanu', delivered 16 March 1923, adapted as 'M.R. James on J.S. Le Fanu.' *Ghosts and Scholars* 7. Web.
34. Thomas Bewick, woodcut, 'The Thief and the Bogles', in *A History of British Land Birds: Vol. 1* (Newcastle: Edward Walker, 1797), 57. Image

courtesy of The Natural History Society of Northumbria, Great North Museum, Hancock.
35. MRJ, 'On J.S. Le Fanu', N.pag.
36. Title quotation from Charles Maturin, *Melmoth the Wanderer* (Oxford: Oxford University Press, 2008), 221. Moncada is here reminded of watching Bermudez de Belmonte's play of the same name, in which the actor playing the devil performed holy devotions at the sound of the monastery bell.
37. Jack Sullivan, *Elegant Nightmares: The English Ghost Story from Le Fanu to Blackwood* (Athens OH: Ohio University Press, 1978), 58, referring to *In a Glass Darkly*.
38. René Girard, *The Scapegoat*, trans. Yvonne Freccero (Baltimore, MD: Johns Hopkins University Press, 1986); *Violence and the Sacred*, trans. Patrick Gregory (Baltimore MD: Johns Hopkins University Press, 1972).
39. Sheridan Le Fanu, 'Borrhomeo the Astrologer', in *Dublin University Magazine*, vol. XXI, January-June (Dublin: William Curry Jun. & co., 1850), 57.
40. Le Fanu, 'Borrhomeo', 58.
41. Le Fanu, 'Borrhomeo', 58.
42. Le Fanu, 'Borrhomeo', 59. Note the allusion to an Augustinian return to Borrhomeo's 'least human' self.
43. Note the similarities of this scene with Lewis' *The Monk*, discussed in chapter 2.
44. Le Fanu, 'Borrhomeo', 59–60.
45. Girard, *Scapegoat*, 165.
46. Girard, *Violence and the Sacred*, 145.
47. Le Fanu, 'Borrhomeo', 56.
48. Le Fanu, 'Borrhomeo', 60, 61.
49. Sheridan Le Fanu, 'Spalatro, A Tale in Two Parts: Part I', in *The Dublin University Magazine*. Vol. XXI, January-June (Dublin: William Curry Jun & Son, 1843), 338.
50. Le Fanu, 'Spalatro', Part I, 341.
51. Le Fanu, 'Spalatro', Part II, 448.
52. Le Fanu, 'Spalatro', Part II, 457.
53. Le Fanu, 'Spalatro', Part II, 451. Note that the theme of paralysis is also repeated here.
54. Aristotle, *Poetics*, 1449b21–29.
55. Todorov, Tzvetan. *The Fantastic: A Structural Approach to a Literary Genre* (Ithaca, NY: Cornell University Press, 1975), 116.
56. Le Fanu, 'Spalatro', Part I, 339. Original emphasis.
57. Le Fanu, 'Sir Robert Ardagh', *Dublin University Magazine*. Vol. XI, (Dublin: James McGlashan, 1838), 313–324. Later reprinted in *The Purcell*

Papers, Vol. 1 (London: Bentley, 1880); 'The Haunted Baronet', in *Chronicles of Golden Friars* (London: Richard Bentley and Son, 1871). The theme is also revisited in 'Sir Dominick's Bargain' (1872).
58. Le Fanu, 'The Haunted Baronet', 61 (from Lord Byron, 'Childe Harold,' canto 4, stanza 1).
59. Le Fanu, 'The Haunted Baronet', 77. Original emphasis.
60. Le Fanu, 'The Haunted Baronet', 77.
61. Le Fanu, 'The Haunted Baronet', 74.
62. Le Fanu, 'The Haunted Baronet', 86.
63. Le Fanu, 'The Haunted Baronet', 74.
64. Le Fanu, 'The Haunted Baronet', 118. Original emphasis.
65. 1 Cor. 15.56, 15.49.
66. Le Fanu, 'Haunted Baronet', 130.
67. Le Fanu, 'Haunted Baronet', 134.
68. Le Fanu, 'Haunted Baronet', 139. See also Arthur Machen's use of the *Vinum Sabatti* motif, chapter 3.
69. Le Fanu, 'Haunted Baronet', 134, 141.
70. See Franckforter, *The Theologia Germanica of Martin Luther*, ed. Bengt Hoffman (Philadelphia: Paulist Press, 1980), 63: 'Even if God would take to himself all humans in the world and become humanised in them and they would become divinised in Him and this did not happen in me, my fall and my apostasy would never be amended.'
71. Job 19:21. Title quotation Sheridan Le Fanu, 'The Evil Guest', *Ghost Stories and Mysteries*, ed. E. F. Bleiler (New York: Dover, 1975). 264.
72. It is interesting for our discussion below that here Satan works not against God, but seemingly on behalf of God.
73. See below for a discussion of my use of the term 'immanent' in this context.
74. Le Fanu, 'The Mysterious Lodger: Part I', in *Dublin University Magazine*, vol. XXXV, January-June (Dublin: James McGlashan, 1850), 65. Original emphasis.
75. Le Fanu, 'The Mysterious Lodger', Part I, 55, Part II, 234.
76. Le Fanu, 'The Mysterious Lodger', Part II, 226.
77. Emanuel Swedenborg, *Heaven and Hell*, trans. George F. Dole (Pennsylvania: Swedenborg Foundation, 2002), §247.
78. Swedenborg, *Heaven and Hell*, §577.
79. 'People who have intended and loved what is evil in the world intend and love what is evil in the other life, and then they no longer allow themselves to be led away from it. This is why people who are absorbed in evil are connected to hell and actually are there in spirit; and after death they crave above all to be where their evil is.' *Heaven and Hell*, §547.
80. Le Fanu, 'The Mysterious Lodger', Part II, 234, Part I, 55.

81. Le Fanu, 'The Mysterious Lodger', Part I, 55.
82. Alister McGrath, *Luther's Theology of the Cross* (Oxford: Basil Blackwell, 1994), 170–1.
83. 'The Familiar', published in the collection of stories *In a Glass Darkly* (1872), is a near identical rewriting of 'The Watcher' published in *Ghost Stories and Tales of Mystery* (Dublin: James McGlashan, 1851). The later text has one substantial change in the addition of a prologue and epilogue by the narrator/collector of the tales of *In a Glass Darkly*, Dr Hesselius. Indeed, the prologue of Dr Hesselius, a self-styled 'metaphysical physician', tries to pre-emptively restore some sense of order to the tale, describing it as some form of spiritual 'disease', in which the internal senses have been accidentally opened. Alison Milbank comments of Hesselius' commentaries that they 'serve only to extend further the sense of mystery' (*Daughters of the House: Modes of the Gothic in the Fiction of Wilkie Collins, Charles Dickens and Sheridan Le Fanu*. Diss. Lancaster: University of Lancaster, 1988, 337.) This is especially pertinent of the reading performed here, as the transparent naiveté of Hesselius' confidence that he 'should have without difficulty referred those phenomena to their proper disease' (42) serves to underscore the theological implications of events. See also Jack Sullivan, *Elegant Nightmares: The English Ghost Story from Le Fanu to Blackwood* (Athens OH: Ohio University Press, 1978), 27sq. Robert Tracy's OUP edition of *In a Glass Darkly* includes marks changes between the two texts in its notes. Dr. Hesselius is further discussed here in chapter 7.
84. For a fuller description of Desmond's concept of 'metaxology', see chapter 2.
85. William Desmond, *God and the Between* (Chennai, India: Blackwell, 2008), 123.
86. Barton's rationalist atheism, for instance, is not radical, but simply inoffensive in the context of his socially respectable behaviour: 'In his personal habits Mr Barton was inexpensive. He occupied lodgings in one of the *then* fashionable streets in the south side of the town—kept but one horse and one servant—and though a reputed free-thinker, yet lived an orderly and moral life.' 'The Familiar', 105. Original emphasis.
87. Le Fanu, 'The Familiar', 148.
88. Le Fanu, 'The Familiar', 150.
89. Augustine, *Confessions*, VII.i.
90. Augustine, *Confessions*, VII.iii.
91. Augustine, *Confessions*, VII.i-ii See 1 Cor. 15:52, Matt. 13:15.
92. Le Fanu, 'The Familiar', 152.
93. Le Fanu, 'The Familiar', 158.
94. Le Fanu, 'The Familiar', 116, 117.
95. Le Fanu, 'The Familiar', 121. Original emphasis.

96. Le Fanu, 'The Familiar', 189. It is implied that this girl is the daughter of the dead sailor. The sailor had forbidden a romantic union between his daughter and Captain Barton, leading the daughter to die from heartbreak, which is what brought about his mistreatment and subsequent death.
97. Title quotation from Christopher Marlowe, 'Doctor Faustus' (B-text), in *Doctor Faustus and Other Plays*, ed. David Bevington and Eric Rasmussen (Oxford: Oxford University Press, 1995), II.iii. Note the addition of the word 'safe' from the A-text.
98. Kierkegaard, *Concept of Dread*, 109.
99. Le Fanu, 'Green Tea', in *In a Glass Darkly*, 89.
100. Marlowe, *Doctor Faustus*, II.iii. Again, in a move which might be said to mirror Le Fanu's journey, note the change from 'can' to 'will' repent between texts A and B.

CHAPTER 6

'He's there from the moment he knows somebody else is': Haunted by Paralysis in the Stories of Henry James

The supernatural tales explored in this book have been shown to be not about hauntings, but about the haunted.[1] The protagonists are haunted by their own potential selves as being, and by the privation of that being. For Arthur Machen, such privation results from a choice to turn away from a Christological teleology, or through the will to power which seeks to create without divine causation. However, through the stories of M. R. James and Sheridan Le Fanu the protagonist of the supernatural tale is given the chance to move back towards such a teleology. In this chapter, I would like to return to the dark 'starting point' of Machen's protagonists, and suggest that Henry James offers an alternative to their teleological potency.

Nearly nowhere is the haunting nature of becoming more poignantly depicted than in the short stories of Henry James. The stories examined in this chapter are tales in which no exchange takes place, and therefore no actualisation. James' protagonists are paralysed and static, and the absence of *becoming* turns the stories from tales of terror to tales of tragedy. Indeed, 'The Beast in the Jungle' is a tale in which the supernatural haunts by its absence. It is through the juxtaposition of these stories with those of previous chapters that I hope to affirm the role of terror as metaphysical process in supernatural fiction.

Henry James' Non-Theology

Henry James' sustained secularism permeates his fiction, refusing to reflect either the spiritual empiricism of his brother or the mystic faith of his father. As Martha Banta notes, 'Henry James seems to have often renounced more than he took.'[2] Edwin Sill Fussell claims that this renunciation left James unable to adequately depict religious faith. Fussell writes:

> For all his skill in the depiction of externals, and for all his liberal and charitable tolerance, James was by his own conviction too remote from that faith to figure it convincingly at the point where it most called for figuration, at the point where human fear and divine revelation collide and hopefully coalesce.[3]

It is true that in those stories in which James' characters are most confronted with their own consciousness, there is seldom a coalescence of fear and revelation. However, contrary to a failure to grasp or to represent a theological component to the supernatural tale, I will argue that James' supernatural tragedies, as I have called them, poignantly explore the condition of human being that undergoes no transformation, those who become conscious of their own static condition, but without the means to break the paralysis.

Though James wrote only seldom about either his father's Swedenborgian mysticism or divinity in general, when he did so it was not, as seems so often to be understood, to reject the concept, but rather to insist of the centrality to it of what he calls 'human fellowship'.[4] In his essay 'Is There a Life after Death', James equates the manifestation of divinity not with the expectation of an afterlife, but in man's response *to* life. He writes:

> In order to contribute in any degree to a discussion of the possibility we have to be consciously in presence of it. I can only see it, the great interrogation or the great deprecation we are ultimately driven to, as a part of our general concern with life and our general, and extremely various—because I speak of each man's general—mode of reaction under it; but to testify for an experience we must have reacted in one way or another.[5]

Indeed, it is this aspect of his father's religion about which James speaks most positively. Henry James senior's relationship with his family's religion seems most striking in its lack of dogmatism or pressure.[6] James' respect for his father's philosophy is clear, however, and he writes that, 'it showed us more intimately still what, in this world of cleft components, one human being can yet be for another'.[7] It is this sense of shared consciousness which I will claim lies at the heart of James' teleological narratives.

Henry James and Teleology

Most investigations into James' depictions of the human condition concern themselves, understandably, with his realist fiction.[8] Here also, James is seen to deliberately disengage with theology. Many critics cannot help, however, recognising T. S. Eliot's perception of James' 'indifference to religious dogma' as belying an 'exceptional awareness of spiritual reality'.[9] Such an acknowledgement, however, has led critics to extend this separation artificially. James' novels are considered sharply spiritual, but vehemently non-religious.[10] To many, this dichotomy manifests itself as a secular aesthetic, and this idea of a Jamesian 'reduction of all experience to the aesthetic level' has come to dominate scholarly discourse on James' fiction.[11] I will argue, however, that any absence of a clearly theological driver in James' tales is not really an absence, but, like the 'ghost of God haunting the despair of nothing', shows an effective presence through its inaccessibility. Indeed, the themes to which I will attend, those of exchange, gift and aesthetics, could just as well be found in James' realist fiction. The idea of sterility also haunts novels such as *The Ambassadors* and *The Sacred Fount*, and themes of giving of self and of exchange permeate *The Golden Bowl* and *The Portrait of a Lady*.

In the stories considered here, themes of teleology and movement become central through their absence. Beyond the *Bildungsroman* of disenchantment that has been used to describe some of James' novels,[12] these tales reinforce the Augustinian journey taken through the previous chapters by depriving their own protagonists of such a journey. Indeed, William Troy, one of the few critics to see religion embedded in James' work, uses his article 'The Altar of Henry James' to trace just such a journey for the author himself, one reflected in his corpus. Troy writes that James' 'most evil book', *The Other House*, was written in

> the depths of what must have been in his life a period of the most tortuous metaphysical panic and moral despair. Without such a sojourn in the abyss

as it represents he would never have attained to the full-bodied affirmation of the last and greatest period. Like Strether, in *The Ambassadors*, he wins through, by a long and difficult 'process of vision'.[13]

BECOMING AND STASIS IN 'THE BEAST IN THE JUNGLE'

John Marcher, the protagonist of 'The Beast in the Jungle', is introduced to the reader through his feeling of anonymity in society.[14] In just such anonymous society, however, he comes across May Bartram, a woman whom he had met ten years before, and to whom he had confided his belief that he feels he is destined for something, an event the likes of which he cannot anticipate. He imagines the event as a beast waiting to spring, although he cannot say whether the outcome will be good or bad; 'possibly', claims Marcher, 'annihilating me; possibly, on the other hand, only altering everything'.[15] The knowledge that he has shared his secret is a wonderful thing for Marcher: 'He had thought himself so long as abominably alone, and, lo, he wasn't alone a bit.'[16] This 'revelation' spurs a fast and lifelong friendship between the two, based on the careful watching and waiting for the beast to spring, whenever and however that should be.

The philosopher William Desmond notes that in our participation in the porous world, there 'is always an excess in astonishment'.[17] He uses the term 'astonishment' in place of 'wonder', to avoid, as he claims, 'sliding into sentimentality'. There is of course a shock in astonishment—it is startling. Most importantly, however, astonishment is receptive. We cannot choose to be astonished, but must simply be open to its possibility. In this way then, astonishment encompasses a sense of patience. This sense of patience is crucial to John Marcher's story, as it permeates, or so it would seem, the duration of the tale. However, Desmond's sense of patience responds to astonishment as gift. By originating beyond the self, it transforms the self:

> There is willingness beyond will to power. Self-transformation is called for but this cannot be a process of self-mediation only. Something from beyond self must be allowed to give itself, if it will give itself at all.[18]

Astonishment acts upon the self then, but this relies upon communication; upon participation. Henry James seems to have shared this understanding of astonishment as agent, and of the role of reception. In his preface to the 1909 edition of 'The Beast in the Jungle', James writes that the supernatural gets its 'character' from its relation to the protagonist's normal life, or their history:

> It's in such connexions as these that they most interest, for what we are then mainly concerned with is their imputed and borrowed dignity. Intrinsic values they have none. [...] Where the indispensible history is absent, where the phenomena evoked, *the moving incidents,* coming straight, [...] the result is that, to my sense, the climax fails—fails because it stops short, and stops short for want of connexions.[19]

For John Marcher, this moving incident, so anticipated and so integral to his sense of purpose, never seems to arrive. He and his friend May Bartram grow older, quietly waiting for the spring of the beast. Throughout, Marcher regards himself as something of a martyr to his fate, withdrawn to contemplate it, much as would a cloistered monk. 'He had disturbed nobody with the queerness of having to know a haunted man. [...] This was why, above all, he could regard himself, in a greedy world, as decently—as, in fact, perhaps even a little sublimely—unselfish.'[20] Only May Bartram seems to realise that in this self-conscious patience Marcher has precluded the possibility for astonishment, to be startled by the supernatural. 'Living with it so long and so closely,' she tells him, 'you've lost your sense of it.'[21] Without the capacity for astonishment to act upon him, Marcher is paralysed, and as May Bartram becomes terminally ill, he starts to realise the emptiness of his patience.

> When the possibilities themselves had, accordingly, turned stale, when the secret of the gods had grown faint, had perhaps even evaporated, that, and that only, was failure. [...] And so, in the dark valley into which his path had taken its unlooked-for twist, he wondered not a little as he groped.[22]

The thought of May Bartram's death haunts Marcher, as her 'vain waiting' with him proves an admonition to his withdrawal.
What Marcher has in fact tragically failed to apprehend, is that the potential agent through which to move him *was* May Bartram. The 'real' May Bartram remains veiled under her role in relation to Marcher and his waiting, 'necessarily crowded out of his consciousness'.[23] When Marcher once asks her why she seems to have dedicated her life to waiting with him for his beast to spring, she answers, 'to help you pass for a man like another'.[24]

Marcher responds to the comment with self-conscious good grace, but in doing so misses another interpretation of the remark, that Bartram can help him *become* more man; more human. Even at her funeral, he relates to her only through her relation to his own (static) position, coming 'face to face with the fact that he was to profit extraordinarily little by the interest May Bartram had taken in him'.[25]

In May Bartram's death, Marcher has been stripped not of a companion in his patient waiting, but of potential. From this point, Marcher is more haunted by his beast than ever before, but now he is haunted by its absence:

> What it presently came to in truth was that poor Marcher waded through his beaten grass, where no life stirred, where no breath sounded, where no evil eye seemed to gleam from a possible lair, very much as if vaguely looking for the Beast, and still more as if missing it.[26]

Marcher goes on to aimlessly travel, wandering the earth. This wandering allows him periodic return, and it is in this returning that he starts to gain a sense of living through connection. May Bartram's grave now wears for him 'the air of conscious greeting that we find, after absence, in things that have closely belonged to us and which seem to confess of themselves to the connection'.[27]

Throughout his waiting, John Marcher has waited for the world to startle and astonish him, but without imagining participation. As William Desmond described above, we cannot go towards astonishment, but we must allow for it. Marcher has ultimately missed not an event but an exchange. Once, frustrated that May Bartram seemed to know something of his fate that he couldn't grasp, Marcher said, 'Why, I thought it the point you were just making—that we *had* looked most things in the face.' 'Including each other?' is Bartam's reply.[28] The answer to this question comes as Marcher, standing by Bartram's grave, notices another mourner at a neighbouring grave, his face stricken with grief and loss. The mourner's grief acts as a mirror to Marcher, who realises the absence of such a connection with another in his own life, 'the proof of which was precisely John Marcher's arid end'. Indeed, it is this exchange which finally moves Marcher, but for James' protagonist it is too late. Marcher's 'revelation' is one of absence and emptiness. 'Now that the illumination had begun, however, it blazed to the zenith, and what he presently stood there gazing at was the *sounded void* of his life.'[29] The impotence of Marcher's life, the loss of potential becoming, becomes overwhelmingly *present*, and Marcher is left in despair.

Both Charles Taylor and William Desmond, in their concept of the supernatural as a signifier of the ultra-natural or as an excess of the natural, highlight its 'givenness' as central to our encounters with it. The supernatural acts as a catalyst to move the protagonist along a teleological journey. The givenness of astonishment, however, relies upon receptivity. Here, where Taylor describes the receptive self as 'porous',[30] Desmond draws from Poros, the mythical father of Eros, and thus relates the 'porosity of being' to communication—porosity as a resource, or a 'way across'.[31] Desmond writes: '*Poros* opens up a way when we seem paralyzed by the perplexity of an insurmountable *aporia* [difficulty, doubt]. A way is opened by *poros* become porous.'[32] This openness, however, demands a response. To be poros/porous means then to give of oneself as well as to be receptive: 'the porosity of love to the other and its communication'. It is this giving of self which Marcher recognises in the grief-stricken mourner:

> Nothing lived but the deep ravage of the features that he showed. He showed them—that was the point; he was moved, as he passed, by some impulse that was either a signal for sympathy or, more possibly, a challenge to another sorrow.[33]

In his discussion on the fall of the devil, Saint Anselm of Canterbury examines this relationship between giving and receiving, recognising that receptivity is a necessary part of gift. Anselm describes the devil's fall as a refusal to participate in God's gift.[34] It is through participation in gifting that openness and receptivity become reciprocity.

From Poros to Eros, the erotic desire to give of oneself which Marcher lacks is explored more hopefully in James' 'The Real Right Thing'. Here, the wife and friend of the recently deceased Ashton Doyne come together to prepare a volume of his life, intending to draw on the papers and materials left in his study. Mrs Doyne establishes George Withermore in his friend's study, giving him free reign and time to research, and it is clear that both characters are motivated by their desire to keep something of Ashton Doyne in being. For Withermore, the chance at intimacy with his friend is 'simply dazzling'. Soon, both characters begin to sense (separately) the presence of Ashton Doyne, and take this as confirmation that they are sharing something with him. However, although Mrs Doyne is careful to leave Withermore to his work, Withermore slowly becomes conscious not only of the ghostly presence of Doyne, but of Doyne's widow as present. 'Though so full of consideration she was at the same time perceptibly *there*: he felt her, through a super subtle sixth sense that the whole connection had already brought into play.'[35]

Meanwhile, however, it is becoming clear that the spirit of Doyne is not present in order to support the biographical work, but in protest. The sadness of this realisation is not, for Mrs Doyne, that he would be against the work, but that in his being gone, she can no longer give of herself: '"It would mean that he won't take from me-" But she dropped for despair.'[36] Unlike John Marcher, however, Mrs Doyne's despair is comforted through her communication with Withermore, and his with her.

Desmond calls this porosity of the self towards the other as 'erotic outreach', a movement beyond ourselves. This erotic outreach is a movement *towards* being as communal, and thus becomes transcendental and agapeic. 'Without this further quickening,' claims Desmond, 'the erotic rebirth can instead be still-born as an idolised autonomy.'[37] It is this movement towards another that marks the crucial difference between Marcher's hopelessness and Withermore and Mrs Doyne's consolation.

Aesthetic Creation in 'The Altar of the Dead'

The givenness of the supernatural event and the movement of response draws us to the creativity inherent in porosity. Indeed, it is through this sense of creativity that the supernatural tale is given an inherently theological framework. In chapter 3, I explored the way in which Arthur Machen's weird tales depict creative nihilism. In 'The Great God Pan' and *The Three Impostors*, Machen's protagonists enact a will to create which bypasses or defies creation as divine gift. The result is the bringing into being of nothingness. The nihil becomes manifest in gruesome and horrific form. In James' 'The Altar of the Dead', we can explore a different version of negative creativity. Where Machen's profane creativity has demonic consequences, for James it is haunting in its reification of absence. Again the crucial difference lies in potency and act. Where Machen's characters choose to turn away from a Christological teleology, for James' characters they perceive no teleology from which to turn.

'Poor Stransom', the protagonist of 'The Altar of the Dead', appears very much in the ilk of John Marcher. Bereaved of his fiancée, he is consumed and paralysed by his self-defined status as 'widower', marking his life by the anniversaries of her death. Indeed, 'it would be more to the point perhaps to say that this occasion kept *him*: it kept him at least effectually from doing anything else'.[38] Slowly Stransom has expanded this role of memory keeper to include anybody whom he knows to have died, collectively calling them 'the Others', and he is bruised and angry when other people seem to let go of them more lightly. Coming across a widowed acquaintance with his new wife, for instance, Stransom is horrified by 'this hired performer Mrs. Creston', and her 'monstrous character'.[39]

To unpack Stransom's failure of participation, we can turn briefly to an analogous tale by May Sinclair, 'Where their Fire is not Quenched' (1923). Sinclair's conception of grace and participation is discussed in chapter 2, and in this tale Sinclair is reminiscent of Henry James by attending to lack of participation as impotence.[40] Sinclair's writings show an acute appreciation of the role of participation in being. In her philosophic work, *The New* Idealism, for instance, she writes: 'To be was to be related, and be related was, *ipso facto*, to be known.'[41] In 'Where their Fire is not Quenched', the protagonist Harriet Leigh has also lost her fiancé, and her life thereafter also has the sense of time passing without her participation. 'Five years passed.' Harriet meets another suitor, who she believes she loves 'with her soul', but he becomes engaged to another. 'Ten years passed.'[42] Eventually Harriet begins an intermittent relationship with a married man, Oscar, although she is never content:

> This was love, the thing she had never had, that she had dreamed of, hungered and thirsted for; but now she had it she was not satisfied. Always she looked for something just beyond it, some mystic, heavenly rapture, always beginning to come, that never came.[43]

The story follows Harriet into death, where she again meets Oscar, and comes to realise that she is doomed to spend eternity with him. Even when she sees her other suitors in the distance, as she approaches them they become Oscar. Because Harriet enacted a lonely and distanced parody of love in life, she is doomed to that same parody in death. Oscar tells her:

> In the last death we shall be shut up in this room, behind that locked door, together. We shall lie here together, for ever and ever, joined so fast that even God can't put us asunder. We shall be one flesh and one spirit, one sin repeated forever and ever; spirit loathing flesh, flesh loathing spirit; you and I loathing each other.[44]

In this story, Sinclair takes the failure of participation evidenced in 'Altar of the Dead' through to an eternal consequence. The hellish repetition which she describes is one in which non-participation and discontent is eternally played out through a claustrophobic distance from another. In James' story, however, he seems at first to offer his protagonist some avenue towards participation. One day Stransom enters a church, seemingly by chance, and like Marcher's experience of his fellow mourner in 'The Beast', Stransom becomes enraptured by a woman sunk in prayers of remembrance. 'He wished he could sink, like her, to the very bottom, be as motionless, as rapt in prostration.'[45] There and then he channels this desire into a plan to create an altar at which he can remember each of his dead with candles. Strikingly, he does not choose to participate in the rituals by lighting candles in the church which he is visiting, but places himself as originator and creator of a new and unique altar:

> He should snatch it from no other rites and associate it with nothing profane; he would simply take it as it should be given up to him and make it a masterpiece of splendour and a mountain of fire.[46]

Fussell sees Stransom's altar as an example of Jamesian 'secularised (aesthetic) consecration', and it is certainly true that the altar brings only empty ritual consolation.[47] However, while Fussell sets up a synonym here of secularisation and the aesthetic, I will argue that it is rather Stransom's *relationship* to the aesthetic which is shown to be theologically empty.

Certainly Stransom's building of his altar of candles is an aesthetic exercise. This is clear in the subjugation of the candles' primary purpose (for the souls of the departed) to aesthetic success:

> There came a day when, for simple exhaustion, if symmetry should really demand one more [candle], he was ready to take symmetry into account. Symmetry was harmony, and the idea of harmony began to haunt him; he said to himself that harmony was of course everything.[48]

Fussell, in equating this aestheticizing with secularisation (on the part of James as well as Stransom), claims that Stransom's treatment of the altar deprives the candles entirely of 'whatever sacred meaning they may still have'.[49] He points to Stransom's relish in the results of the altar to highlight his point, claiming that in the following passage, 'the prose grows more resplendent still and the content still more banal—transcendence defers to infantility'[50]:

> He lost himself in the large lustre, which was more and more what he had from the first wished it to be—as dazzling as the vision of heaven in the mind of a child. He wandered in the fields of light; he passed, among the tall tapers, from tier to tier, from fire to fire, from name to name, from the white intensity of one clear emblem, of one saved soul, to another.[51]

I would argue that here, however, Fussell's dichotomy of aesthetic and religious, and moreover his equating 'childlike' with 'infantile', causes him to miss the point. Indeed, this very passage is arguably one in which Stransom comes closest (although without reaching it) to what might be called aesthetic transcendence.

Perhaps Fussell's rejection of Stransom's *potential* transcendence is Aristotelean in understanding 'beauty' as motionless, in contrast to 'good' as action.[52] Likewise Stransom's appreciation of his own altar does not depict a theophanic response to divine creation. However, Stransom's response reflects the *potential* movement towards transcendence *through* beauty. As William Desmond writes: 'The aesthetics of happening awakens us to the glory of creation—offered both in given beauty and sublimity, and in what we ourselves create.'[53] For Desmond, aesthetic creativity becomes transcendent when it takes form to be communicated outside ourselves. Again transcendence is rooted in exchange and movement, and Stransom begins such a move as he 'loses himself' in the lights of the 'other saved souls'. The breakdown in this potential participation comes in fact as James' passage proceeds:

> It was in the quiet sense of having saved his souls that his deep strange instinct rejoiced. This was no dim theological rescue, no boon of a contingent world; they were saved better than faith or works could save them, saved for the warm world they had shrunk from dying to, for actuality, for continuity, for the certainty of human remembrance.[54]

No sooner has Stransom 'lost himself' than he has reasserted his centrality to the whole project. *He* has 'saved' the souls himself by mourning them. Stransom thinks of himself as 'the shepherd of a huddled flock', a Christ-like identification which mirrors the tragic saviour complex of James' more famous protagonist in *The Turn of the Screw*.[55] Indeed, Stransom's delusion of himself as divine creator and saviour brings the story to its painful crisis. Having befriended the mourning woman with her single candle, he discovers that this candle burns for a man with whom he had quarrelled, and has judged unworthy of redemptive remembrance: 'There was a strange sanctification in death, but some characters were more sanctified by being forgotten than by being remembered.'[56] Stransom's inability to accept the deceased Acton Hague into his 'flock' causes tension with his only living friend, bringing the entire project into crisis.

Rather than a schism of aesthetic and transcendence then, the aesthetic *as* transcendent is shown again to be inextricable to participation and exchange. Dionysius (Pseudo-Denys) identifies beauty within the context of several of the Divine Names, describing it as the principle of unity.[57] Fittingly to Stransom's altar of candles, Dionysius examines the unifying purpose of the transcendent aesthetic under the 'Name of Light'. Spiritual light, given out as divine creation and experienced in Beauty, enlightens, 'so the presence of spiritual light is collective and unifying of those being enlightened, both perfecting and further turning them towards the true Being'.[58] In this way Dionysius draws analogous human creation into divine Beauty, claiming that the beautiful participates in divine Beauty:

> But the beautiful and Beauty are not to be divided, as regards the Cause which has embraced the whole in one. For, with regard to all created things, by dividing them into participations and participants, we call beautiful that which participates in Beauty.[59]

Again in Dionysius the themes of participation and movement come together in the aesthetic. Pre-existing in the Good, aesthetic participation 'returns to the good'; erotic participation returns to agapeic participation.[60] For Dionysius, however, the communal aspect of this is crucial. The unity which he describes is not only a unity of return to the Good, but a movement together. Distinctions and diversities participate in 'communions of contraries, the commingling of things unified'.[61] Indeed, any participation is for Dionysius identical to Beauty and the Good, because of its moving power: 'there is no existing thing which does not participate in the Beautiful and the Good'.[62] How then, do I come to argue that Stransom's altar is one of non-participation?

Dionysius' statement above links, as has this book, participation in the Good with being. 'There is no *existing* thing', he notes, which does not participate. For this connection between participation and being it is worth returning to the Thomist anthropology which was so useful in interpreting Arthur Machen's tales. Dionysius anticipates Aquinas by embedding being in natural law—all things exist, or *should* exist, in keeping with their nature.[63] Aquinas explains that God is the exemplary 'template' of all things in creation, and so the more a thing 'participates' in this template, the more complete it is.[64] In this way Dionysius' 'return' to divine creation mirrors this fullness of being.

In Machen's story *The Three Impostors*, we saw that Machen's characters attempt to create outside of, or independent from, divine creation. The results are horrific manifestations of non-being. Machen himself distinguished in this way between 'art' and 'artifice', and this distinction goes some way to understanding why Stransom's aesthetic endeavours are read by scholars as spiritually empty.

By establishing himself as 'shepherd', Stransom fails to participate in his own altar. Rather, the remembered dead should participate in *his* being. Of Acton Hague, to whom he refuses a candle, he claims, 'He's one of the world's, if you like—he's one of yours. But he's not one of mine. Mine are only the Dead who died possessed of me. They're mine in death because they were mine in life.'[65] The irony that this self-positioning causes his alienation from his one living friend is compounded when we notice that his initial entering of the church and his early relationship with her had given him just such a glimpse into communal participation:

> This one was almost empty and the other altars were dim; a verger shuffled about, an old woman coughed, but it seemed to Stransom there was hospitality in the thick, sweet air. Was it only the savor of the incense, or was it something larger and more guaranteed? He had at any rate quitted the great gray suburb and come nearer to the warm centre. He presently ceased to feel an intruder—he gained at last even a sense of community with the only worshipper in his neighborhood, the sombre presence of a woman, in mourning unrelieved, whose back was all he could see of her, and who had sunk deep into prayer at no great distance from him.[66]

Likewise his relationship with this fellow mourner builds not through social conversation, but 'only their perfect practice and common need'.

Stransom's alienation derives from the immovability of his position. There is no movement towards another which can be accommodated in his self-conscious creator role. Stransom only realises the privation of this alienation once he has lost his relationship with the fellow mourner. In this realisation, Stransom becomes melancholic, and his health starts to fail. Only now does he come, like John Marcher, to at least recognise his position:

> All the lights had gone out—all his Dead had died again. He couldn't exactly see at first how it had been in the power of his late companion to extinguish them, since it was neither for her nor by her that they had been called into being. Then he understood that it was essentially in his own soul the revival had taken place, and that in the air of this soul they were now unable to breathe. The candles might mechanically burn, but each of them had lost its lustre. The church had become a void; it was his presence, her presence, their common presence, that had made the indispensable medium.[67]

Moreover, Stransom has come to see his altar as an empty creation—without communal participation the transcendent possibilities of its aesthetic have been extinguished. Still now, however, Stransom comforts himself with his creator role, sinking further into the delusions of his saviour complex:

> It was in the quiet sense of having saved his souls that his deep, strange instinct rejoiced. This was no dim theological rescue, no boon of a contingent world; they were saved better than faith or works could save them, saved for the warm world they had shrunk from dying to, for actuality, for continuity, for the certainty of human remembrance.[68]

Stransom finally makes one last visit to the church which holds his altar, where he is visited by a vision of his dead fiancée Mary Antrim. With the joy of the vision, however, is 'communicated knowledge that had the force of a reproach', and Stransom repents his refusal to remember Acton Hague. In the next instant, Stransom realises that his female friend has also returned to the church, and he dies, seemingly reconciled, in her arms. True to James' persistent ambiguity, however, this reconciliation is also complicated. Their meeting is one in which one completely gives to the other, participating in the creative aesthetic of the altar. However, it is *the friend* who declares this gift, just like May Bartram to John Marcher. 'It was as if I suddenly saw something,' she explains, 'as if it all became possible. I could come for what you yourself came for: that was enough.'[69] Stransom himself dies reminding her that there is a gap left to fill amongst the candles on the altar—an aesthetic imperfection, as it were. One more candle will fill it, but as the story ends it remains unclear whether this will be the candle for Acton Hague, as Stransom's repentance would promise, or, as he had wished all along, his own.

Conclusion

Henry James' supernatural stories, far from denying a spiritual teleology, reinforce it by poignantly depicting the effect when it is not apprehended.[70] The very equivocation of internal and external haunting is what gives James' supernatural stories their power. Martha Banta describes this equivocation as 'self-hauntedness', and locates it in the nineteenth-century *Angst* of modern man. In terms extremely close to Taylor's porous and buffered description of self, Banta calls James' literary use of this *Angst* 'a reverse transference'—not reducing supernaturalism to psychology, but pouring psychological insights into 'the receptacles of the early romancers, gothicisers, and tellers of fashionable tales'.[71] I would go further, and claim that these stories haunt their protagonists not simply with their own *psychological* anxiety, but with their own porosity.

The sense of stagnancy and alienation felt by John Marcher and Stransom emphasise the role of gift and exchange in the actualisation of porosity. The necessary movement of the self is not only along a teleological journey, but towards participation in teleological being. The journey which has progressed through the previous chapters relies on the supernatural acting as a catalyst for movement. The confrontation of the *actual* self as fallen brings with it the promise of the potential self. By calling James' stories 'supernatural tragedies', I hope to show that they reaffirm the journey of the other tales discussed in this book, by revealing to their protagonists a fallen self, but without the promise of actualisation.

The juxtaposition of James' stories against those with teleological potential also highlights the vehicles necessary for that potential, those of gift, exchange and community. Like M. R. James' characters, these protagonists are surrounded by voices which guide and effect actualisation, and, like those of MRJ, their success depends on their ability to listen. In these tales, it is May Bartram and Stransom's mourning friend who represent a faithful community. Aesthetic excess is given meaning when handed over to another. The equivocity of James' tales is therefore potentially positive; Marcher and Stransom's companions give them the opportunity to pass *through* aesthetic transcendence into agapeic communication.

In the face of such gifted opportunity, however, Stransom and Marcher's position becomes more than just inertia or ennui. The nature of the gifted exchange is its givenness. For Marcher and Stransom, therefore, their paralysis is a *refusal* of gift. The epiphanic climaxes of 'The Beast in the Jungle' and 'The Altar of the Dead' have no redemptive or reconciliatory conclusion because the realisation is not that a gift of exchange is offered, but that they have *already refused* that gift.

Notes

1. Title quotation Henry James, 'The Private Life', in *The Private Life, The Wheel of Time, Lord Beaupre, The Visits, Collaboration, Owen Wingrave* (London: James R. Osgood, McIlvaine & Co., 1893), 42.
2. Martha Banta, *Henry James and the Occult* (Bloomington, IN: Indiana University Press, 1972), 37.
3. Edwin Sill Fussell, *The Catholic Side of Henry James* (Cambridge: Cambridge University Press, 1993), 109.
4. Henry James, *Notes of a Son and Brother* (London: Macmillan & co., 1914), 152. Both Leon Edel and Fred Kaplan point to James' essay 'Is There a Life after Death' to support claims that he rejected a religious or spiritual position. Kaplan declares that as to an afterlife, James 'found it unlikely' (*Henry James: The Imagination of Genius*, New York: Morrow, 1992, 563), and Edel states that James 'believed there was none. Death was absolute'. (*The Life of Henry James, vol. 2*, New York: Penguin, 1975), 819.
5. Henry James, 'Is There a Life After Death?' in *In After Days: Thoughts on the Future Life* (New York and London: Harper and Brothers, 1910) 200–1.
6. James, *Notes of a Son and Brother*, 146–7, 156–7.
7. James, *Notes of a Son and Brother*, 167.
8. Title quotation from James, 'Is There a Life after Death?', 204.
9. Cited in F.O. Matthiessen, *Henry James: The Major Phase* (New York: Oxford University Press, 1944), 145.
10. For readings of James' secularism in his novels, see Martha Banta, *Henry James and the Occult*, 42, 134sqq.; Peter Brooks, *The Melodramatic Imagination: Balzac, Henry James, Melodrama and the Mode of Excess* (New Haven, CT: Yale University Press, 1976), 11; Sarah B. Daugherty, 'James, Renan, and the Religion of Consciousness', *Comparative Literature Studies*,16. 4 (1979): 318–331; Stuart P. Sherman, "The Aesthetic Idealism of Henry James", in *The Question of Henry James*, ed. F. W. Dupee (New York: Henry Holt and Co., 1945), 70–91.
11. Sherman, 'Aesthetic Idealism', 79. This acceptance of the Jamesian aesthetic has led to a dominance of lenses such as psychoanalysis (for instance Shoshanah Felman, 'Turning the Screw of Interpretation', *Yale French Studies*, 55/56, 1977, 94–207) or social theory (such as Van Wyck Brooks,

The Pilgrimage of Henry James. New York: Octagon, 1972) through which to scrutinise James' works.
12. Leon Edel, *Henry James, a Life* (London: Collins, 1987), 587.
13. William Troy, 'The Altar of Henry James', in *The Question of Henry James*, ed. F. W. Dupee (New York: Henry Holt and Co., 1945), 269–70.
14. Title quotation Henry James, 'The Beast in the Jungle', in *The Better Sort* (New York: Charles Scribner's Sons, 1903), 219.
15. James, 'Beast', 198.
16. James, 'Beast', 197.
17. William Desmond, *The Intimate Strangeness of Being: Metaphysics After Dialectic* (Washington, DC: Catholic University of America Press, 2012), 8.
18. Desmond, *Intimate Strangeness*, 34.
19. James, Preface, *The Altar of the Dead, The Beast in the Jungle, The Birthplace, and other Tales*, (New York: Charles Scribner's Sons, 1909), xix. My emphasis.
20. James, 'Beast', 203.
21. James, 'Beast', 213.
22. James, 'Beast', 218.
23. James, 'Beast', 207.
24. James, 'Beast', 214.
25. James, 'Beast', 234.
26. James, 'Beast', 235.
27. James, 'Beast', 238.
28. James, 'Beast', 222. Original emphasis.
29. James, 'Beast', 242. My emphasis.
30. See chapter 2.
31. Desmond, *Intimate Strangeness*, 109. Also *God and the Between*, p. 41.
32. Desmond, *Intimate Strangeness*, 109.
33. James, 'Beast', 241.
34. Saint Anselm of Canterbury, *De Casu Diaboli*, 3.
35. James, 'The Real Right Thing', in *The Soft Side* (New York: Macmillan, 1900), 75.
36. James, 'The Real Right Thing', 84.
37. Desmond, *God and the Between*, 43.
38. James, 'The Altar of the Dead', in *Terminations* (New York: Harper and Sons, 1895), 185.
39. James, 'Altar', 191.
40. May Sinclair had a standing friendship with Henry James, and wrote to Charlotte Mew in 1915 that he had 'influenced me considerably.' Letter 22nd April 1915, quoted in Raitt, *May Sinclair*, 69. Original emphasis. Letter archived at the Berg Collection of English and American Literature, New York Public Library.
41. May Sinclair, *The New Idealism* (New York: Macmillan, 1922), 235.

42. May Sinclair, 'Where Their Fire is not Quenched', in *Uncanny Stories*, 28–29.
43. Sinclair, 'Fire', 31. It is worth noting that this story does not seem to be a comment particularly on extramarital affairs in themselves, a topic with which Sinclair deals with some complexity in her novel *The Helpmate* (New York: Henry Holt and Company, 1907).
44. Sinclair, 'Fire', 44.
45. James, 'Altar', 196.
46. James, 'Altar', 197–8.
47. Fussell, *The Catholic Side of Henry James*, 55.
48. James, 'Altar', 237.
49. Fussell, *Catholic Side*, 107.
50. Fussell, *Catholic Side*, 107.
51. James, 'Altar', 235–6. Also quoted in Fussell, *Catholic Side*, 107–8.
52. See Aristotle, *Metaphysics*, 1078a, 31–2.
53. Desmond, *God and the Between*, 135.
54. James, 'Altar', 236. Fussell also continues his quotation to this point.
55. James, 'Altar', 201. See James, 'The Turn of the Screw', in *The Two Magics* (London: William Heinemann, 1898), 124, 150.
56. James, 'Altar', 202.
57. Dionysius the Aereopagite, *On Divine Names*, capita 4, 7.
58. Dionysius, *Divine Names*, 4.6.
59. Dionysius, *Divine Names*, 4.7.
60. Dionysius, *Divine Names*, 4.14, 4.12.
61. Dionysius, *Divine Names*, 4.7.
62. Dionysius, *Divine Names*, 4.7.
63. Dionysius, *Divine Names*, 6.2.
64. Aquinas, *Summa*, 1a2ae q.93. See also 'Arthur Machen's Thomist Anthropology', chapter 3.
65. James, 'Altar', 220–1.
66. James, 'Altar', 196.
67. James, 'Altar', 234.
68. James, 'Altar', 236.
69. James, 'Altar', 241.
70. Title quotation: Dante, *The Divine Comedy, Purgatorio*, Ed. David H. Higgins, trans. C. H. Sisson (Oxford: Oxford University Press), 18.
71. Banta, *James and the Occult*, 136.

CHAPTER 7

Conclusion: 'This supernatural soliciting cannot be ill, cannot be good'

Wolfgang Iser describes the process of reading as the actualisation of what is given by the text: 'the text represents a potential effect that is realised in the reading process'.[1] Indeed, the dominant theme of this book has been that of potency and act, of bringing into being what is promised in the tales. For Machen, MRJ and Le Fanu, the demonic or terrifying appears as a manifestation of the world as porous. Moreover, it is a catalyst for the emergence of the porous self. For both the haunted characters and the reader, apparitions contribute to a repositioning of this self by opening out a suspended space between the natural, supernatural, and super-natural.

Iser calls such spaces 'gaps', writing that: 'These gaps give the reader a chance to build his own bridges, relating the different aspects of the object which have thus far been revealed to him. It is quite impossible for the text itself to fill the gaps.'[2] For the journey through this suspended space to be teleological, as I have described in the introduction, relies on what Iser observes: that it is *impossible for the text itself to fill the gaps*. The journey must be participatory. In this chapter I will suggest that Iser's theory of reading can be expanded and developed to describe a participatory mode of reading theologically.[3] I will suggest a reappropriation of our understanding of 'response' in light of gift. In this way I would like to return to the theme of reading theologically which I discussed in chapter 2, and thus frame the supernatural journey in the reader's participation of it.

The Catholic philosopher William Desmond makes very much the same claim as Iser for the seemingly demonic or evil apparition. For Desmond the supernatural itself is neither good nor evil, but equivocal. The weird sisters of *Macbeth*, for instance, tell prophecies mixed with half-truths and half-lies.[4] This equivocity reveals the purpose of the supernatural event not as evil agency, nor as good, but as startling us into astonishment. As Desmond writes:

> We do not first go towards something, but find ourselves going out of ourselves because something has made its way, often in startling communication, into the very depths of roots of our being, beyond our self-determination.[5]

While the weird tales of Arthur Machen depicted the demonic as Augustinian privation of good, Desmond's claim of equivocity takes this beyond evil as pure negation, and reintroduces potentiality. It is this catalyst for the potentiality of being 'beyond self-determination' which reveals itself in Le Fanu's supernatural tales.

The Greek writer Nikos Kazantzakis draws all these elements of startling potentiality and opposing forces together in *The Saviors of God*. In this poetic essay he explores the struggle of human-being to go beyond the primordial through creativity. He writes:

> As soon as we are born we begin the struggle to create, to compose, to turn matter into life; we are born in every moment. In the temporary living organism these two streams collide: (a) the ascent toward composition, toward life, toward immortality; (b) the descent toward decomposition, toward matter, toward death. Both streams well up from the depths of primordial essence. Life startles us at first; it seems somewhat beyond the law, somewhat contrary to nature, somewhat like a transitory counteraction to the dark eternal fountains; but deeper down we feel that Life is itself without beginning, an indestructible force of the Universe. But both opposing forces are holy. It is our duty, therefore, to grasp that vision which can embrace and harmonise these two enormous, timeless, and indestructible forces, and with this vision to modulate our thinking and our action.[6]

This passage can be thought of as a fitting description of the journey through which this book has travelled with Machen, MRJ and Le Fanu. Firstly, Kazantzakis recognises the Augustinian journey itself as one of not just coming into being, but coming *more* into being. Secondly, he acknowledges the conflicting forces upon man as fallen, those of ascent and descent. Most important, however, are the two final statements of this extract. *Both opposing forces are holy*. As Kazantzakis explains, it is the momentum of both of these forces which charge human agency into human being. The startling astonishment of perceiving the world in its breadth, beyond what Kazantzakis calls nature, propels us into participation of being in that world.

In the supernatural tales, the protagonists are doubled, mirrored and followed by versions of themselves which are catalysts for self-recognition. However, they are also doubled and followed by the reader. The position and potential repositioning of the reader when accompanying the haunted protagonist on his journey frames this book. To conclude then, I return to my 'non-theological' reader who has been inhabiting the suspended space of supernatural fiction, and will examine the relationship that the reader has with this journey.

Return to the Gap

In Arthur Machen's story 'Opening the Door', the Reverend Secretan Jones, amongst experience of other strange disturbances of time and place, walks through a gate in his garden for a moment, only to return to find that he has in fact been gone for over six weeks.[7] He tells the narrator of the tale that although he cannot remember where he was in that time, he has the sense that it was somewhere benign:

> At first [I remembered] nothing at all. I could not believe that more than a few seconds came between my opening the garden door and shutting it. Then in a day or two there was a vague impression that I had been somewhere where everything was absolutely right. I can't say more than that. No fairyland joys, or bowers of bliss or anything of that kind; no sense of anything strange or unaccustomed. But there was no care there at all. *Est enim magnum chaos.*[8]

The narrator notes his strange use of Latin description, however, commenting, 'But that means "For there is a great void," or "A great gulf."' Jones' sense of a void is notable as this gulf is neither an abyss nor an idyll. Several weeks later Jones returns to his home country of the Welsh borderlands (Machen's own location of spiritual borderlands), and disappears again, this time leaving a note with the Latin inscription repeated. It seems that Jones has chosen to return to the void.

As discussed in the introduction, literary criticism has commonly interpreted the equivocity of Victorian supernatural fiction as an indication of agnostic anxiety—ambiguity reflects an absence of religious truth claims. However, the equivocity shown here demonstrates not a neither/nor ambiguity, but both/and. The void, or gap, contains promise. William Desmond again imbues the gap with momentum, writing that 'equivocity thrusts us along this passageway of danger and hope'.[9]

Iser's Reader-Response model describes such a void in the reader/text relationship in his notion of a 'gap' or a 'blank'. The reader, claims Iser, actualises this gap, participating in an act of exchange with the text. I have argued throughout, however, that the gap, or the 'suspended space', as I have called it, is one which reveals the potency of gift as integral to exchange and communication. Thus I would extend Iser's claim, and argue that when reading theologically, the reader does not simply fill the gap in response to an emptiness, but *responds to* the potency of the gap. Specifically, the reader responds with porosity.

When bringing together five of his magazine stories into book form for *In a Glass Darkly*, Sheridan Le Fanu introduced the character of Dr Hesselius as a literary device to frame the tales. The haunted narratives thus become cases from the notes of this self-styled 'metaphysical physician', whose claims to metaphysics belie an attempt in each case to contain the story within medicalised or empiricist narratives. Of 'Green Tea', for instance, Dr Hesselius is confident that he would have imposed order on the experiences of the protagonist. 'I have not,' he claims, 'the slightest doubt that I should have first dimmed and ultimately sealed that inner eye which Mr Jennings had inadvertently opened.'[10] James Walton argues that Dr Hesselius occupies the gap between protagonist and reader, claiming that 'as a surrogate for the author he holds an indispensible place in the chain that links the character's subjectivity to the reader's.'[11] However, far from providing a guide through the 'gap', Walton concedes that Dr Hesselius' attempts to impose a metaphysical order on the tales produce only 'a Shandyesque parody of the confusion of "spirit" and "matter"— the secularisation or emptying of the concept of spirit—that characterises a whole line of post-Cartesian discourse.'[12] It is this distinction between imposing order on the gap or responding to it which illustrates my extension of Iser's role of the reader. In this way I will build on Iser's recognition that the text is a 'dynamic happening' whose actualisation is one of interaction.[13]

The vehicle for this response to gift is recognition or *anamnesis*. For Iser the dynamic happening relies on the aesthetic event having no accessible a priori meaning. The reader turns the aesthetic event into something discursive as its meaning is extended to relate to something outside itself. Iser writes:

> The aesthetic effect is robbed of this unique quality the moment one tries to define what is meant in terms of other meanings that one knows. [...] For one automatically seeks to relate it to contexts that are familiar. The moment one does so, however, the effect is extinguished, because the effect is in the nature of an experience and not an exercise in explanation.[14]

Iser's reader must be active in this creative process as there is no 'common code' in the message.[15] It is *anamnesis*, however, which provides just such a common code.

In Henry James' unfinished novel *A Sense of the Past*, Ralph Pendrell, living in 1910, is given the opportunity to swap places with his ancestor cum alter ego from 1820. However, the more time he spends in 1820, the more he comes to see that his friends there are ghostly. Their relationship is haunted by the feeling that something is not quite right:

> It was for all the world as if his own interpretation grew, under this breath of a crisis, exactly by the lapse of theirs, lasting long enough to suggest that his very care for them had somehow annihilated them, or had at least converted them to the necessarily void and soundless state. He could understand that they didn't, and that this would have made them take him for mad, the chill and the dismay of which—felt for that matter by Ralph too—turned them to stone or wood or wax, or whatever it was they momentarily most resembled.[16]

Much more importantly, however, he comes to see *himself* as ghostly. James' notes for the rest of the novel declare his intention that Pendrell would be returned to his own time eventually, and that this return would perform a salvation from the ghostliness of his existence in 1820, 'saved from all the horror of the growing fear of *not* being saved, of being lost, of being *in* the past to stay, heart-breakingly to stay and never know his own original precious Present again.'[17] Pendrell's actualisation is here bound in a return to himself.

Recognition and return, then, become integral to an understanding of self. Narrative theologians ascribe such an *anamnesis* to biblical narrative. The stories are universal narratives of a people, in which sin is made universal, as is suffering. The recognition of this universal story, then, is a recognition of self. Augustine extends this to a recognition of the divine in the self, writing that God is 'more inward than my most inward part and higher than the highest element within me'[18] (*interior intimo meo et superior summo meo*). This can be interpreted more literally as 'more intimate', or perhaps 'closer to'. The divine presence within the self is more intimate than the perceived-self built by experience. For the non-theological reader, the Judeo-Christian myths of self provide an analogous structure within which he can participate in this *anamnesis*.

To Paul Ricœur, the role of myth as symbol is crucial to the configuration of self. In order to understand this use of myth as symbol, Ricœur gives the example of the Adamic myth, describing it as the 'anthropological myth *par excellence*'.[19] This myth recognises man's narrative as one of being in relation to the Good. In this way we understand being as becoming. The myth thus becomes a hermeneutical symbol which anticipates interpretation and exploration. In this way Judeo-Christian myth as a story of being becomes recognisable.[20] This act of recognition constitutes reader participation in the theological journey of the supernatural tale. It indicates that the reader has begun to navigate the suspended space.

Reader Doubling

Pendrell's haunting is of course itself caused by doubling, and it is doubling which facilitates that feature central to haunting—that of return.[21] Indeed, each of the stories in this thesis contain a doubling of sorts, and the confrontation of the supernatural reveals the protagonist to himself as doubled—both actually fallen but potentially saved. The apparitions serve as mirrors, albeit with dark glass.

At this point, I return to the final doubling of this book, that of the doubling of protagonist and reader. In chapter 2, I used Desmond's metaxology to describe the suspended space as a doubled space: The in-between is both immanent (in the midst of) and transcendent. It is this double status which allows the in-between space to contain both the possibility of a journey 'through' and a monstrous quality. The doubleness of being allows for monstrous possibilities, as man becomes a counterfeit double of God. However, when the doubleness of the in-between contains recognition and return, this potency becomes positive. The horror of recognising the self *as* double is precursor to recognizing the potency of the double.

To actualise this potency, the protagonists of our stories must recognise their own story. This is vividly explored in Henry James' story 'The Jolly Corner', in which Spencer Brydon encounters his alter ego with just this double sensation of something 'so intimate and so strange'.[22] Spencer Brydon is haunted by what he is not—the lives which he has not led, the selves which he has not become. Confronted, however, by this other self, Brydon's response is one of horror: 'for the bared identity was too hideous as *his*, and his glare was the passion of his protest. The face, *that* face, Spencer Brydon's?' The horror progresses for Brydon, however, in ultimately recognising this alter ego as alter:

> It was unknown, inconceivable, awful, disconnected from any possibility!—he had been 'sold,' he inwardly moaned, stalking such game as this: the presence before him was a presence, the horror within him a horror, but the waste of his nights had been only grotesque and the success of his adventure an irony. Such an identity fitted his at no point, made its alternative monstrous. A thousand times yes, as it came upon him nearer now, the face was the face of a stranger.[23]

Reconciliation comes for Brydon as he wakes from the experience in the arms of the woman he loves, who helps him to respond to the vision with pity as well as horror. By recognising the apparition as at once intimate and other, Brydon is able to affirm and actualise his own self:

> 'Ah!' Brydon winced—whether for his proved identity or for his lost fingers. Then, 'He has a million a year,' he lucidly added. 'But he hasn't you.'
> 'And he isn't—no, he isn't—*you*!' she murmured, as he drew her to his breast.[24]

In 'reading' the apparition, Brydon is moved to 'read' his own story. The intimacy of this doubling both dissolves dualism and restores unity of self.

M. R. James most strongly explores the textuality of doubling, his characters literally finding their own stories in libraries and old books. For MRJ, documents provide clarity and explanation to relationships which have until then only been sensed. Mr Humphries, for instance, learns from an inscription above the maze that he is not only an inheritor of land, but a 'son of the house', and the fullness of this inheritance is revealed to him grotesquely in his uncle's library. Documents provide a frame through which the porous world can be interpreted, for characters whose ontological commitments have been shattered.

In a similar way Iser ascribes such an agency to text in his theory of reading, but claims that it is the texts themselves which cause such an ontological shattering, arguing that the removal of norms from textual material instigates movement in the reader. Iser writes that when such norms are negated, 'the familiar appears to [the reader] to be obsolescent—it belongs to the "past", and he is suddenly moved into a position beyond it, without having command of this new situation'.[25] Just like the protagonist, the reader of the supernatural tale is catapulted into movement.

However, while Iser uses the term 'negation' to describe this removal of norms, using such a negation to place the reader in the suspended space, I would suggest that the doubling experience of reading theologically moves the reader, like MRJ's protagonists, not only to the suspended space of negation, but through it, by recognition and return. To read theologically, that is to say teleologically, the reader must, like MRJ's characters, read himself in the story. To recognise the confronted protagonist as teleological is to recognise *being* as teleological. Such a movement *through* the suspended space requires responding to the double with porosity.

Response as Participation

For the characters of our tales to successfully navigate the porous world with which they are confronted, they need to both respond to and participate in it. Henry James' supernatural tragedies show the stagnation and paralysis which results from a failure to do this. At most, such a refusal can bring about despairing realisation of that stagnancy. In many ways, the same demands are made of the reader of the supernatural tale. Iser's Reader-Response theory relies on the premise that the reader actualises the text. For the purposes of theological reading, I would describe this actualisation as taking place in two stages.

Firstly, the teleological possibilities of the text are realised as the protagonist is recognised as a potent and doubled being. The reader thus experiences re-cognition of the Adamic myth. The fictional ghost story plays into the equivocity inherent in this potency by necessarily remaining open-ended. Even those short stories with epilogues serve mostly to inform us of the protagonist's disappearance or a death shrouded in mystery as to the condition of his soul. The second stage, the actualisation of these possibilities, thus takes place as the reader repositions himself *in light* of being as becoming. By recognising the story of human being in the tales, the reader most fully actualises the supernatural tale as confrontation. In responding to a porous world, the reader responds with porosity.

The value of fictional literature to theological thinking is well established. What is literature if not an exploration of the human condition, and a depiction of the world as an excess of being? With this in mind, this book has not claimed to attempt either definitive literary readings of the texts, nor a definitive theology for them. The theological framework is intended to be consistent and sound, but its specifically Augustinian and at times orthodox perspective makes no claims to encompass 'theology' as a literary hermeneutic. However, the ghost story or supernatural tale takes up a specific and privileged space in this relationship, which hopefully takes the value of the readings performed here beyond an exercise in theological commentary. The momentary confrontations of these tales suspend ontology, and open a space in which theological truth claims are at once immanent and strange.

The supernatural tale provides a space in which the non-theological reader can participate in the theological journey. For the literary scholar, theological readings of the ghost story provide a recovery of a specific ontological vocabulary, and for theologians, they provide a reminder that 'the divine is there in the grotesque'.[26] The supernatural tale as theological experience is a moment of suspension expanded into a journey, along which travel both the protagonist and reader. As Dorothy L. Sayers realised: 'Nobody but a god can pass unscathed through the searching ordeal of incarnation.'[27]

NOTES

1. Wolfgang Iser, *The Act of Reading: A Theory of Aesthetic Response* (Baltimore: Johns Hopkins University Press, 1978), ix. Title quotation William Shakespeare, *Macbeth*, 1.3.137–8.
2. Wolfgang Iser, *Prospecting: From Reader Response to Literary Anthropology* (Baltimore: Johns Hopkins University Press, 1989), 9.
3. Anthony Thiselton has already turned to Iser's Reader-Response theory for utilisation in biblical studies. The insights that he offers are useful in reversing this process here, bringing theology into literary study. Cf. Thiselton, *New Horizons in Hermeneutics* (Grand Rapids MI: Zondervan, 1992), 516–529.
4. William Desmond, 'Sticky Evil: Macbeth and the Karma of the Equivocal', in *God, Literature and Process Thought*, ed. Darren J. N Middleton (Aldershot: Ashgate, 2002), 133.

5. Desmond, *Intimate Strangeness*, 106.
6. Nikos Kazantzakis, *The Saviors of God: Spiritual Exercises*, trans. Kimon Friar (New York: Simon and Schuster, 1960), 43–44.
7. Title quotation: Jacques Derrida, *Spectres of Marx*, trans. Peggy Kumef (New York: Routledge, 1994), 11.
8. Arthur Machen, 'Opening the Door', in *Holy Terrors* (Harmondsworth: Penguin, 1946), 65.
9. Desmond, *God and the Between*, 74.
10. Sheridan Le Fanu, 'Green Tea', in *In a Glass Darkly* (London: R. Bentley and Son, 1872), 94.
11. James Walton, *Vision and Vacancy: The Fictions of J.S. Le Fanu* (Dublin: University College Dublin Press, 2007), 47.
12. Walton, *Vision and Vacancy*, 30. See chapter 5 for Alison Milbank and Jack Sullivan's elaborations of this point.
13. Iser, *The Act of Reading*, 22.
14. Iser, *The Act of Reading*, 22.
15. Iser, *The Act of Reading*, 21. See also 112.
16. Henry James, *The Sense of the Past* (New York: Charles Scribner's Sons, 1917), 213.
17. James, *The Sense of the Past*, 294 (notes). Original emphasis. Note that *The Sense of the Past* repeats the theme of a female companion who *gives* of herself that he may return.
18. Augustine, *Confessions*, III.iv (11).
19. Paul Ricœur, *The Symbolism of Evil* (Boston MA: Beacon Press, 1967), 233.
20. Compare this to the child's narrative in Machen's 'The White People': 'I had remembered the story I had quite forgotten before, and in the story the two figures are called Adam and Eve, and only those who know the story understand what they mean.' See Chap. 2.
21. Title quotation: E.T.A. Hoffmann, *The Devil's Elixir* (Edinburgh: William Blackwood, 1829), 36.
22. Henry James, *The Jolly Corner* (London: Martin Secker, 1918), 35.
23. James, *The Jolly Corner*, 60–1. Original emphasis.
24. James, *The Jolly Corner*, 72. Original emphasis.
25. Iser, *The Act of Reading*, 212–3.
26. Desmond, *God and the Between*, 197.
27. Dorothy L. Sayers, *The Mind of the Maker* (London: Continuum, 1994), 74.

Bibliography

Allen, Grant. 1893. *Ivan Greet's Masterpiece*. London: Chatto and Windus.
Anselm of Canterbury. 2000. The Fall of the Devil. In *The Complete Philosophical and Theological Treatises of St Anselm of Canterbury*. Trans. Jasper Hopkins and Herbert Richardson, 213–261. Minneapolis, MN: Arthur J. Banning.
Aquinas, Thomas. 1915. *The "Summa Theologica" of St. Thomas Aquinas*. Trans. Fathers of the English Dominican Province. London: Burns Oates and Washbourne.
Aquinas, Thomas. 1952. *Quaestiones Disputatae De Veritate: Questions 1–9*. Trans. Robert W. Mulligan, S.J. Chicago: Henry Regnery Company.
Aquinas, Thomas. 1998. *Selected Writings*. Trans. Ralph McInerny. London: Penguin Books.
Aristotle. 1924. *Metaphysics*. Trans. W.D. Ross. Oxford: Clarendon.
Aristotle. 1997. *Poetics*. Trans. George Whalley. Montreal: McGill-Queens Press.
Armstrong, A.H. 1953. *Plotinus*. London: George Allen & Unwin.
Augustine. 1957. *Against Julian: The Writings of Saint Augustine*, vol. 16. Trans. Michael A. Schumacher. New York: Fathers of the Church.
Augustine. 1982. *The Literal Meaning of Genesis* [De Genesi ad litteram.]. Trans. John Hammond Taylor. New York: Paulist Press.
Augustine. 1991. *Confessions*, ed. Henry Chadwick. Oxford: Oxford University Press.
Augustine. 2002a. *On the Trinity: Books 8–15*, ed. Gareth B. Matthews. Cambridge: Cambridge University Press.
Augustine. 2002b. *On the Trinity: Books 1–7*, ed. Gareth B. Matthews. Cambridge: Cambridge University Press.
Augustine. 2003. *Concerning the City of God Against the Pagans*. Trans. Henry Bettenson. London: Penguin Books.

Bakhtin, M.M. 1986. *Speech Genres and Other Late Essays*, ed. Carl Emerson and Michael Holquist. Trans. Vern W. McGee. Austin: University of Texas Press.

Banta, Martha. 1972. *Henry James and the Occult*. Bloomington: Indiana University Press.

Barth, Karl. 1968. *The Epistle to the Romans*. Trans. Edwyn C. Hoskyns. Oxford: Oxford University Press.

Benson, Robert Hugh. 2004. The Watcher. In *The Light Invisible*, 6–10. Falls Church, VA: Universal Values Media.

Bequette, John P. 2004. *Christian Humanism: Creation, Redemption and Reintegration*. Lanham, MD: University Press of America.

Bewick, Thomas. 1797. *A History of British Land Birds: Vol. 1*. Newcastle: Edward Walker.

Boyiopoulos, Kostas. 2010. "Esoteric Elements": The Judeo-Christian Scheme in Arthur Machen's *the Great God Pan*. *Neophilologus* 94: 363–374.

Briggs, Julia. 1977. No Mere Antiquary: M.R. James. In *Night Visitors: The Rise and Fall of the English Ghost Story*, 124–142. London: Faber and Faber.

Brooks, Peter. 1976. *The Melodramatic Imagination: Balzac, Henry James, Melodrama and the Mode of Excess*. New Haven, CT: Yale University Press.

Brooks, Van Wyck. 1972. *The Pilgrimage of Henry James*. New York: Octagon.

Browne, Thomas, Stephen Greenblatt, and Ramie Targoff. 1964. *Religio Medici and Other Works*, ed. L.C. Martin. Oxford: Oxford University Press.

Bruns, Gerald L. 1992. *Hermeneutics Ancient and Modern*. New Haven, CT: Yale University Press.

Carroll, Anthony J. 2010. The Philosophical Foundations of Catholic Modernism. In *George Tyrrell and Catholic Modernism*, ed. Oliver Rafferty, 38–55. Dublin: Four Courts Press.

Cavaliero, Glen. 1995. An Iconography of Fear. In *The Supernatural and English Fiction*, 23–51. Oxford: Oxford University Press.

Chadwick, Owen. 1960. *The Mind of the Oxford Movement*. Stanford, CA: Stanford University Press.

Chesterton, G.K. 1905. *Heretics*. London: Bodley Head.

Coleridge, Samuel Taylor. 1816. *The Statesman's Manual; Or, the Bible the Best Guide to Political Skill and Foresight, a Lay Sermon. With an Appendix [Statesman's manual]*. London: Gale and Fenner.

Coleridge, Samuel Taylor. 1853. On Poesy or Art. In *The Complete Works of Samuel Taylor Coleridge*, vol. IV, ed. William G.T. Shedd, 328–336. New York: Harper and Brothers.

Collins, Wilkie. 1977. Mrs. Zant and the Ghost. In *Little Novels*, 1–22. New York: Dover Publications.

Connors, Scott. 2007. 'What is this that I have done?' The Scapegoat Figure in the Stories of M.R. James. In *Warnings to the Curious: A Sheaf of Criticism on*

M.R. James, ed. S.T. Joshi and Rosemary Pardoe, 215–224. New York: Hippocampus Press.

Cox, Michael. 1983. *M.R. James: An Informal Portrait*. Oxford: Oxford University Press.

Daly, Gabriel. 2000. Theological and Philosophical Modernism. In *Catholicism Contending with Modernity: Roman Catholic Modernism and Anti-Modernism in Historical Context*, ed. Darrell Jodock, 88–112. Cambridge: Cambridge University Press.

Dante. 1993. *The Divine Comedy*, ed. David H. Higgins. Trans. C.H. Sisson. Oxford: Oxford University Press.

Daugherty, Sarah B. 1979. James, Renan, and the Religion of Consciousness. *Comparative Literature Studies* 16: 318–331.

Davies, Brian. 1992. *The Thought of Thomas Aquinas*. Oxford: Clarendon Press.

de Certeau, Michel. 1970. Is There a Language of Unity? *Concilium* 1: 73–93.

de Certeau, Michel. 2000. Walking in the City. In *The Certeau Reader*, ed. Graham Ward, 101–118. Malden, MA: Blackwell.

Derrida, Jacques. 1983. The Time of a Thesis: Punctuations. In *Philosophy in France Today*, ed. Alan Montefiore. Trans. Kathleen McLaughlin, 34–50. Cambridge: Cambridge University Press.

Derrida, Jacques. 1994. *Spectres of Marx*. Trans. Peggy Kumef. New York: Routledge.

Descartes, René. 1990. *Meditations on First Philosophy*. Trans. John Cottingham. Cambridge: Cambridge University Press.

Desmond, William. 1995. *Being and the Between*. Albany, NY: SUNY Press.

Desmond, William. 2002. Sticky Evil: Macbeth and the Karma of the Equivocal. In *God, Literature and Process Thought*, ed. Darren J.N. Middleton, 133–157. Aldershot: Ashgate.

Desmond, William. 2008. *God and the Between*. Chennai, India: Blackwell.

Desmond, William. 2012a. *The Intimate Strangeness of Being: Metaphysics After Dialectic*. Washington, DC: Catholic University of America Press.

Desmond, William. 2012b. *The William Desmond Reader*, ed. Christopher Ben Simpson. Albany, NY: SUNY.

Dickens, A.G. 1967. *Martin Luther and the Reformation*. New York: English Universities Press.

Dionysius the Areopagite. 1897. *Works: Part One*. Trans. John Parker. London: James Parker.

Eckhart. 2009. *The Complete Mystical Works of Meister Eckhart*, ed. Maurice O'Connell Walshe. Trans. Maurice O'Connell Walshe. New York: Crossroad.

Edel, Leon. 1975. *The Life of Henry James*, vol. 2. New York: Penguin.

Edel, Leon. 1987. *Henry James, a Life*. London: Collins.

Eden, Kathy. 1997. *Hermeneutics and the Rhetorical Tradition*. New Haven, CT: Yale University Press.

Edmundson Makala, Melissa. 2013. *Women's Ghost Literature in Nineteenth-Century Britain*. Cardiff: University of Wales Press.
Eliade, Mircea. 1968. *The Sacred and the Profane: The Nature of Religion*. Trans. Willard R. Trask. New York: Harvest.
Eliot, George. 1865. The Influence of Rationalism. *Fortnightly Review* 1: 43–55.
Eliot, George. 1895. The Lifted Veil. In *Silas Marner, The Lifted Veil, Brother Jacob*, 252–313. Boston, MA: Estes and Lauriat.
Felman, Shoshanah. 1977. Turning the Screw of Interpretation. *Yale French Studies* 55–56: 94–207.
Foucault, Michel. 1988. *Madness and Civilization: A History of Insanity in the Age of Reason*. Trans. Richard Howard. New York: Vintage Books.
Franckforter. 1980. *The Theologia Germanica of Martin Luther*, ed. Bengt Hoffman. Philadelphia, PA: Paulist Press.
Fraser, Hilary. 1986. *Beauty and Belief: Aesthetics and Religion in Victorian Literature*. Cambridge: Cambridge University Press.
Freeman, Nicholas. 2010. Arthur Machen: Ecstasy and Epiphany. *Literature and Theology* 24: 242–255.
Frye, Northrop. 1981. *The Great Code: The Bible and Literature*. Orlando, FL: Harcourt Brace Jovanovich.
Frye, Northrop. 1990. *Anatomy of Criticism*. Princeton, NJ: Princeton University Press.
Fusell, Edwin Sill. 1993. *The Catholic Side of Henry James*. Cambridge: Cambridge University Press.
Gadamer, Hans-Georg. 2013. *Truth and Method*. Trans. Joel Weinsheimer and Donald G. Marshall. Chennai, India: Bloomsbury.
Girard, René. 1972. *Violence and the Sacred*. Trans. Patrick Gregory. Baltimore, MD: Johns Hopkins University Press.
Girard, René. 1986. *The Scapegoat*. Trans. Yvonne Freccero. Baltimore, MD: Johns Hopkins University Press.
Grant, Helen. 2007. The Nature of the Beast: The Demonology of "Canon Alberic's Scrap-Book". In *Warnings to the Curious: A Sheaf of Criticism on M.R. James*, ed. S.T. Joshi and Rosemary Pardoe, 227–238. New York: Hippocampus Press.
Green, Thomas Hill. 1883. *Prolegomena to Ethics*, ed. A.C. Bradley. Oxford: Clarendon.
Habermas, Jürgen. 2002. On Hermeneutics' Claim to Universality. In *The Hermeneutics Reader*, ed. Kurt Mueller-Vollmer, 294–319. New York: Contiuum.
Habermas, Jürgen. 2010. An Awareness of What Is Missing. In *An Awareness of What Is Missing: Faith and Reason in a Post-Secular Age*, ed. Jürgen Habermas et al. Trans. Ciaran Cronin, 15–23. Cambridge: Polity Press.

Hägglund, Bengt. 1961. *The Background of Luther's Doctrine of Justification in Late Medieval Theology.* Philadelphia, PA: Fortress Press.
Harrison, Jane. 1916. The Head of John Baptist. τίνος πρόσωπον δη τ' ἐν ἀγκάλαις ἔχεις; (Eur. Bacch. 1277). *The Classical Review* 30: 216–219.
Hauerwas, Stanley. 1981. *A Community of Character: Toward a Constructive Christian Social Ethic.* Notre Dame, IN: University of Notre Dame Press.
Hauerwas, Stanley. 1983. *The Peaceable Kingdom: A Primer in Christian Ethics.* Notre Dame, IN: University of Notre Dame Press.
Hay, Simon. 2011. *A History of the Modern British Ghost Story.* Basingstoke: Palgrave Macmillan.
Heidegger, Martin. 1982. *Nietzsche*, vol. IV, ed. David Farrell Krell. Trans. Frank A. Capuzzi. San Francisco, CA: Harper and Row.
Heidegger, Martin. 1985. *Schelling's Treatise on the Essence of Human Freedom.* Trans. Joan Stambough. Athens: Ohio University Press.
Hibbs, Thomas S. 2007. *Aquinas, Ethics, and Philosophy of Religion: Metaphysics and Practice.* Bloomington: Indiana University Press.
Hoffman, Bengt. 1976. *Luther and the Mystics.* Minneapolis, MN: Augsburg.
Hoffmann, E.T.A. 1829. *The Devil's Elixir*, vol. II. Edinburgh: William Blackwood.
Hopkins, Gerard Manley. 1918. *Poems*, ed. Robert Bridges. London: Humphrey Milford.
Hughes, Martin. 2007. A Maze of Secrets in a Story by M.R. James. In *A Warning to the Curious: A Sheaf of Criticism on M.R. James*, 258–278. New York: Hippocampus Press.
Huxley, Thomas Henry. 1869. On the Physical Basis of Life. *Fortnightly Review* 11: 129–145.
Hylton, Raymond. 2005. *Ireland's Huguenots and Their Refuge, 1662–1745.* Brighton: Sussex Academic Press.
Hyman, Gavin. 2001. *The Predicament of Postmodern Theology: Radical Orthodoxy Or Nihilist Textualism?* Louisville, KT: Westminster John Knox Press.
Irenaeus. 2010. *Against Heresies*, ed. Alexander Roberts and James Donaldson. Oxford: Ex Fontibus.
Irwin, W.R. 1961. The Survivial of Pan. *Pmla* 76: 159–167.
Iser, Wolfgang. 1978. *The Act of Reading: A Theory of Aesthetic Response.* Baltimore, MD: Johns Hopkins University Press.
Iser, Wolfgang. 1989. *Prospecting: From Reader Response to Literary Anthropology.* Baltimore, MD: Johns Hopkins University Press.
Jacobs, Alan. 2001. *A Theology of Reading.* Boulder, CO: Westview Press.
James, Henry. 1881. *The Portrait of a Lady.* London: Macmillan.
James, Henry. 1893. The Private Life. In *The Private Life, the Wheel of Time, Lord Beaupre, the Visits, Collaboration, Owen Wingrave*, 1–56. London: James R. Osgood, McIlvaine.

James, Henry. 1895. The Altar of the Dead. In *Terminations*, 185–242. New York: Harper and Brothers.
James, Henry. 1897. *The Other House*. London: William Heineman.
James, Henry. 1898. The Turn of the Screw. In *The Two Magics*, 3–169. London: William Heinemann.
James, Henry. 1900. The Real Right Thing. In *The Soft Side*, 71–86. New York: Macmillan.
James, Henry. 1901. *The Sacred Fount*. New York: Scribner's Sons.
James, Henry. 1903a. *The Ambassadors*. London: Harper and Brothers.
James, Henry. 1903b. The Beast in the Jungle. In *The Better Sort*, 189–244. New York: Charles Scribner's Sons.
James, Henry. 1905. *The Golden Bowl*. London: Methuen.
James, Henry. 1909. Preface. In *The Altar of the Dead, the Beast in the Jungle, the Birthplace, and Other Tales*, v–xxviii. New York: Charles Scribner's Sons.
James, Henry. 1910. Is there a Life After Death. In *In After Days: Thoughts on the Future Life*, ed. W.D. Howells, 199–233. New York: Harper and Brothers.
James, Henry. 1914. *Notes of a Son and Brother*. London: Macmillan.
James, Henry. 1917. *The Sense of the Past*. New York: Charles Scribner's Sons.
James, Henry. 1918. *The Jolly Corner*. London: Martin Secker.
James, Herbert. 1890. *The Country Clergyman and His Work: Six Lectures on Pastoral Theology Delivered in the Divinity School, Cambridge, May Term, 1889*. London: Macmillan.
James, M.R. 1899. The Testament of Solomon. *Guardian Church Newspaper*, March 15.
James, M.R. 1905a. Canon Alberic's Scrapbook. In *Ghost Stories of an Antiquary*, 1–28. London: Edward Arnold.
James, M.R. 1905b. Count Magnus. In *Ghost Stories of an Antiquary*, 149–180. London: Edward Arnold.
James, M.R. 1905c. Lost Hearts. In *Ghost Stories of an Antiquary*, 29–52. London: Edward Arnold.
James, M.R. 1905d. Oh Whistle and I'll Come to You, My Lad. In *Ghost Stories of an Antiquary*, 181–226. London: Edward Arnold.
James, M.R. 1905e. Preface. In *Ghost Stories of an Antiquary*, vii–viii. London: Edward Arnold.
James, M.R. 1905f. The Treasure of Abbot Thomas. In *Ghost Stories of an Antiquary*, 227–270. London: Edward Arnold.
James, M.R. 1913. *Old Testament Legends*. London: Longmans, Green.
James, M.R. 1917. Some Remarks on 'the Head of John Baptist'. *The Classical Review* 31: 1–4.
James, M.R. 1923. Prologue. In *Joseph Sheridan Le Fanu:Madam Crowl's Ghost and Other Tales of Mystery*, ed. M.R. James, vii–viii. London: G. Bell & Sons.

James, M.R. 1980. *The Apocryphal New Testament: Being the Apocryphal Gospels, Acts, Epistles, and Apocalypses.* Oxford: Clarendon Press.
James, M.R. 2009. Mr Humphreys and His Inheritance. In *Casting the Runes and Other Ghost Stories*, ed. Michael Cox, 172–198. Oxford: Oxford University Press.
James, M.R. 2011. *Eton and Kings.* Cambridge: Cambridge University Press.
James, M.R. 2013. M.R. James on J.S. Le Fanu. *Ghosts and Scholars 7*, October 10.
Jerome. 1845. Commentariorum in Zahariam Liber Secundus. In *Patriologiae Cursus Completus XXV*, 1415–1541. Maine: Garnier fratres et J.-P. Migne successores.
Jodock, Darrell. 2000. *Catholicism Contending with Modernity: Roman Catholic Modernism and Anti-Modernism in Historical Context.* Cambridge: Cambridge University Press.
Joshi, S.T. 1990. *The Weird Tale: Arthur Machen, Lord Dunsany, Algernon Blackwood, M.R. James, Ambrose Bierce, H.P. Lovecraft.* Austin: University of Texas Press.
Kant, Immanuel. 1960. *Religion within the Limits of Reason Alone.* Harper Torchbooks. Cloister Library. Trans. Theodore Meyer Greene, Hoyt H. Hudson, and John R. Silber. New York: Harper & Brothers.
Kaplan, Fred. 1992. *Henry James: The Imagination of Genius.* New York: Morrow.
Kazantzakis, Nikos. 1960. *The Saviors of God: Spiritual Exercises.* Trans. Kimon Friar. New York: Simon and Schuster.
Keats, John. 1899. Endymion. In *The Complete Poetical Works*, 46–109. Boston, MA: Houghton, Mifflin.
Kenney, John Peter. 2005. *The Mysticism of Saint Augustine: Rereading the Confessions.* Abingdon: Routledge.
Kierkegaard, Søren. 1946. *The Concept of Dread.* Trans. Walter Lowrie. Princeton, NJ: Princeton University Press.
Kierkegaard, Søren. 1989. *The Sickness Unto Death.* Trans. Alastair Hannay. New York: Penguin.
Knight, Mark, and Emma Mason. 2006. *Nineteenth-Century Religion and Literature.* Oxford: Oxford University Press.
Landy, Joshua, and Michael Sale. 2001. Introduction. In *The Re-Enchantment of the World: Secular Magic in a Rational Age*, ed. Joshua Landy and Michael Sale, 1–9. Stanford, CA: Stanford University Press.
Lang, Andrew. 1894. *Cock Lane and Common-Sense.* Cambridge: Cambridge University Press.
Larsen, Timothy. 2004. *Contested Christianity: The Political and Social Contexts of Victorian Theology.* Waco, TX: Baylor University Press.
Larsen, Timothy. 2006. *Crisis of Doubt.* Oxford: Oxford University Press.

Larsen, Timothy. 2011. *A People of One Book: The Bible and the Victorians*. Oxford: Oxford University Press.
Le Fanu, Sheridan. 1838. The Fortunes of Sir Robert Ardagh. In *Dublin University Magazine, Vol. XI*, 313–324. Dublin: James McGlashan.
Le Fanu, Sheridan. 1839. Strange Events in the Life of Shalken the Painter. In *Dublin University Magazine, Vol. XIII*, 579–590. Dublin: James McGlashan.
Le Fanu, Sheridan. 1843a. Spalatro, A Tale in Two Parts: Part I. In *The Dublin University Magazine. Vol. XXI, January–June*, 338–351. Dublin: William Curry Jun & Son.
Le Fanu, Sheridan. 1843b. Spalatro, A Tale in Two Parts: Part II. In *The Dublin University Magazine. Vol. XXI, January–June*, 446–458. Dublin: William Curry Jun. & Son.
Le Fanu, Sheridan. 1850a. Borrhomeo the Astrologer. In *Dublin University Magazine, Vol. XXI, January–June*, 54–71. Dublin: William Curry Jun.
Le Fanu, Sheridan. 1850b. The Mysterious Lodger: Part I. In *Dublin University Magazine, Vol. XXXV, January–June*, 54–71. Dublin: James McGlashan.
Le Fanu, Sheridan. 1850c. The Mysterious Lodger: Part II. In *Dublin University Magazine, Vol. XXXV, January–June*, 225–235. Dublin: James McGlashan.
Le Fanu, Sheridan. 1851. The Watcher. In *Ghost Stories and Tales of Mystery*, 9–60. Dublin: James McGlashan.
Le Fanu, Sheridan. 1871. The Haunted Baronet. In *Chronicles of Golden Friars*, 61–177. London: Richard Bentley and Son.
Le Fanu, Sheridan. 1872a. The Familiar. In *In a Glass Darkly*, 97–205. London: R. Bentley and Son.
Le Fanu, Sheridan. 1872b. Green Tea. In *In a Glass Darkly*, 3–95. London: R. Bentley and Son.
Le Fanu, Sheridan. 1872c. Sir Dominick's Bargain. Chap. 181–286. In *All the Year Round Vol. 8*, ed. Charles Dickens, 181–286. Vol. 8, 186–461. London: Chapman and Hall.
Le Fanu, W.R. 1893. *Years of Irish Life*. London: Edward Arnold.
Leo XIII. 1879. *Aeterni Patris*. http://www.papalencyclycals.net/Leo13/l13cph.htm
Lewis, Matthew. 1797. *The Monk: A Romance in Three Volumes*. London: J. Bell.
Lightman, Bernard. 1987. *The Origins of Agnosticism: Victorian Unbelief and the Limits of Knowledge*. Baltimore, MD: Johns Hopkins University Press.
Lilley, A. Leslie. 1907. *What we Want: An Open Letter to Pius X from a Group of Priests*. London: John Murray.
Livingston, James C. 2006. *Religious Thought in the Victorian Age: Challenges and Reconceptions*. London: T&T Clark.
Lovecraft, H.P. 2000. *The Annotated Supernatural Horror in Literature*, ed. S.T. Joshi. New York: Hippocampus Press.

Lozes, Jean. 1974. Fragment d'Un Journal Intime De J.S. Le Fanu: Document Inédit En Date Du 18 Mai 1858. *Caliban* 10: 153–164.
Luther, Martin. 1961. Two Kinds of Righteousness. In *Martin Luther: Selections from His Writings*, ed. John Dillenberger, 86–96. New York: Anchor.
Luther, Martin. 2006. *Lectures on Romans*. Trans. Wilhelm Pauck. Louisville, KY: Westminster John Knoxville Press.
Machen, Arthur. 1895. *The Three Impostors or the Transmutations*. London: John Lane.
Machen, Arthur. 1902. *Hieroglyphics*. London: Grant Richards.
Machen, Arthur. 1906. *Dr. Stiggins: His Views and Principles, a Series of Interviews*. Westminster: Francis Griffiths.
Machen, Arthur. 1908a. Modernism. *The Academy* 74: 686–689.
Machen, Arthur. 1908b. Realism and Symbol. *The Academy* 75: 109–110.
Machen, Arthur. 1922a. *The Hill of Dreams*. New York: Alfred A. Knopf.
Machen, Arthur. 1922b. *The Secret Glory*. New York: Alfred A. Knopf.
Machen, Arthur. 1926. *Notes and Queries*. London: Spurr & Swift.
Machen, Arthur. 1906a. A Fragment of Life. In *The House of Souls*, 3–112. London: E. Grant Richards.
Machen, Arthur. 1906b. The Great God Pan. In *The House of Souls*, 169–246. London: E. Grant Richards.
Machen, Arthur. 1906c. The Red Hand. In *The House of Souls*, 475–514. London: E. Grant Richards.
Machen, Arthur. 1906d. The White People. In *The House of Souls*, 113–168. London: E. Grant Richards.
Machen, Arthur. 1922/1915. *Far Off Things*. London: M. Secker.
Machen, Arthur. 1946. Opening the Door. In *Holy Terrors*, 54–65. Harmondsworth: Penguin.
Machen, Arthur. 1988. *Selected Letters: The Private Writings of the Master of the Macabre*, ed. Godfrey Brangham, Roger Dobson, and R.A. Gilbert. Wellingborough: Aquarian.
Machen, Arthur. 1997/1992. The Gift of Tongues. In *Ritual and Other Stories*, 209–214. Lewes: Tartarus.
Machin, James. 2015. Arthur Machen and J.S. Le Fanu. *The Green Book* 5: 34–39.
MacIntyre, Alasdair C. 1981. *After Virtue: A Study in Moral Theory*. London: Duckworth.
Maritain, Jacques. 1942. *Saint Thomas and the Problem of Evil (the Aquinas Lecture 1942)*. Aquinas Lecture. Trans. Mabelle Louise Cunningham Andison, vol. 1942. Milwaukee: Marquette University Press.
Marlowe, Christopher. 1995. *Doctor Faustus and Other Plays*, ed. David Bevington and Eric Rasmussen. Oxford: Oxford University Press.
Mason, Michael A. 1982. On Not Letting them Lie: Moral Significance in the Ghost Stories of M.R. James. *Studies in Short Fiction* 19: 253–260.

Matthews, W.H. 1922. *Mazes and Labyrinths: Their History and Development.* London: Longmans, Green.
Matthiessen, F.O. 1944. *Henry James: The Major Phase.* New York: Oxford University Press.
Maturin, Charles. 2008. *Melmoth the Wanderer.* Oxford: Oxford University Press.
McCormack, W.J. 1980a. *Sheridan Le Fanu.* Oxford: Clarendon Press.
McCormack, W.J. 1980b. *Sheridan Le Fanu and Victorian Ireland.* Oxford: Clarendon Press.
McCorristine, Shane. 2010. *Spectres of the Self: Thinking About Ghosts and Ghost-Seeing in England, 1750–1920.* Cambridge: Cambridge University Press.
McFarland, Ian A. 2010. *In Adam's Fall: A Meditation on the Christian Doctrine of Original Sin.* Chichester: Wiley-Blackwell.
McGrath, Alister. 1994. *Luther's Theology of the Cross.* Oxford: Basil Blackwell.
Merivale, Patricia. 1969. *Pan, the Goat-God, His Myth in Modern Times*, Harvard Studies in Comparative Literature, vol. 30. Cambridge, MA: Harvard University Press.
Migne, J.P. 1884. *Patriologiae Latinae Tomus* apud Garnier fratres et J.-P. Migne successores.
Milbank, Alison. 1988. Daughters of the House: Modes of the Gothic in the Fiction of Wilkie Collins, Charles Dickens and Sheridan Le Fanu. PhD thesis, University of Lancaster.
Milbank, Alison. 2007. Gothic Femininities. In *The Routledge Companion to Gothic*, 155–163. Abingdon: Routledge.
Milbank, Alison. 2008. Sacrificial Exchange and the Gothic Double in *Melmoth the Wanderer* and *the Picture of Dorian Gray*. In *Shaping Belief: Culture, Politics and Religion in Nineteenth-Century Writing*, ed. Victoria Morgan and Clare Williams, 113–128. Liverpool: Liverpool University Press.
Milbank, Alison. 2010a. Joseph Sheridan Le Fanu: Gothic Grotesque and the Huguenot Inheritance. In *A Companion to Irish Literature*, vol. 1, ed. Julia M. Wright, 362–376. Oxford: Wiley-Blackwell.
Milbank, Alison. 2010b. The Sleep of Reason: Reason, Gothic and the Grotesque. In *The Grandeur of Reason: Religion, Tradition and Universalism*, ed. Conor Cunningham and Peter M. Chandler, 432–443. London: SCM Veritas.
Milbank, John. 1996. The End of Dialogue. In *Christian Uniqueness Reconsidered: The Myth of a Pluralistic Theology of Religions*, ed. Gavin D'Costa, 174–191. Maryknoll, NY: Orbis.
Milbank, John. 1997. *The Word made Strange.* Cambridge, MA: Blackwell.
Milbank, John. 1999. The Theological Critique of Philosophy in Hamann and Jacobi. In *Radical Orthodoxy: A New Theology*, ed. John Milbank, Catherine Pickstock, and Graham Ward, 21–37. London: Routledge.

Milbank, John. 2015. Fictioning Things: Gift and Narrative. In *Theology and Literature After Postmodernity*, ed. Lehmann Imfeld, Alison Milbank Zoë, and Peter Hampson, 215–252. London: Bloomsbury T&T Clark.

Milbank, John, Graham Ward, and Catherine Pickstock. 1999. Introduction. In *Radical Orthodoxy: A New Theology*, ed. John Milbank, Graham Ward, and Catherine Pickstock, 1–20. London: Routledge.

Milbank, John, Simon Oliver, Zoë Lehmann Imfeld, and Peter Hampson. 2013. Interview and Conversation with John Milbank and Simon Oliver: Radical Orthodoxy and Christian Psychology I—Theological Underpinnings. *Edification* 6: 44–52.

Moseley, James G. 1975. Conversion through Vision: Puritanism and Transcendentalism in "the Ambassadors". *Journal of the American Academy of Religion* 43: 473–484.

Mozley, J.B. 1865. *Eight Lectures on Miracles: Preached before the University of Oxford in the Year M.DCCC.LXV. On the Foundation of the Late Rev. John Bampton, M.A. Canon of Salisbury*, Bampton Lectures. Vol. 1865. London: Rivingtons.

Muir, Edwin. 1960. *Collected Poems 1921–1958*. London: Faber & Faber.

Myers, Frederic W.H. 1903. *Human Personality and Its Survival of Bodily Death*, vol. 2, Abridgth ed. New York: Longmans, Green.

Navarette, Susan J. 1998. *The Shape of Fear: Horror and the Fin De Siècle Culture of Decadence*. Lexington: University Press of Kentucky.

Nesbit, Edith. 1893. The Mystery of the Semi-Detached. In *Grim Tales*, 67–76. London: A.D. Innes.

Newman, John Henry. 1901. *The Via Media of the Anglican Church Illustrated in Lectures, Letters and Tracts Written Between 1830 and 1841*, vol. I. London: Longman, Greens.

Nicholas of Cusa. 1978. De Possest. In *A Concise Introduction to the Philosophy of Nicholas of Cusa*. Trans. Jasper Hopkins, 914–954. Minneapolis: University of Minnesota Press.

Nietzsche, Friedrich. 2001. *The Gay Science*, ed. Bernard Williams. Trans. Josefine Nauckhoff. Cambridge: Cambridge University Press.

Novalis. 2003. *Fichte Studies*, ed. Jane Kneller. Cambridge: Cambridge University Press.

Otto, Rudolf. 1931. *The Philosophy of Religion*. Trans. E.B. Dicker. New York: Richard R. Smith.

Otto, Rudolf. 1950. *The Idea of the Holy: An Inquiry into the Non-Rational Factor in the Idea of the Divine and Its Relation to the Rational* [Heilige.]. Trans. John W. Harvey, 2nd ed. London: Oxford University Press.

Paige, Nicholas. 2001. Permanent Re-Enchantments: On some Literary Uses of the Supernatural from Early Empiricism to Modern Aesthetics. In *The Re-Enchantment of the World: Secular Magic in a Rational Age*, ed. Joshua Landy and Michael Sale, 159–180. Redwood City: Stanford University Press.

Pardoe, Rosemary, and Jane Nicholls. 2001. The Black Pilgrimage. In *Some Thoughts on M.R. James's World View*, ed. Christopher Roden and Barbara Roden, 601–608. Ashcroft: Ash-Tree.

Pardoe, Rosemary. 1994. Some Thoughts on M.R. James's World View. *Ghosts and Scholars*. *18:* 43–44.

Pardoe, Rosemary and Jane Nicholls. 1997. James Wilson's Secrets. *Ghosts and Scholars* 24: NP.

Pasi, Marco. 2007. Arthur Machen's Panic Fears: Western Esotericism and the Irruption of Negative Epistemology. *Aries 7:* 63–83.

Pfaff, Richard William. 1980. *Montague Rhodes James*. London: Scolar Press.

Pickstock, Catherine. 2013. *Repetition and Identity*. Oxford: Oxford University Press.

Pittion, Jean-Paul. 1987. The Question of Religious Conformity and Non-Conformity in the Irish Refuge. In *The Huguenots and Ireland: Anatomy of an Emigration*, ed. C.E.J. Caldicott, H. Gough, and J.-P. Pittion, 285–296. Dublin: The Glendale Press.

Pius X. 1907. *Pascendi Dominici Gregis.* http://www.papalencyclicals.net/Pius10/p10pasce.htm

Plotinus. 1956. *The Enneads*. Trans. Stephen MacKenna. London: Faber and Faber.

Poe, Edgar Allan. 1857. The Imp of the Perverse. In *The Works of the Late Edgar Allan Poe: Volume 1 Tales*, ed. Rufus Wilmot Griswald, 353–359. New York: Redfield.

Porter, Jean. 2005. Right Reason and the Love of God: The Parameters of Aquinas' Moral Theology'. In *The Theology of Thomas Aquinas*, ed. Rik Van Nieuwenhove and Joseph Peter Wawrykow, 167–191. Notre Dame, IN: University of Notre Dame Press.

Powell, Baden. 1860. On the Study of the Evidences of Christianity. In *Essays and Reviews*, ed. John W. Parker, 94–144. London: J. W. Parker.

Prudentius. 1949a. *Works Vol. I.* Trans. H.J. Thomson. Cambridge, MA: Harvard University Press.

Prudentius. 1949b. *Works Vol. II.* Trans. H.J. Thomson. Cambridge, MA: Harvard University Press.

Radcliffe, Ann. 1826. On the Supernatural in Poetry. *New Monthly Magazine* 16: 145–151.

Rafferty, Oliver P. 2010. Introduction. In *George Tyrrell and Catholic Modernism*, ed. Oliver Rafferty, 9–20. Dublin: Four Courts Press.

Raitt, Suzanne. 2000. *May Sinclair: A Modern Victorian*. Oxford: Clarendon Press.

Rapinchuk, Mark. 1999. Universal Sin and Salvation in Romans 5:12–21. *Jets. 42/3:* 427–441.

Reynolds, Aidan, and William Charlton. 1963. *Arthur Machen: A Short Account of His Life and Work*. London: Published by J. Baker for Richards Press.
Ricoeur, Paul. 1991. *From Text to Action: Essays in Hermeneutics II*. London: Continuum.
Ricoeur, Paul. 1969. *The Symbolism of Evil*. Trans. Emerson Buchanan. Boston, MA: Beacon.
Ruskin, John. 1881. *Stones of Venice*, vol. 3. New York: Wiley.
Sage, Victor. 1988. *Horror Fiction in the Protestant Tradition*. New York: St Martin's Press.
Sage, Victor. 2004. *Le Fanu's Gothic: The Rhetoric of Darkness*. New York: Palgrave Macmillan.
Sayers, Dorothy L. 1941. *The Mind of the Maker*. London: Methuen.
Schleiermacher, Friedrich. 1963. *The Christian Faith*, ed. H.R. Mackintosh and J.S. Stewart. New York: Harper & Row.
Sewell, Brocard. 1997. Arthur Machen: His Ideas and Beliefs. *Avallaunius: The Journal of the Arthur Machen Society*: 3–10.
Shakespeare, William. 1982. *Hamlet*. ed. Harold Jenkins. London: Methuen Drama.
Shakespeare, William. 1984. *Macbeth*, ed. Kenneth Muir. London: Methuen Drama.
Sherman, Stuart P. 1945. The Aesthetic Idealism of Henry James. In *The Question of Henry James*, ed. F.W. Dupee, 70–91. New York: Henry Holt.
Sinclair, May. 1907. *The Helpmate*. New York: Henry Holt and Company.
Sinclair, May. 1917. *A Defence of Idealism: Some Questions and Conclusions*. London: Macmillan.
Sinclair, May. 1922. *The New Idealism*. New York: Macmillan.
Sinclair, May. 2006a. The Finding of the Absolute. In *Uncanny Stories*, 161–176. Ware: Wordsworth.
Sinclair, May. 2006b. Where Their Fire is Not Quenched. In *Uncanny Stories*, 27–46. Ware: Wordsworth.
Smith, Andrew. 2010. *The Ghost Story, 1840–1920*. Manchester: Manchester University Press.
Starrett, Vincent. 1996. *Arthur Machen: A Novelist of Ecstasy and Sin*. Caerleon: Tartarus.
Steiner, George. 1979. "Critic"/"Reader". *New Literary History* 10: 423–452.
Stevenson, Robert Louis. 2005. *The Strange Case of Dr Jekyll and Mr Hyde*, ed. Martin A. Danahay. Plymouth: Broadview.
Sullivan, Jack. 1978. *Elegant Nightmares: The English Ghost Story from Le Fanu to Blackwood*. Athens: Ohio University Press.
Swedenborg, Emanuel. 2002. *Heaven and Hell*. Trans. George F. Dole. West Chester, PA: Swedenborg Foundation, 2002.
Taylor, Charles. 2007. *A Secular Age*. Cambridge, MA: Harvard University Press.

The New Oxford Annotated Bible, with the Apocryphal/Deuterocanonical Books, 3rd ed, ed. Michael David Coogan. Oxford: Oxford University Press, 2001.
Thiselton, Anthony C. 1992. *New Horizons in Hermeneutics*. Grand Rapids, MI: Zondervan.
Todorov, Tzvetan. 1975. *The Fantastic: A Structural Approach to a Literary Genre*. Trans. Richard Howard. Ithica, NY: Cornell University Press.
Torchio, Natale Joseph. 1999. *'Creatio Ex Nihilo' and the Theology of St Augustine: The Anti-Manichaean Polemic and Beyond*. New York: Peter Lang.
Troy, William. 1945. The Altar of Henry James. In *The Question of Henry James*, ed. F.W. Dupee, 267–272. New York: Henry Holt.
Valentine, Mark. 1995. *Arthur Machen*, Border Lines. Bridgend: Seren.
Varnado, S.L. 1987. *Haunted Presence: The Numinous in Gothic Fiction*. Tuscaloosa: University of Alabama Press.
Wallace, Diana. 2004. Uncanny Stories: The Ghost Story as Female Gothic. *Gothic Studies* 6: 57–68.
Wallace, Diana, and Andrew Smith. 2009. Introduction: Defining the Female Gothic. In *The Female Gothic: New Directions*, ed. Diana Wallace and Andrew Smith, 1–12. Basingstoke: Palgrave Macmillan.
Walton, James. 2007. *Vision and Vacancy: The Fictions of J.S. Le Fanu*. Dublin: University College Dublin Press.
Walz, Robin. 2001. The Rocambolesque and the Modern Enchantment of Popular Fiction. In *The Re-Enchantment of the World: Secular Magic in a Rational Age*, ed. Joshua Landy and Michael Sale, 130–148. Stanford, CA: Stanford University Press.
Weber, Max. 1963. *The Sociology of Religion*. London: Beacon Press.
Weber, Max. 1946. *From Max Weber: Essays in Sociology*. Trans. H.H. Gerth and C. Wright Mills. Oxford: Oxford University Press.
Weighell, Ron. 2007. Dark Devotions: M.R. James and the Magical Tradition. In *Warnings to the Curious: A Sheaf of Criticism on M.R. James*, ed. S.T. Joshi and Rosemary Pardoe, 124–137. New York: Hippocampus Press.
Wheeler, Michael. 1994. *Heaven, Hell, and the Victorians [Death and the future life in Victorian literature and theology]*, Abridgth ed. Cambridge: Cambridge University Press.
Wiley, Tatha. 2002. *Original Sin: Origins, Developments, Contemporary Meaning*. New York: Paulist Press.
Williams, Rowan. 2000. *On Christian Theology*. Oxford: Blackwell.
Wright, Craig. 2001. *The Maze and the Warrior: Symbols in Architecture, Theology and Music*. Cambridge, MA: Harvard University Press.

INDEX

A
Adam, 79, 84
   Adamic myth, 164, 166
   Northrop Frye on, 89
aesthetics, 49
   Machen on, 34, 35, 41, 70
   James on, 142–4, 149, 155
   Le Fanu on, 110, 134n1
   Iser on, 159
agnostic. *See* agnosticism
agnosticism, 1–3, 39, 43
Allen, Grant
   'Pallinghurst Barrow,' 24, 37n28
anamnesis, 25–6, 162, 163
Anglicanism
   Anglo-Irish Protestantism, 110
   Broad Church, 42
   Church of Ireland, 109
   Irish Huguenots, 109
   James, Herbert, 80
Anselm, 147
apocalypse, 6, 81, 83
Apocrypha, 80, 82

Aquinas, Thomas, 27, 34, 40, 41, 47–50, 58, 60, 69, 72n5, 74n25, 75n36, 77n63, 78n93, 112, 135n20, 152
   eternal law, 40, 46–7
   grace, 112
   habitus, 46
   knowledge, 49–50
   natural law, 46–7
   potency and act, 49, 50, 148, 159
   Summa Theologicae, 46, 72n5
Aristotle, 89
   metaphysics, 27
   potency and act, 27, 49
Augustine, 27, 29, 34, 42, 46, 56, 58, 69, 75n35, 76n57, 84, 87, 93, 104n47, 107, 111, 112, 130, 131, 135n21
   on causation, 56
   City of God, 29
   Confessions, 28, 112, 130
   on evil, 29
   grace, 111–12
   On the Trinity, 56
   telos, 87

Note: Page number followed by 'n' refers to endnotes

B

Bakhtin, M.M., 19, 22, 37n23
  dialogue, 22
Barth, Karl, 29–30
  on terror, 29
Benson, Robert Hugh, 28
  'The Watcher,' 28
Bewick, Thomas, 114
black pilgrimage, 87
Blondel, Maurice, 43

C

Calvinism, 110
  election, 110
  predestination, 112
Cartesian hermeneutics, 19
Catholic emancipation in Ireland, 109
Chesterton, G. K., 41
cogito, 14, 15, 82
Coleridge, Samuel Taylor, 44, 61
Collins, Wilkie
  'Mrs Zant and the Ghost,' 16

D

Decadent movement, 9, 39, 40, 62, 82
de Certeau, Michel, 21
  'Walking in the City,' 21
Demonic, 29–31, 100, 107, 114, 159
Derrida, Jacques, 17
Desmond, William, 15, 16, 19, 24, 129, 138n84, 144, 146–8, 151, 157n17, 159–60, 162, 167n4
  astonishment, 144–7, 160
  on evil, 159
  immanence, 130
  in-between, 19, 24
  metaxology, 24, 129, 164
  otherness of God, 15

poros, 129, 147
porous self, 159
porous world, 144
potency, 19
devil (antichrist), 40, 55, 58, 76n54, 97, 107, 147
  Anselm on, 147
  Pan as, 45, 76n54
  Prudentius on, 97
  Todorov on, 25
Dionysius (Pseudo-Denys), 152
  beauty, 152
  Divine Names, 152
dread, 107
  Kierkegaard, Søren, 113

E

Eckhart, Meister, 68
Eliot, George
  'The Lifted Veil,' 2
Eliot, T.S.
  on Henry James, 143
empiricism, 2, 3, 43, 82, 142
Enlightenment, 2, 31, 32, 46, 65, 71, 82
evil, 28, 29, 47, 67, 70, 93
  Augustine on, 28
  Desmond on, 159
  Kierkegaard on, 114
  Maritain on, 57
  as negation, 56, 57, 67
  as privation, 29, 40, 55
  radical, 17, 44

F

fantastic. *See* Todorov, Tzvetan
Frye, Northrop, 4
pharmakos, 88
  on revelation, 6

G

Girard, René
  mimetic crisis, 116–17
  mimetic desire, 117
  scapegoat, 88
Gnosis, 96
Gnosticism, 84, 85, 98, 118
Gothic
  Female Gothic, 5
grace
  Aquinas on, 112
  Augustine on, 112, 113
  Luther on, 111, 120
Gregory of Nyssa, 99

H

Habermas, Jürgen, 17, 18, 23
habitus, 46, 74n28
Hay, Simon, 4
Hopkins, Gerard Manley, 41, 167n1
  'The Wreck of the Deutschland,' 41

I

Imago Christi, 27, 58, 89, 91
Imago Dei, 27, 32, 58, 94, 108, 131, 133
immanence, 127, 130
  Desmond, William, 129
Irenaeus, 84, 85, 93, 98, 101, 103n23, 105n64, 113
  Against Heresies, 85
  universal sin, 84
Irish Huguenots, 109
  and Anglicanism, 109
Irish Protestantism, 110
Iser, Wolfgang, 159, 162, 163, 166, 167n1, 168n13
  aesthetics, 163
  gaps, 159
  reader-response model, 162, 166

J

James, Henry, 2
  aesthetics, 143, 150–4, 162
  'The Altar of the Dead,' 148, 156
  The Ambassadors, 143, 144
  'The Beast in the Jungle,' 111, 144, 145
  The Golden Bowl, 143
  'Is There a Life After Death,' 142
  'The Jolly Corner,' 165
  The Other House, 143
  The Portrait of a Lady, 143
  The Sacred Fount, 143
  secularism, 82, 142
  A Sense of the Past, 163
  on Swedenborg, 142
  T.S. Eliot on, 143
  The Turn of the Screw, 151
James, Herbert
  conservative Anglicanism, 80
James, M.R., 34, 80–3, 111, 114, 133
  Apocrypha, 80, 85
  The Apocryphal New Testament, 81
  'Canon Alberic's Scrapbook,' 86–94
  'Count Magnus,' 86–94
  Ghost Stories of an Antiquary, 79, 86
  'John Humphreys,' 99
  'Mr Humphreys and his Inheritance,' 94–100
  'The Novels and Stories of J.S. Le Fanu,' 104
  'Oh Whistle and I'll Come to You, my Lad,' 83
  Old Testament Legends, 92
  priesthood, 81
  Testament of Solomon, 92
Job, 98, 126, 129, 130

K

Kant, Emmanuel, 27, 59
Kazantzakis, Nikos, 160, 161
   The Saviors of God, 160
Kierkegaard, Søren, 15, 30, 31, 107, 113, 114, 133
   The Concept of Dread, 113
   demonic, 30
   dread, 107
   on evil, 114
   shut-upness, 30

L

Lang, Andrew, 1
Larsen, Timothy, 2–3, 5, 7
Le Fanu, Sheridan, 15, 133
   Anglo-Irish Protestantism, 108
   '*Borrhomeo the Astrologer*,' 115–20
   Calvinist election, 110
   Dr. Hesselius, 138n83
   'The Familiar,' 126
   'The Fortunes of Sir Robert Ardagh,' 120, 125
   In a Glass Darkly, 162
   'The Haunted Baronet,' 120–6
   'The Mysterious Lodger,' 126–32
   '*Schalken the Painter*,' 119
   'Spalatro,' 115–20
Le Fanu, Susanna, 110
Le Fanu, Thomas, 114
Leo XIII, 41
   Aeterni Patris, 41
Lewis, Matthew, 34
   The Monk, 33, 34
Loisy, Alfred, 43
Lovecraft, H.P., 7
   Supernatural Horror in Literature, 7
Luther, Martin
   Anfechtung, 107, 110, 129
   grace, 111, 130
   justification in faith, 107
   sola fide, 128

M

Machen, Arthur, ix, 148
   'The Adventure of the Gold Tiberius,' 60
   'The Adventure of the Missing Brother,' 63
   aesthetics, 40, 46, 59
   Anglo-Catholicism, 41–6
   artifice, 61, 62, 65, 68, 69
   'The Decadent Imagination,' 62
   Dr Stiggins, 45
   on evil as absence, 29
   'A Fragment of Life,' 45, 47, 70
   'The Gift of Tongues,' 42
   'The Great God Pan,' 40, 55–9, 148
   'great sacrament,' 40, 41, 51, 53, 55, 70
   Hieroglyphics, 39, 40, 44, 47, 61, 73n14
   The Hill of Dreams, 45
   'History of the Young Man in Spectacles,' 62
   'Inmost Light,' 59
   on Modernism, 42–3
   'Modernism' (article), 42
   mystic experience, 45, 51, 75n34
   Notes and Queries, 73n19
   'Novel of the Black Seal,' 63–6
   'Novel of the Iron Maid,' 62
   'Novel of the White Powder,' 65–7
   'Opening the Door,' 161
   'The Red Hand,' 59, 71
   The Recluse of Bayswater,' 63
   The Secret Glory, 47, 48, 70
   'The Statement of William Gregg, F.R.S. etc.,' 64
   'The Strange Occurrence in Clerkenwell,' 60

The Three Imposters, 60
The Three Impostors, 40, 44, 46, 47,
   59–70, 87, 148, 153
   Vinum Sabbati, 40, 41, 66
   'The White People,' 40, 46–55, 67, 71
Marlowe, Christopher, 133
   Doctor Faustus, 133
mazes
   as Christian symbol, 95
McGrath, Alister
   Luther, *Anfechtung,* 129
Milbank, Alison, 10n14
Milbank, John, 19, 36n18
   dialogue, 19, 20
   'Fictioning Things,' 52
Modernism, 42, 43, 65, 73n13,
   78n86
   modernist theology, 43

N

Nesbit, Edith, 5
   'The Mystery of the Semi-
      Detached,' 5
Newman, John Henry, 35
Nicholas of Cusa, 15
   possest, 3
Nietzsche, Friedrich, 61, 68, 69,
   78n92
   The Gay Science, 68n92
nihilism, 31–5, 54, 59, 61, 68,
   71, 148
numinous. *See* Otto, Rudolf; Otto,
   Rudolf, numinous

O

oral tradition, 82, 87, 88, 93
original sin, 84
   Aquinas, 46
   Augustine, 84
   Kierkegaard, Søren, 113

Otto, Rudolf, 31, 32, 34, 38n45
   The Idea of the Holy, 32
   numinous, 31–2
Oxford Movement, 34

P

Pan, 36, 40, 47, 83
   as devil, 40
   Panic fear, 83
Pauline resurrection, 108, 109, 113, 126
pharmakos, 78, 89
Pickstock, Catherine, 82, 88, 102n16
Pius X, 43, 78n85
   Pascendi Domini Gregis, 43
Plotinus, 87
porosity, 147, 155
porous world, 14, 23, 144, 165–7
   Desmond, William, 147
   See also Taylor, Charles, porous self
potency, 24, 70, 141, 148, 162, 164,
   165
   and act, 27, 49, 50, 148, 159
Prudentius, 97
psychoanalysis, 1, 4

R

Radcliffe, Ann, 34, 108
   horror and terror, 108
Radical Orthodoxy, 19, 34
reader, 13–15, 18–22, 52, 68, 128,
   161
   literary scholar, 13, 19
   non-theological, 13, 14, 17, 18,
      37n25, 161, 164, 167
   participation, 19, 30, 164
   reading process, 159
   secular reader, 22
Ricœur, Paul, 18, 22, 37n30, 164
   Adamic myth, 164
Roman Catholicism, 65

S

Sage, Victor, 108, 109
Satan. *See* devil (antichrist)
Sayers, Dorothy, 6, 167
   The Mind of the Maker, 6
scapegoat, 88
   Girard, René, 117
   pharmakos, 88
Sinclair, May, 5, 27, 149
   'The Finding of the Absolute,' 27
   The New Idealism, 149
   'Where their fire is not Quenched,' 149
Society for Psychical Research, 1, 144
Solomon, 91–3
   Testament of Solomon, 92
Stevenson, Robert Louis, 30, 31
   The Strange Case of Dr Jekyll and Mr Hyde, 30
Swedenborg, Emanuel, 128, 129, 133, 137n77
   Heaven and Hell, 137n78
   James, Henry Snr, 142

T

Taylor, Charles, 13
   buffered self (bounded self), 14, 23, 100
   immanent frame, 14, 15, 23, 30, 129, 130, 132
   on orthodoxy, 83
   porous self, 23, 159
   secular reader (*see* reader)
   semantic readjustment, 18
telos, 27, 34, 38n37, 87–9, 94, 98, 103n29, 112, 116, 119
   Augustine, 87
The Testament of Solomon, 92
Thomism, 40, 46–7, 49–52, 54, 56, 61, 88, 152, 158n64
Todorov, Tzvetan, 25, 119
   fantastic, 25
Tyrrell, George, 43

U

universal sin, 27, 84
   See also original sin

V

Vatican I, 41

W

Williams, Rowan, 20
   'The Finality of Christ,' 20

Printed by Printforce, the Netherlands